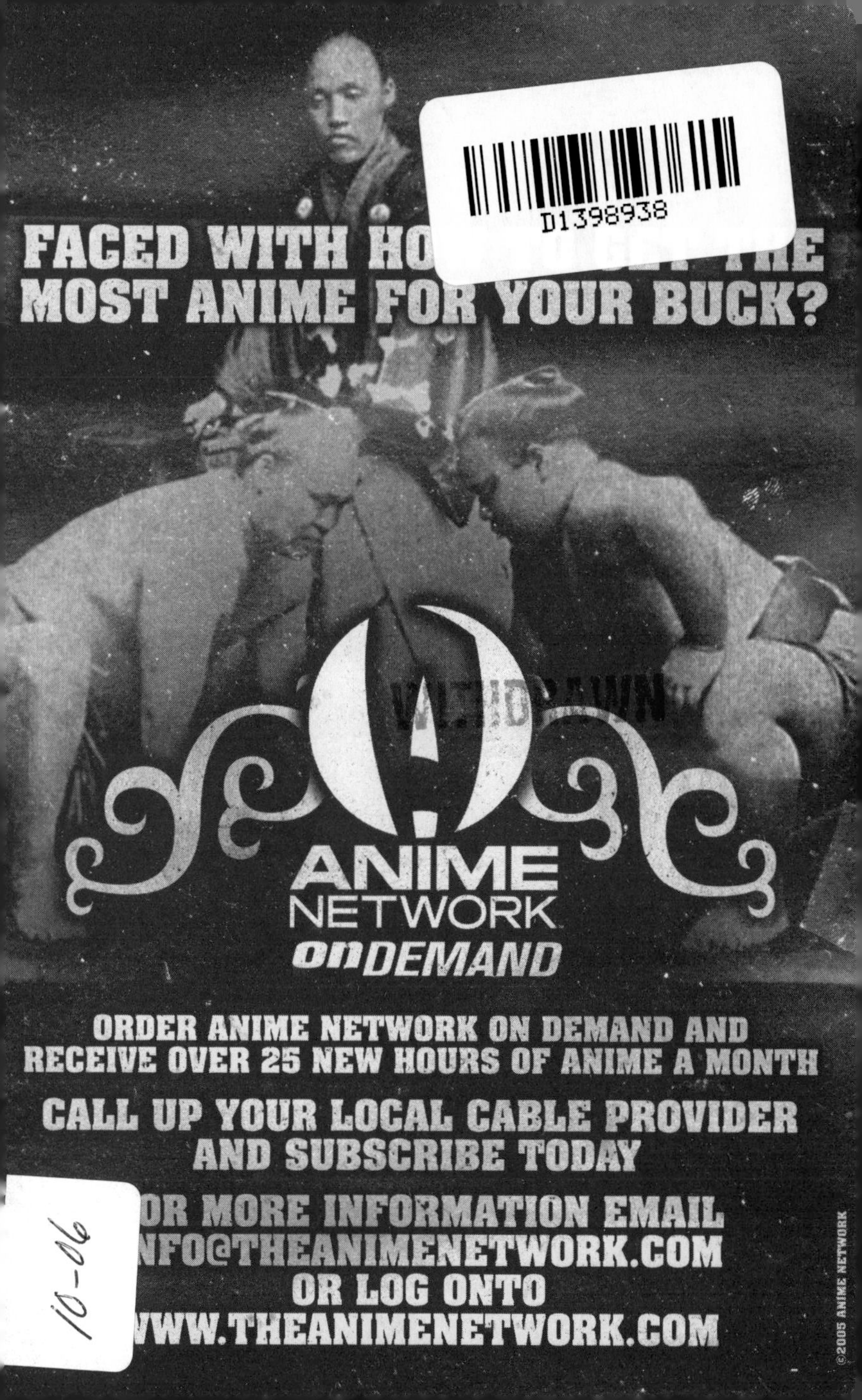
FACED WITH HO THE
MOST ANIME FOR YOUR BUCK?
ANIME
NETWORK
onDEMAND
ORDER ANIME NETWORK ON DEMAND AND RECEIVE OVER 25 NEW HOURS OF ANIME A MONTH
CALL UP YOUR LOCAL CABLE PROVIDER AND SUBSCRIBE TODAY
OR MORE INFORMATION EMAIL
NFO@THEANIMENETWORK.COM
OR LOG ONTO
WWW.THEANIMENETWORK.COM
©2005 ANIME NETWORK

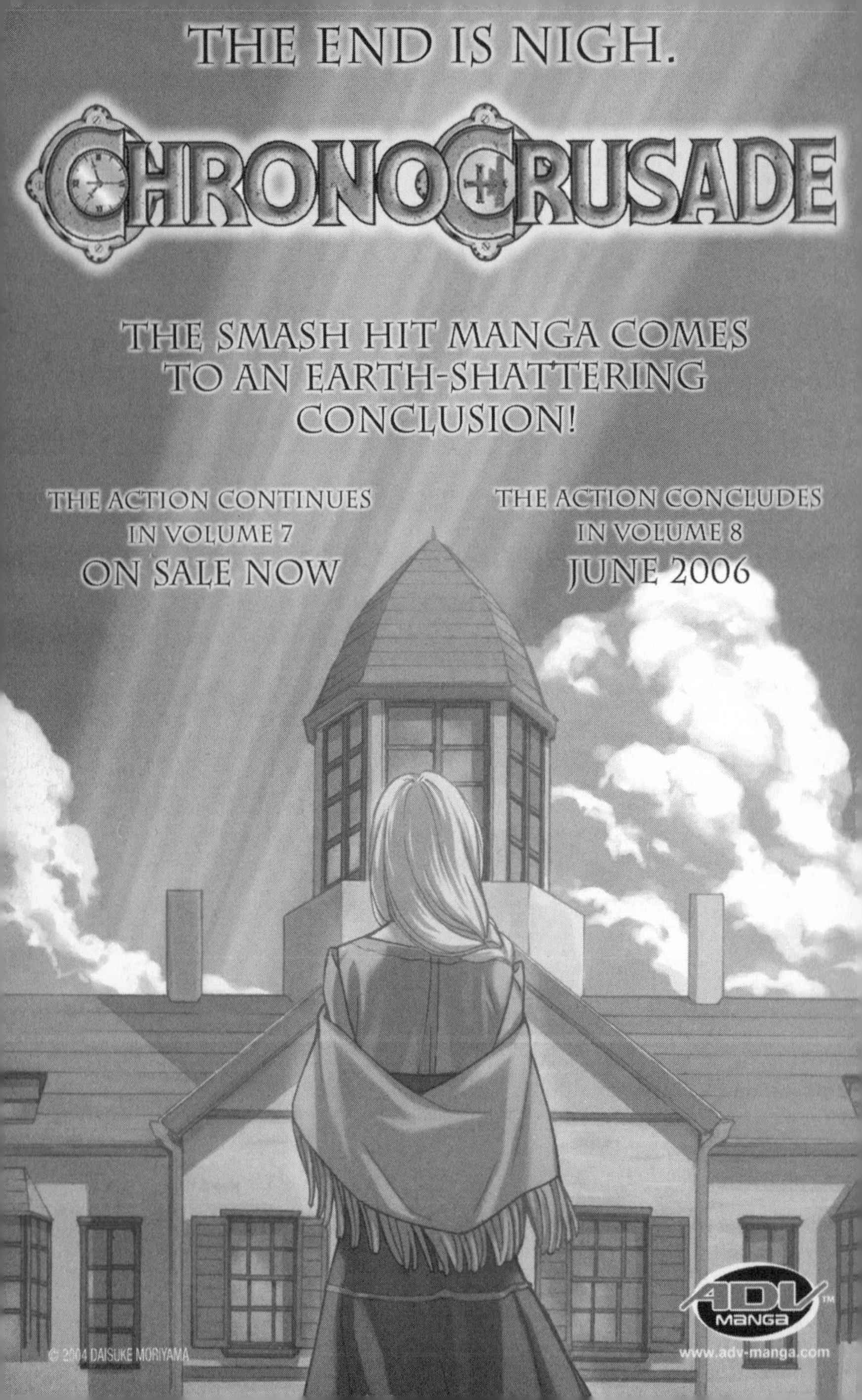
THE END IS NIGH.
CHRONO CRUSADE
THE SMASH HIT MANGA COMES TO AN EARTH-SHATTERING CONCLUSION!
THE ACTION CONTINUES IN VOLUME 7
ON SALE NOW
THE ACTION CONCLUDES IN VOLUME 8
JUNE 2006
© 2004 DAISUKE MORIYAMA
ADV Manga™
www.adv-manga.com

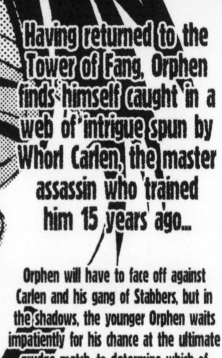

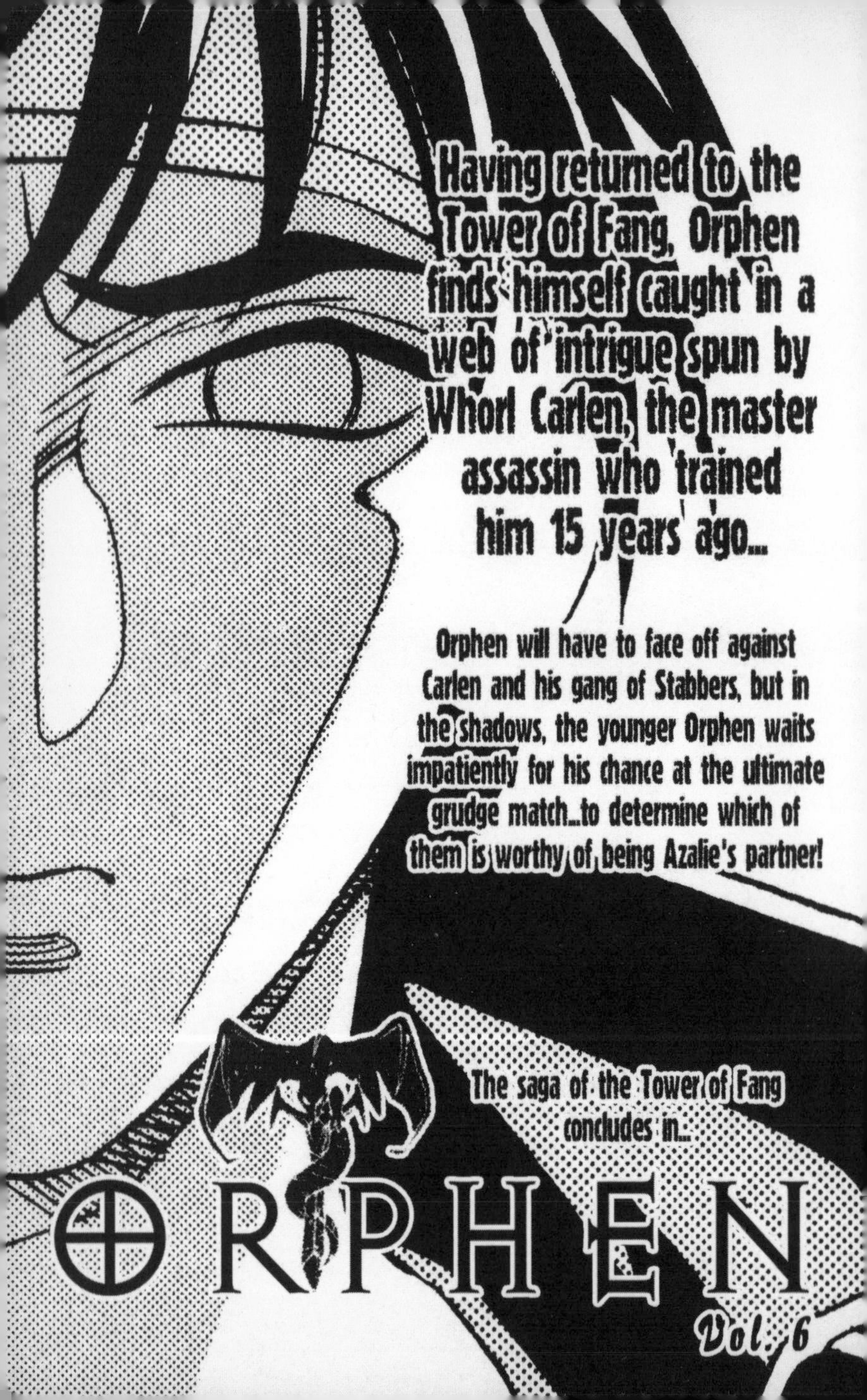

Having returned to the
Tower of Fang, Orphen
finds himself caught in a
web of intrigue spun by
Whorl Carlen, the master
assassin who trained
him 15 years ago...

Orphen will have to face off against
Carlen and his gang of Stabbers, but in
the shadows, the younger Orphen waits
impatiently for his chance at the ultimate
grudge match...to determine which of
them is worthy of being Azalie's partner!

The saga of the Tower of Fang
concludes in...

⊕RPHEN

Vol. 6

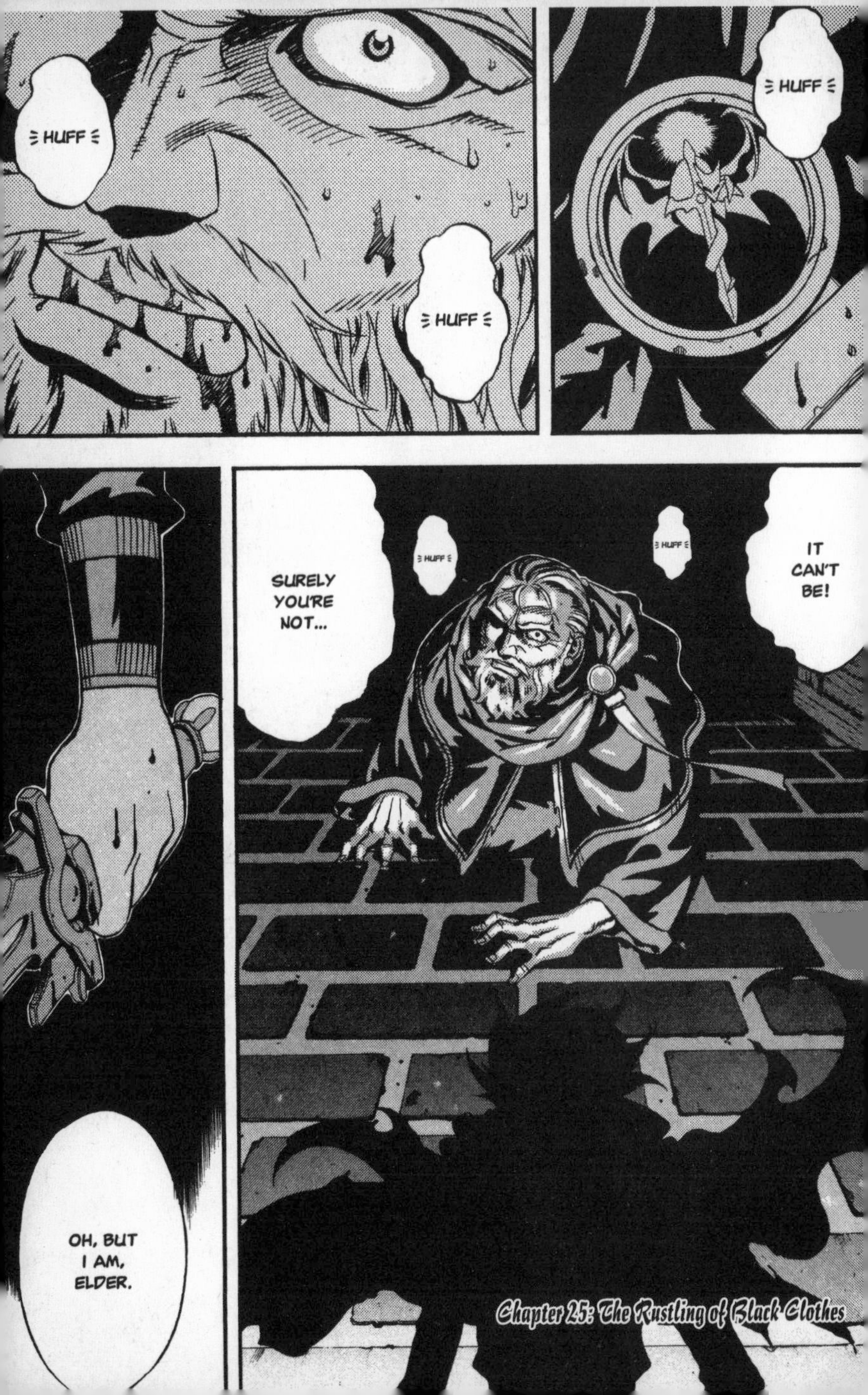
HUFF
HUFF
HUFF
IT CAN'T BE!
HUFF
HUFF
SURELY YOU'RE NOT...
OH, BUT I AM, ELDER.
Chapter 25: The Rustling of Black Clothes

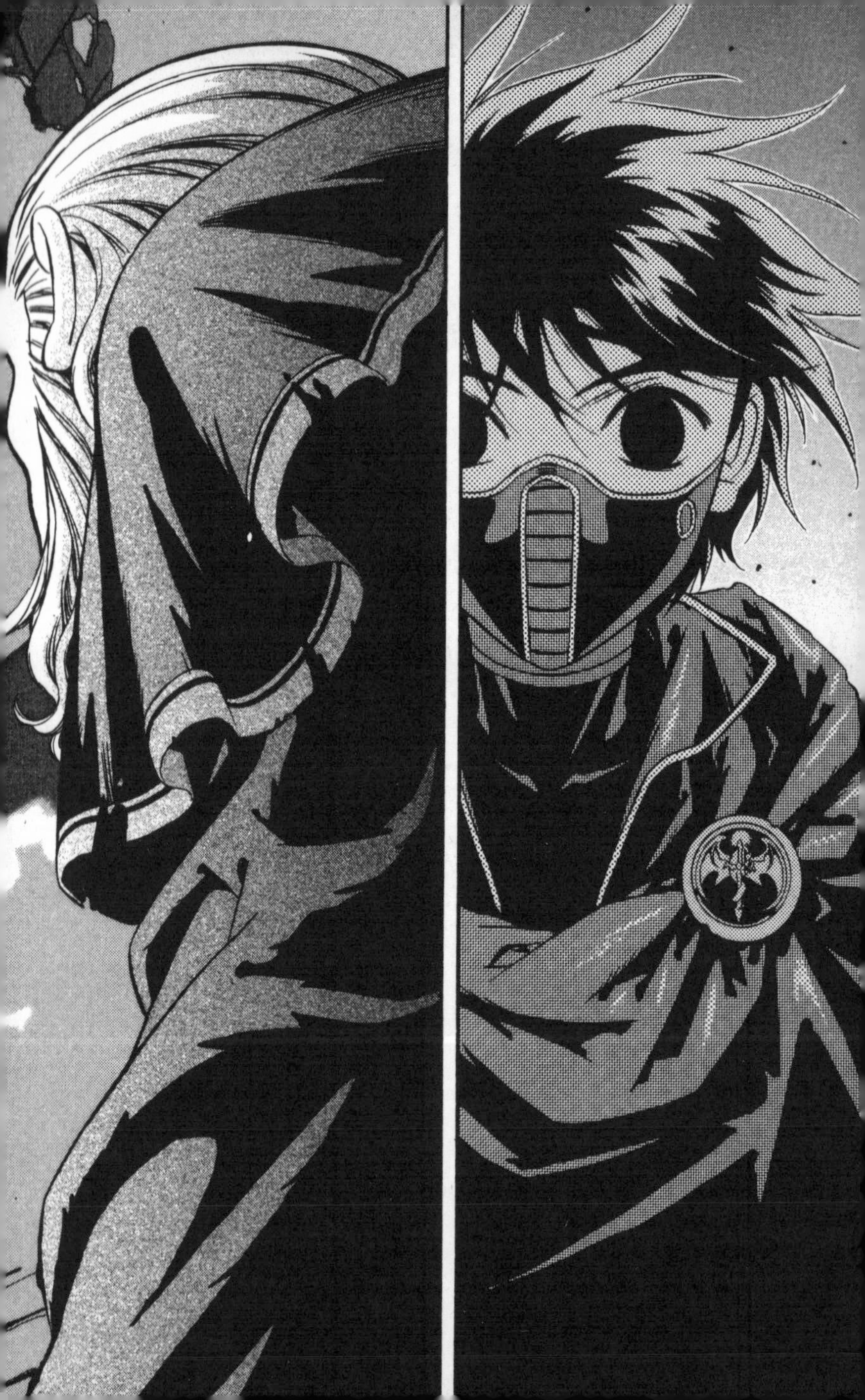

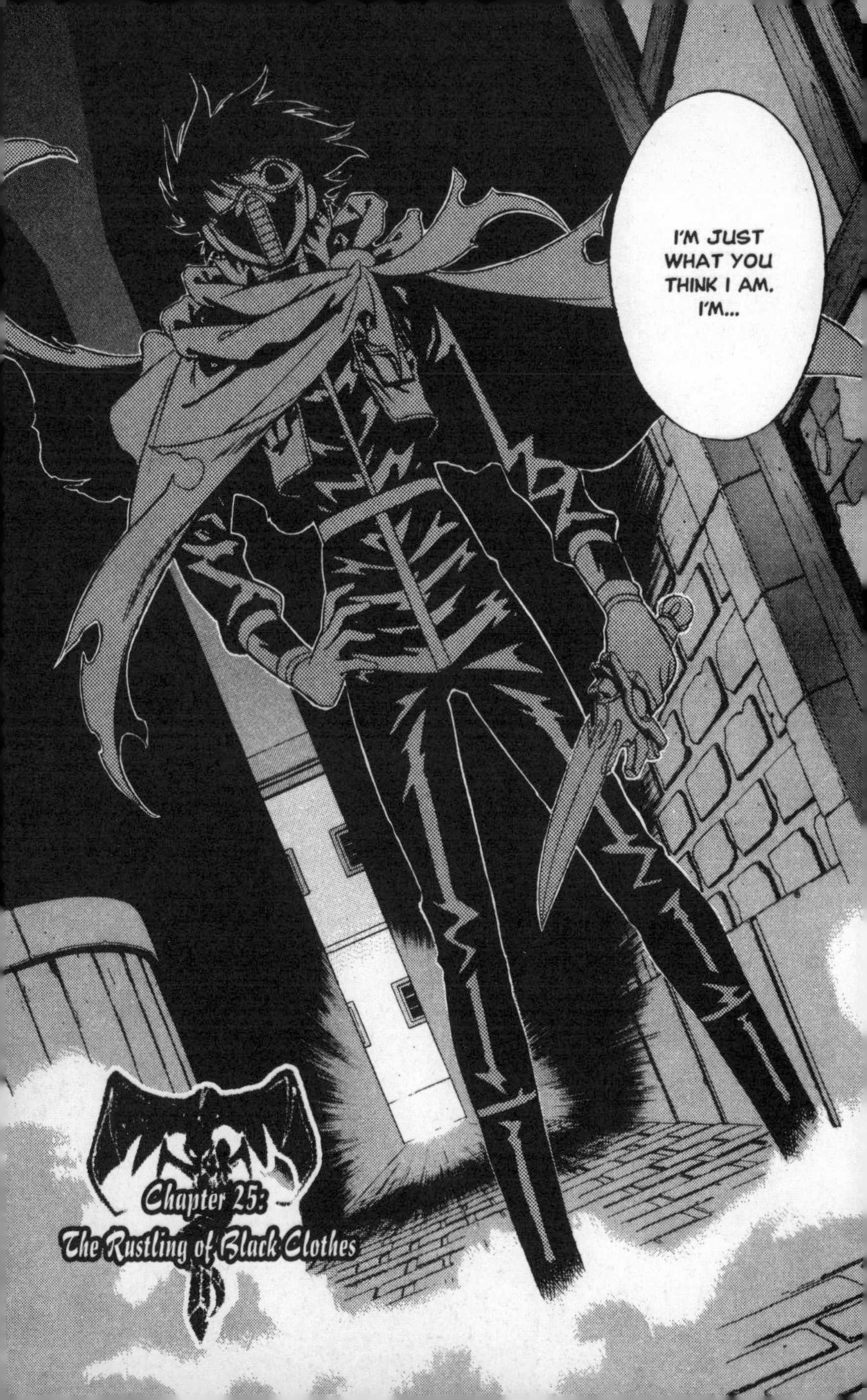
I'M JUST WHAT YOU THINK I AM. I'M...
Chapter 25:
The Rustling of Black Clothes

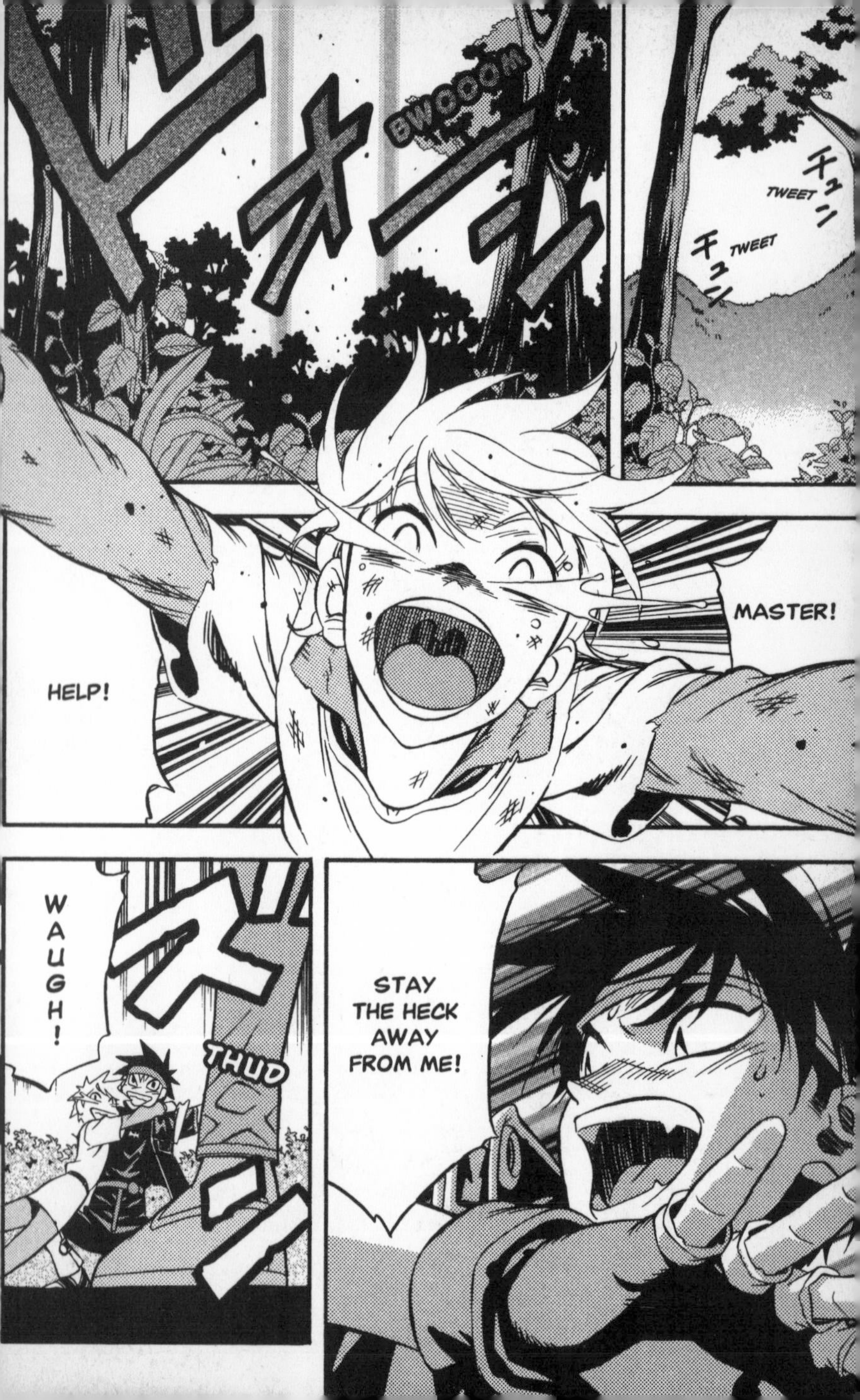
BWOOOM
チュン
TWEET
チュン
TWEET
MASTER!
HELP!
STAY THE HECK AWAY FROM ME!
WAUGH!
THUD

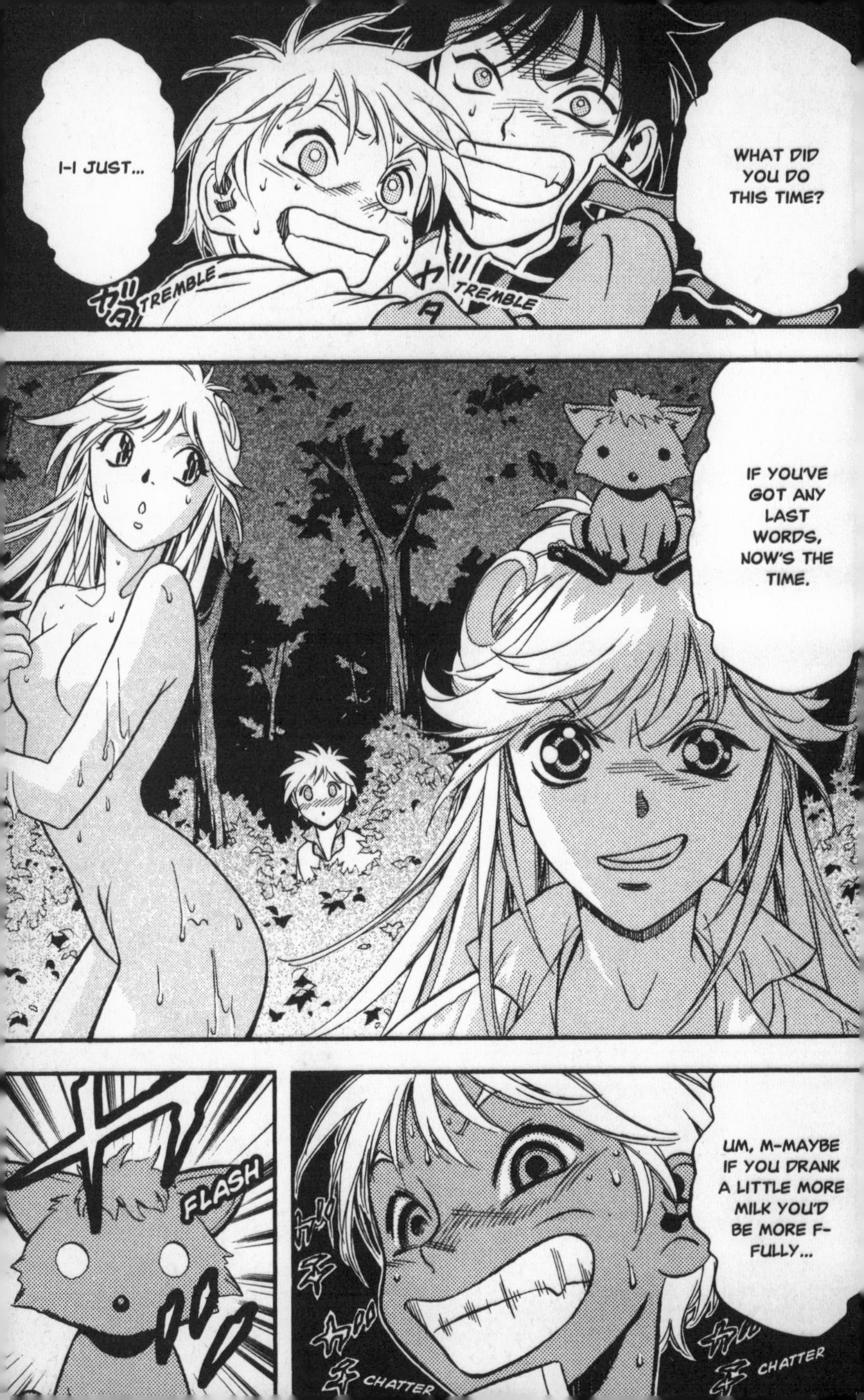
WHAT DID YOU DO THIS TIME?
I-I JUST...
TREMBLE
TREMBLE
IF YOU'VE GOT ANY LAST WORDS, NOW'S THE TIME.
UM, M-MAYBE IF YOU DRANK A LITTLE MORE MILK YOU'D BE MORE F-FULLY...
CHATTER
CHATTER
FLASH

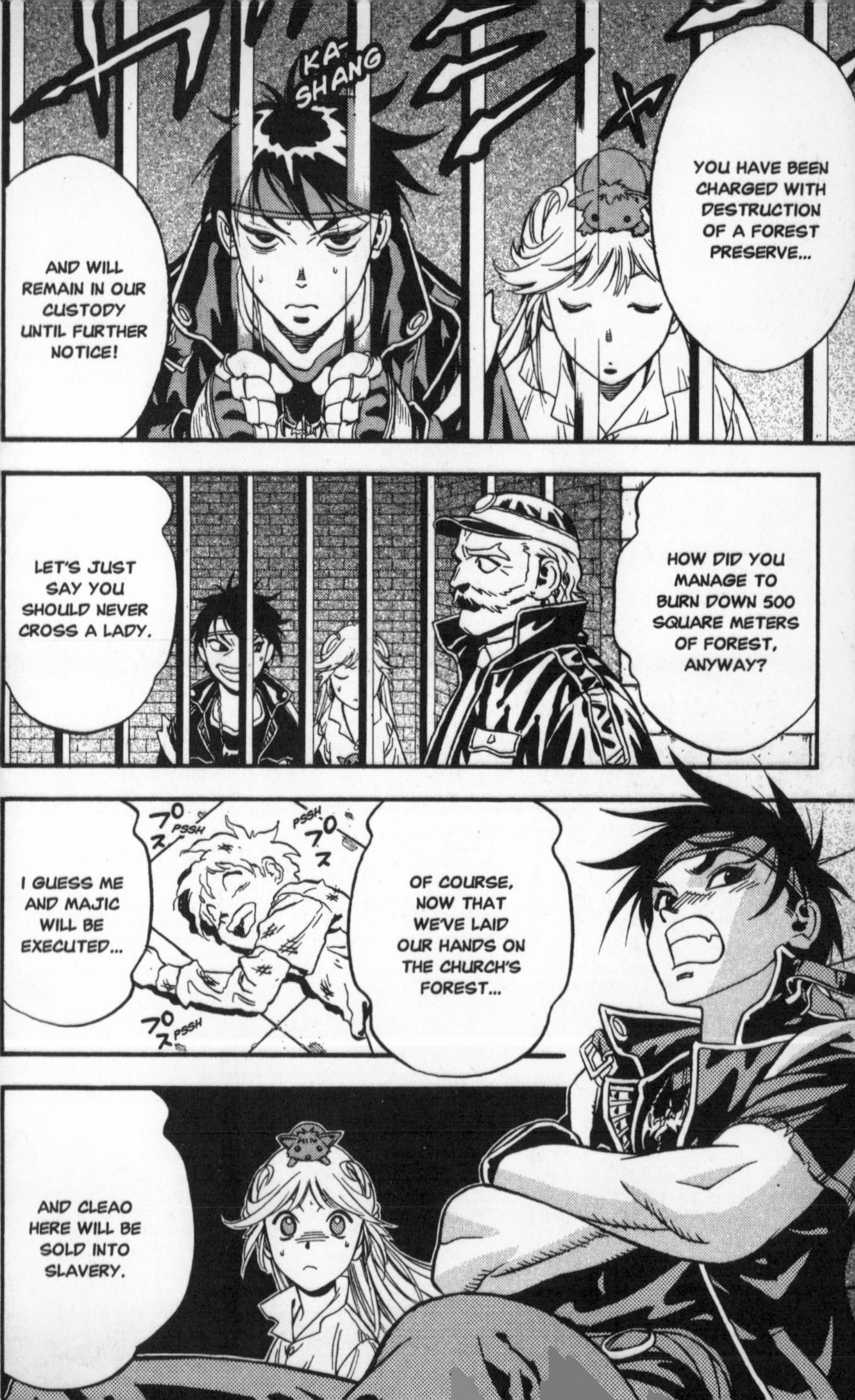
KA-SHANG
YOU HAVE BEEN CHARGED WITH DESTRUCTION OF A FOREST PRESERVE...
AND WILL REMAIN IN OUR CUSTODY UNTIL FURTHER NOTICE!
HOW DID YOU MANAGE TO BURN DOWN 500 SQUARE METERS OF FOREST, ANYWAY?
LET'S JUST SAY YOU SHOULD NEVER CROSS A LADY.
OF COURSE, NOW THAT WE'VE LAID OUR HANDS ON THE CHURCH'S FOREST...
PSSH
PSSH
I GUESS ME AND MAJIC WILL BE EXECUTED...
PSSH
AND CLEAO HERE WILL BE SOLD INTO SLAVERY.

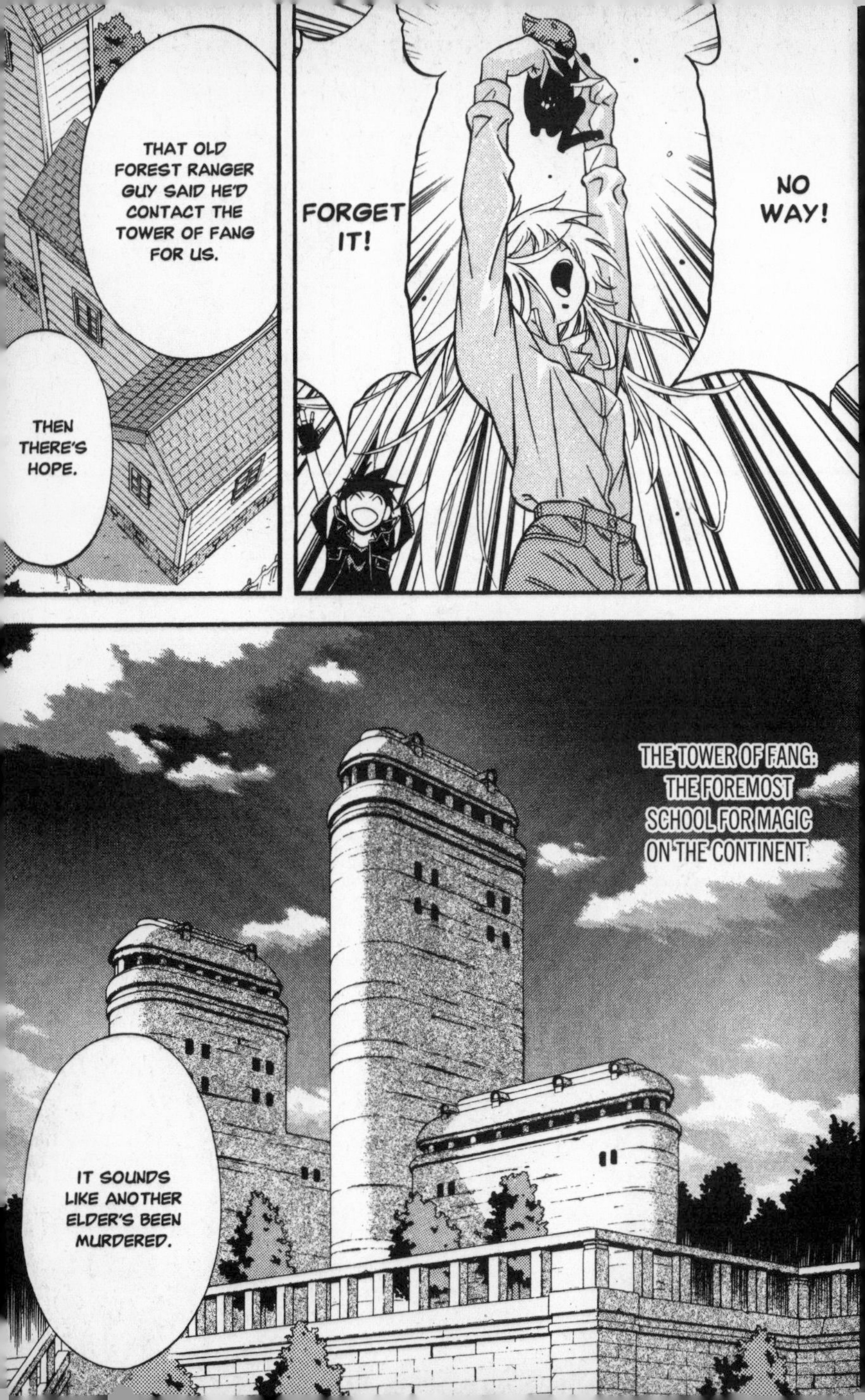
THAT OLD FOREST RANGER GUY SAID HE'D CONTACT THE TOWER OF FANG FOR US.
THEN THERE'S HOPE.
FORGET IT!
NO WAY!
THE TOWER OF FANG: THE FOREMOST SCHOOL FOR MAGIC ON THE CONTINENT.
IT SOUNDS LIKE ANOTHER ELDER'S BEEN MURDERED.

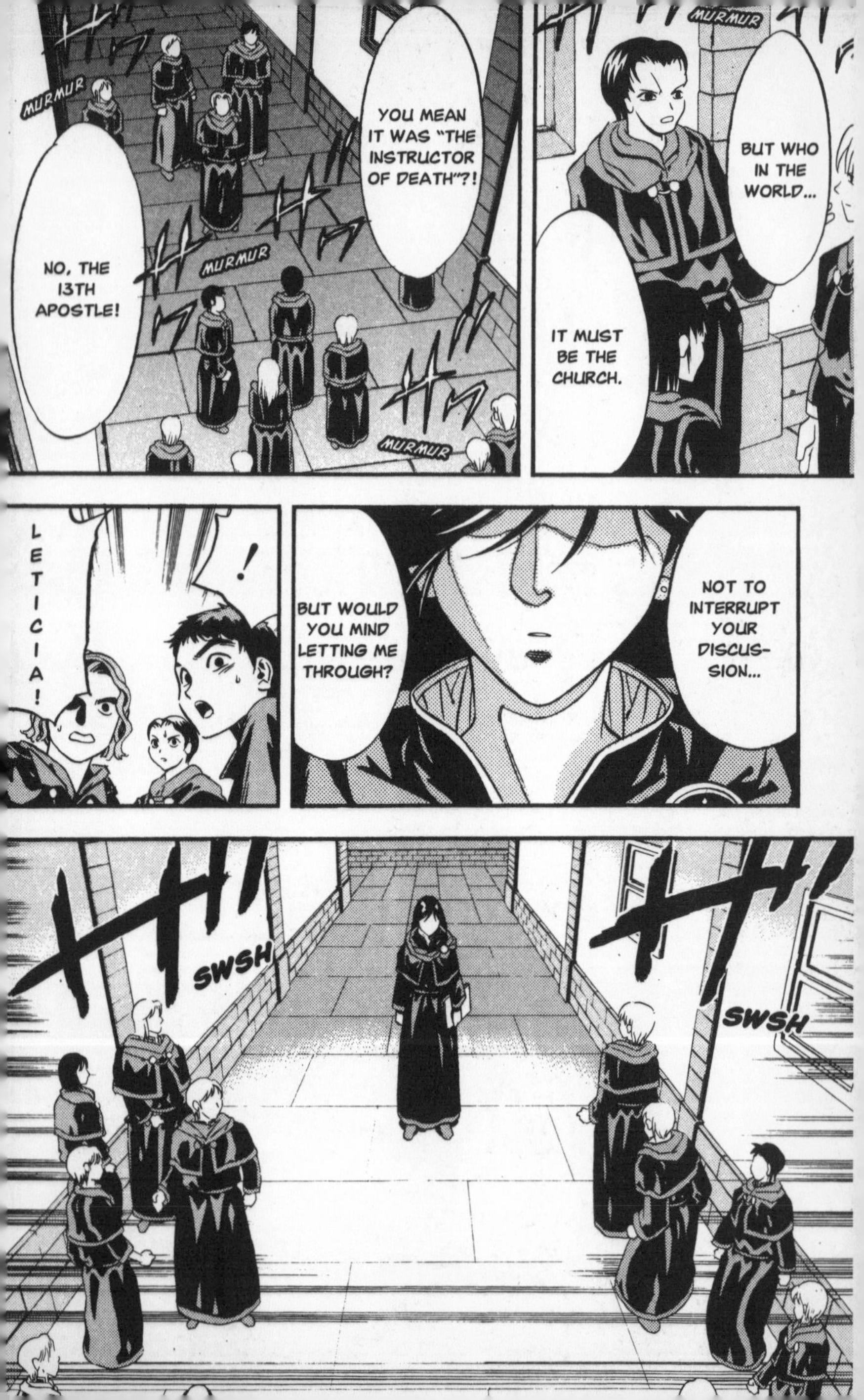
MURMUR
BUT WHO IN THE WORLD...
IT MUST BE THE CHURCH.
YOU MEAN IT WAS "THE INSTRUCTOR OF DEATH"?!
MURMUR
NO, THE 13TH APOSTLE!
MURMUR
MURMUR
NOT TO INTERRUPT YOUR DISCUSSION...
BUT WOULD YOU MIND LETTING ME THROUGH?
!
LETICIA!
SWSH
SWSH

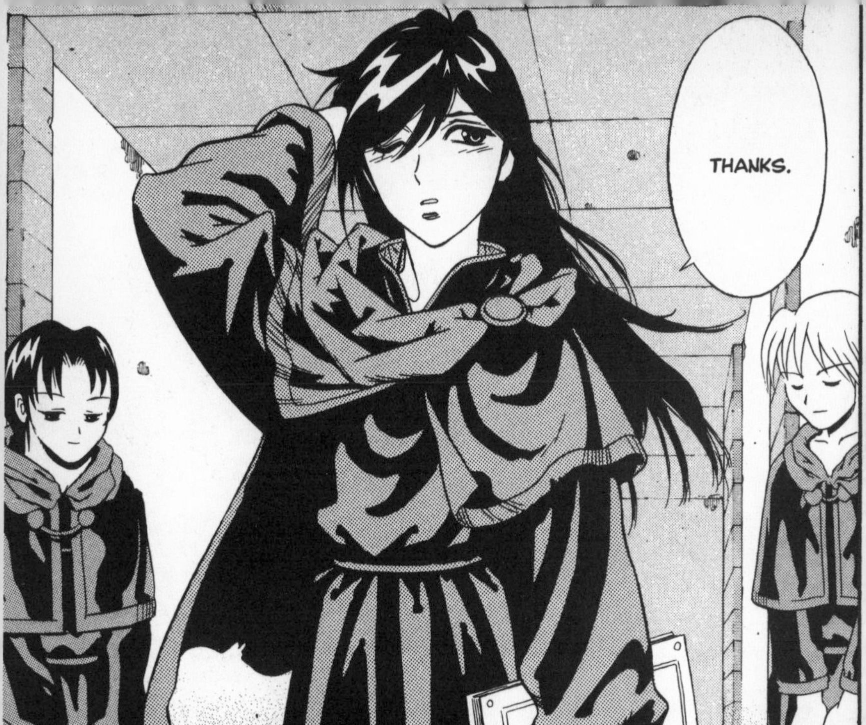
THANKS.

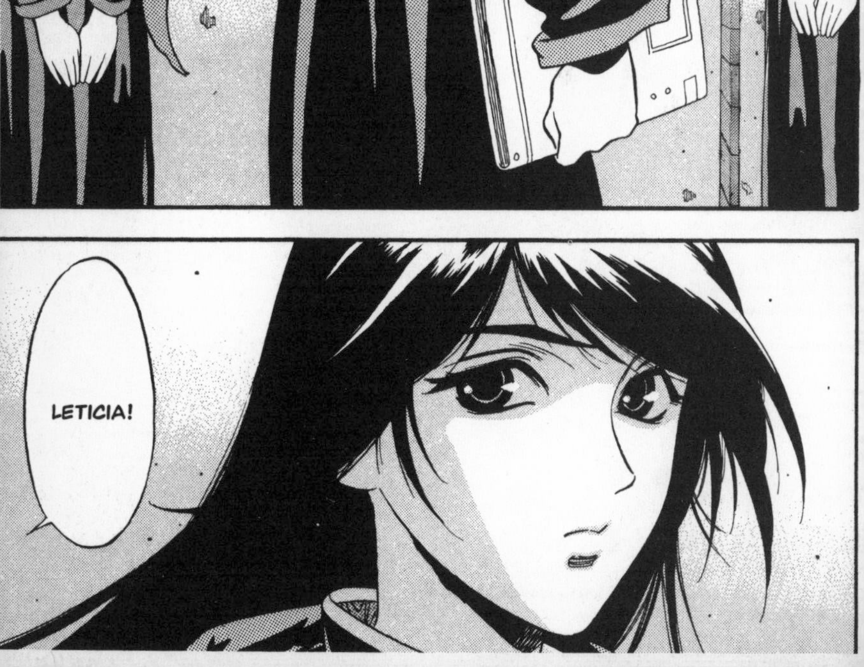
LETICIA!

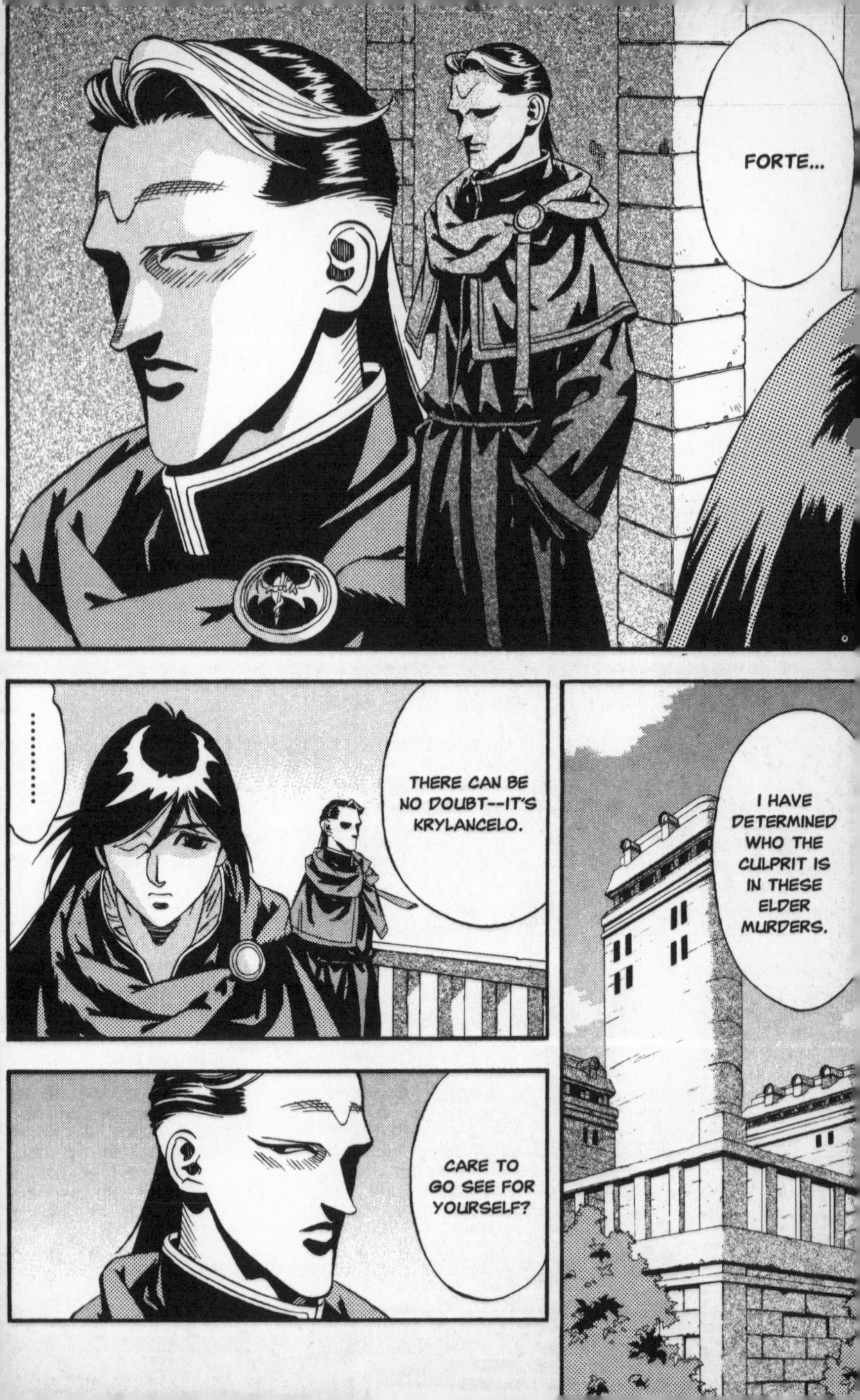
FORTE...
I HAVE DETERMINED WHO THE CULPRIT IS IN THESE ELDER MURDERS.
THERE CAN BE NO DOUBT--IT'S KRYLANCELO.
....
CARE TO GO SEE FOR YOURSELF?

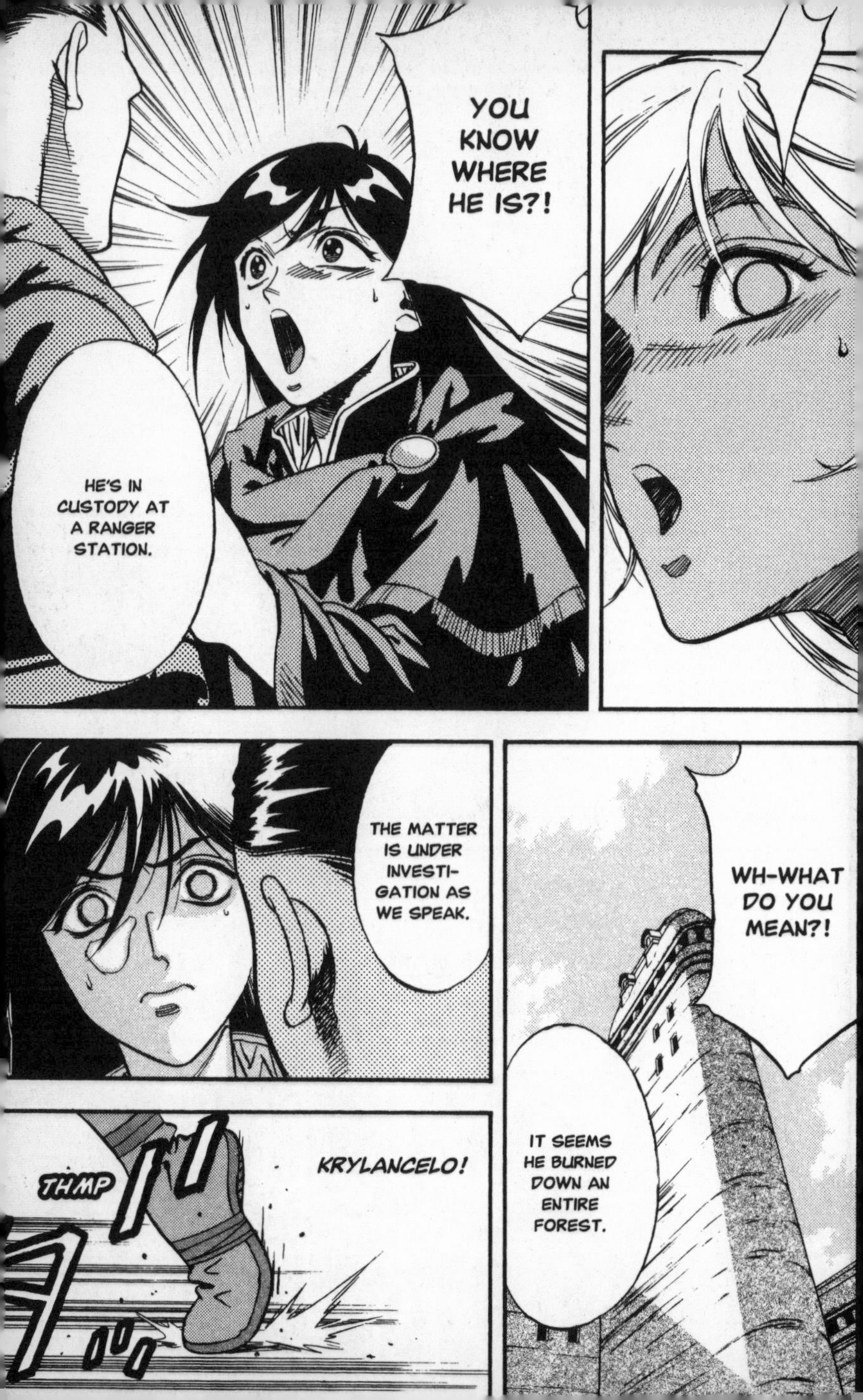
YOU KNOW WHERE HE IS?!
HE'S IN CUSTODY AT A RANGER STATION.
WH-WHAT DO YOU MEAN?!
IT SEEMS HE BURNED DOWN AN ENTIRE FOREST.
THE MATTER IS UNDER INVESTIGATION AS WE SPEAK.
KRYLANCELO!
THMP

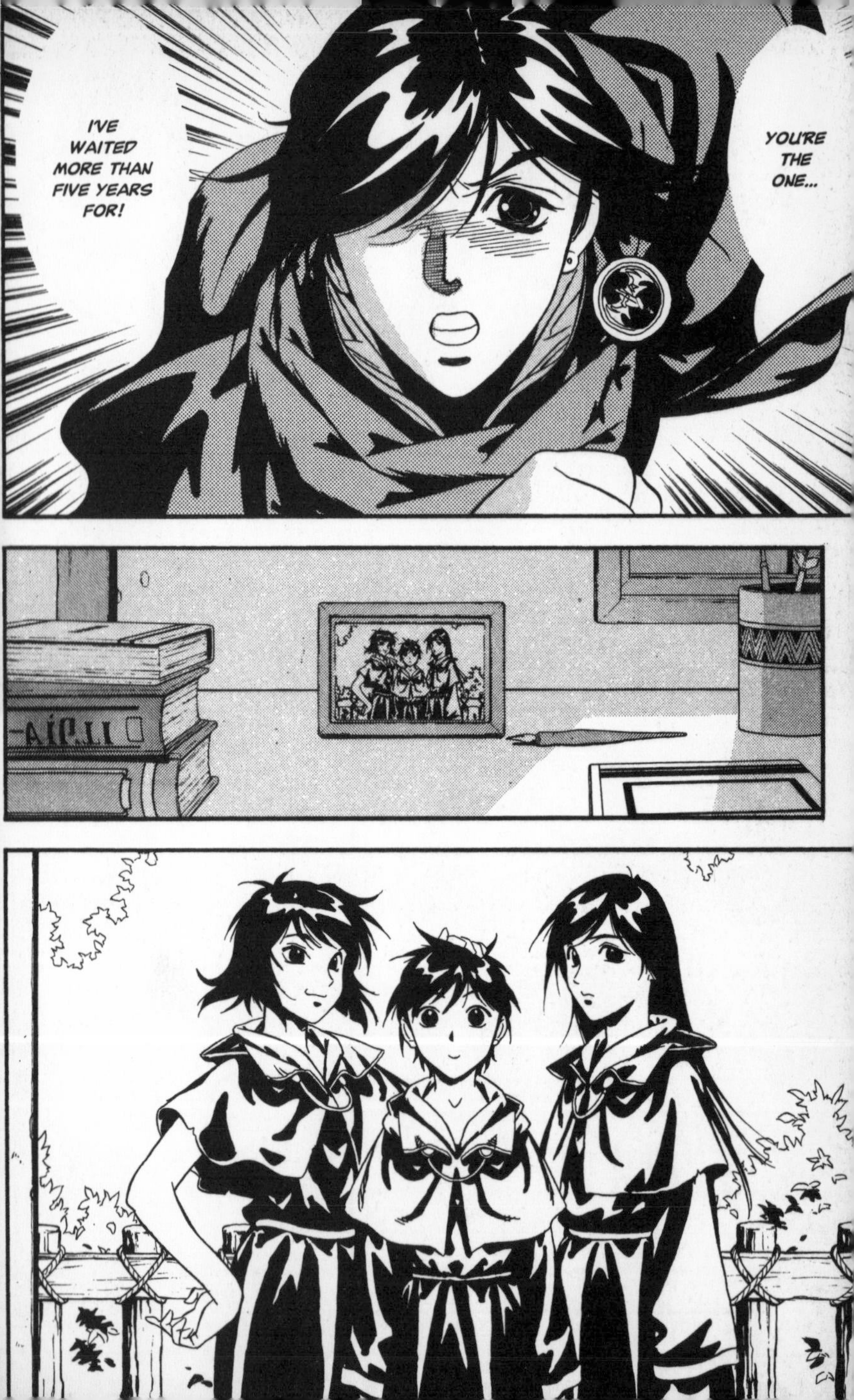
YOU'RE THE ONE...
I'VE WAITED MORE THAN FIVE YEARS FOR!

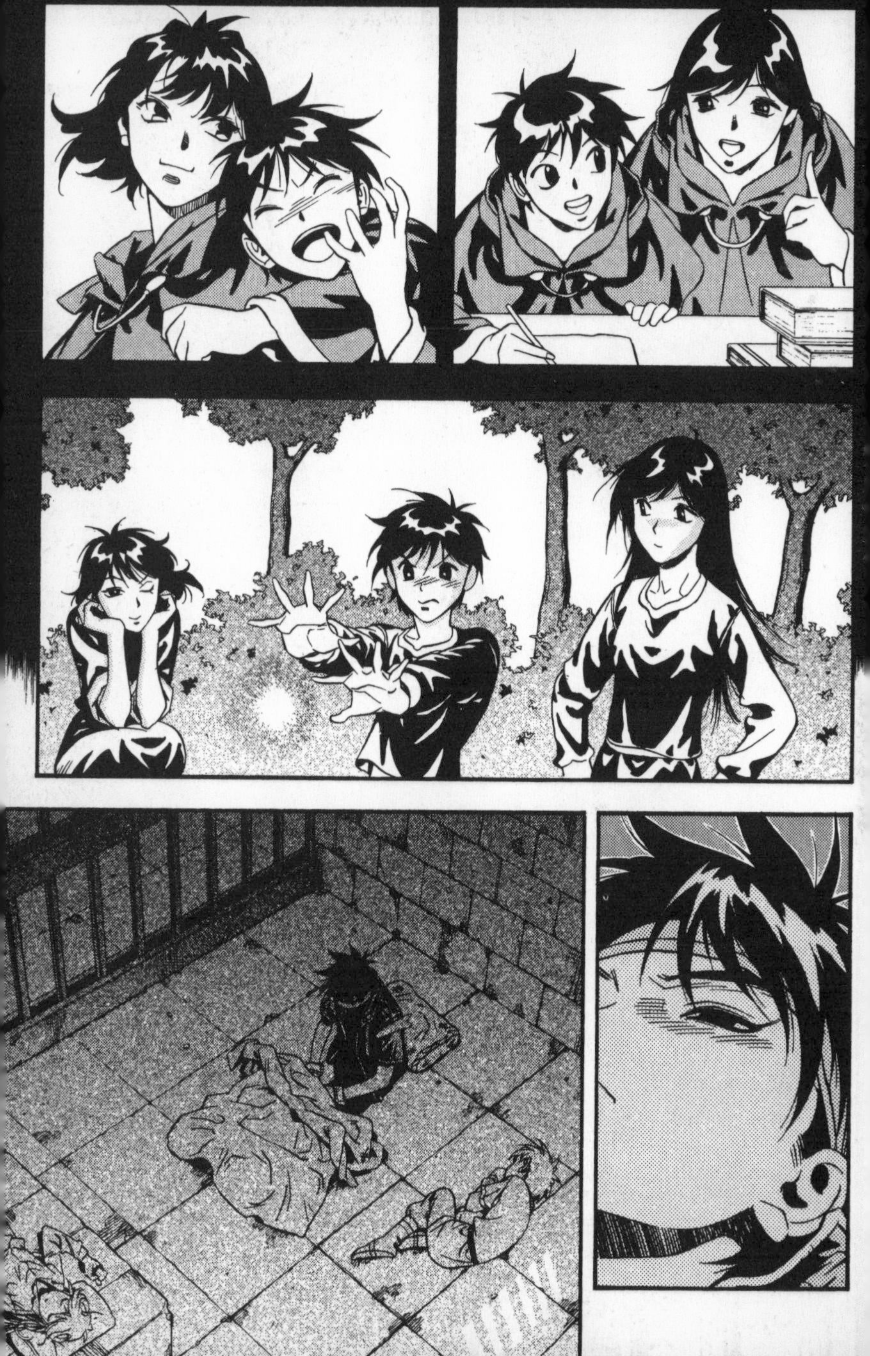

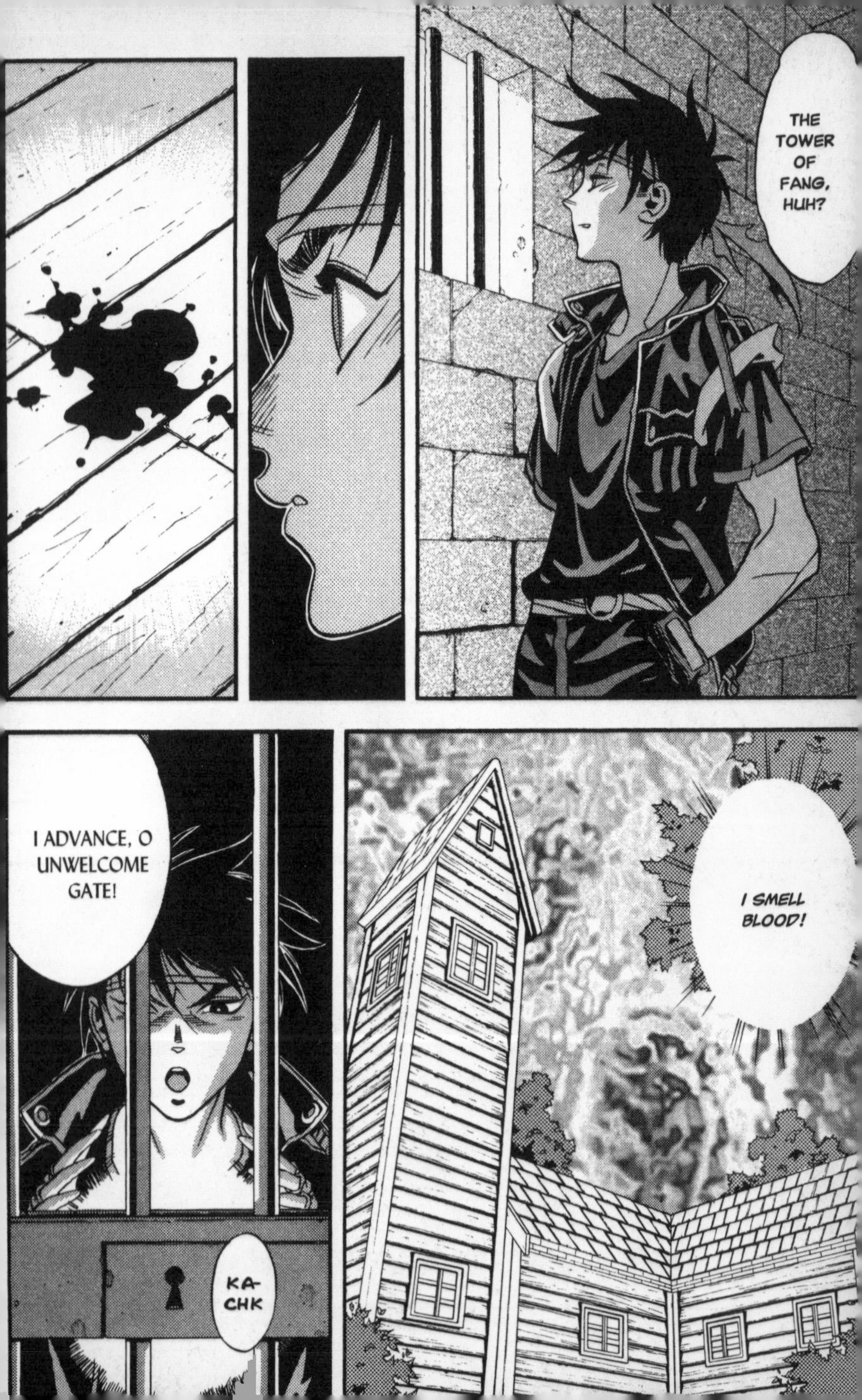
THE TOWER OF FANG, HUH?
I ADVANCE, O UNWELCOME GATE!
KA-CHK
I SMELL BLOOD!

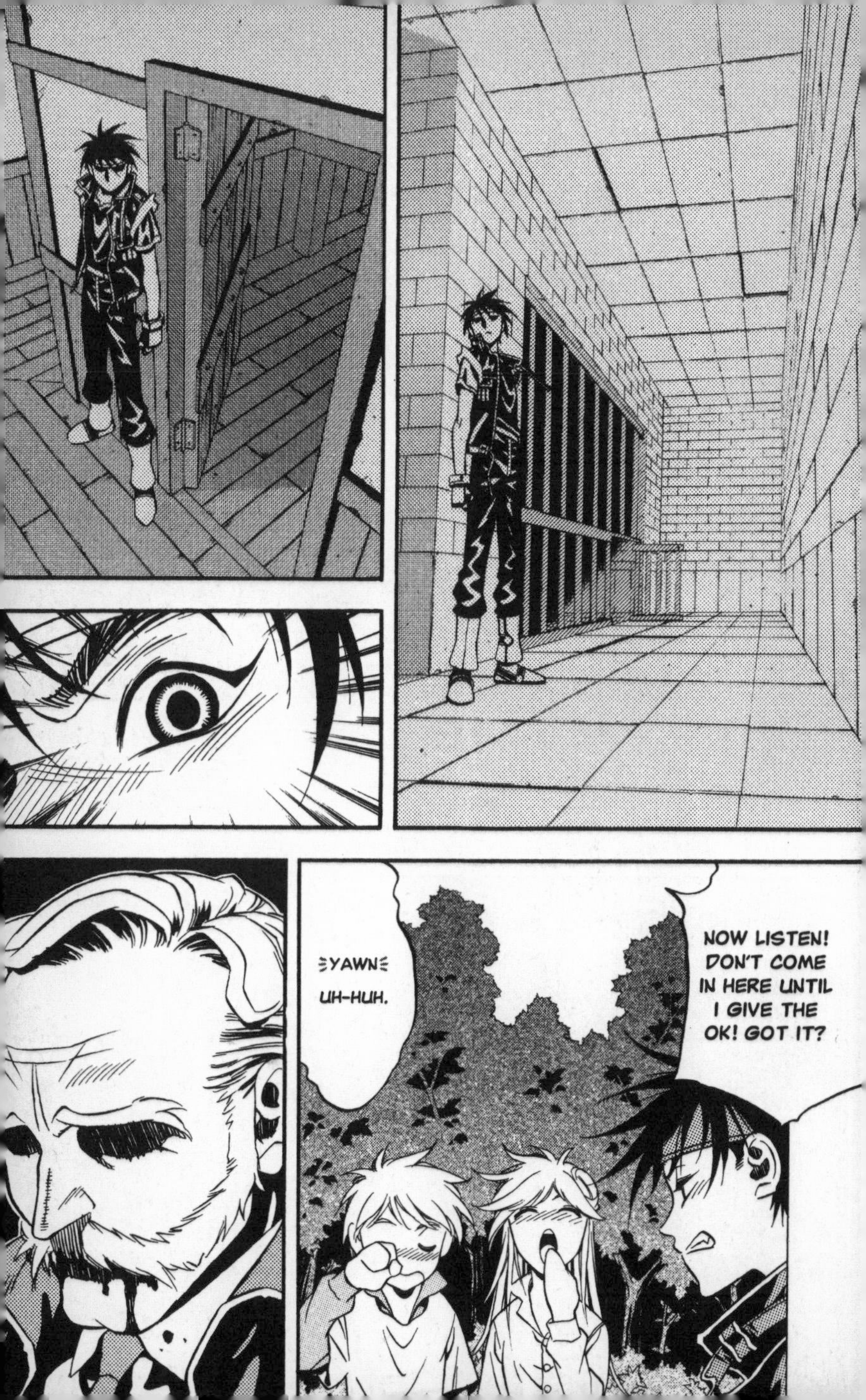

NOW LISTEN! DON'T COME IN HERE UNTIL I GIVE THE OK! GOT IT?
YAWN
UH-HUH.

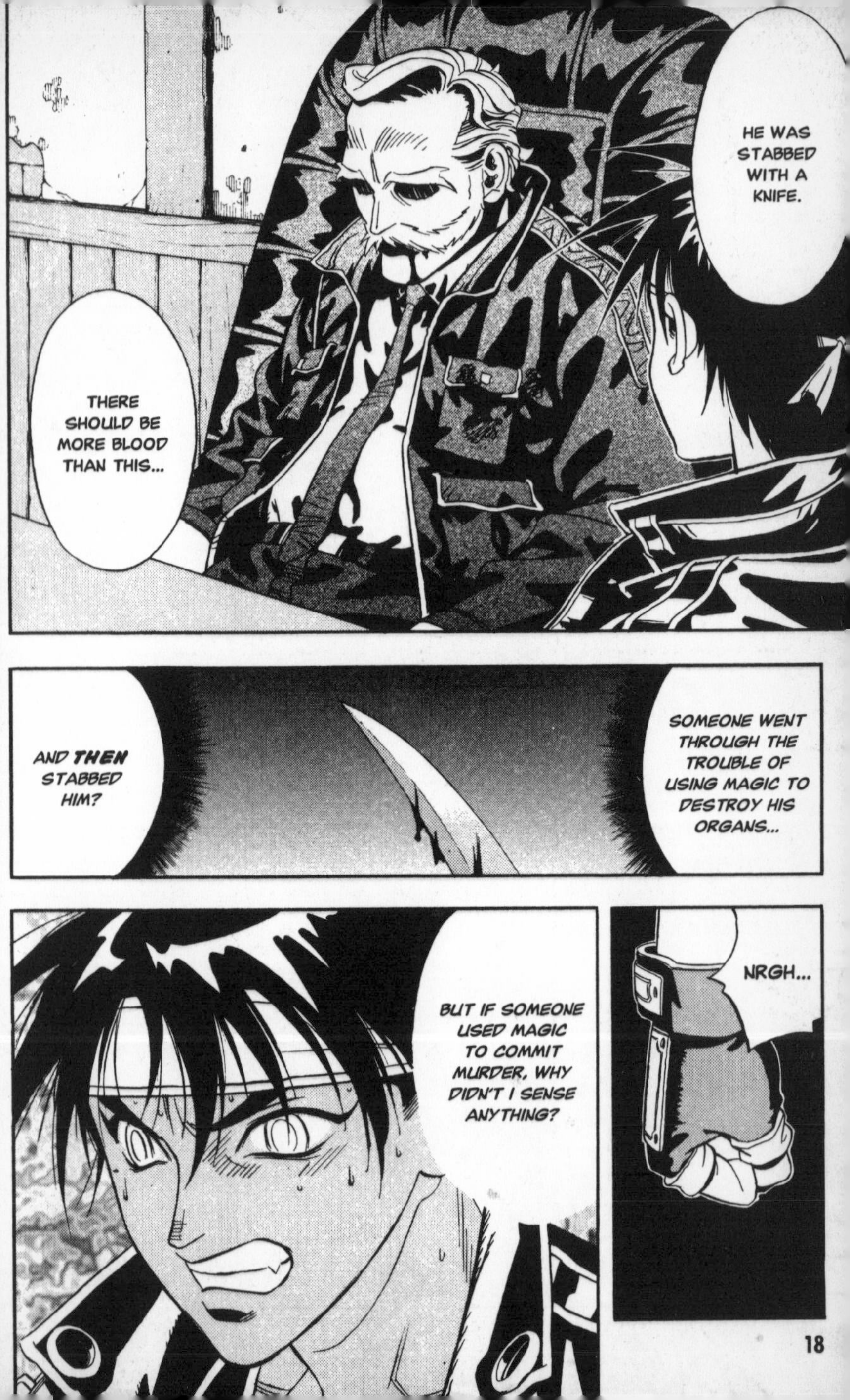
HE WAS STABBED WITH A KNIFE.
THERE SHOULD BE MORE BLOOD THAN THIS...
SOMEONE WENT THROUGH THE TROUBLE OF USING MAGIC TO DESTROY HIS ORGANS...
AND **THEN** STABBED HIM?
NRGH...
BUT IF SOMEONE USED MAGIC TO COMMIT MURDER, WHY DIDN'T I SENSE ANYTHING?

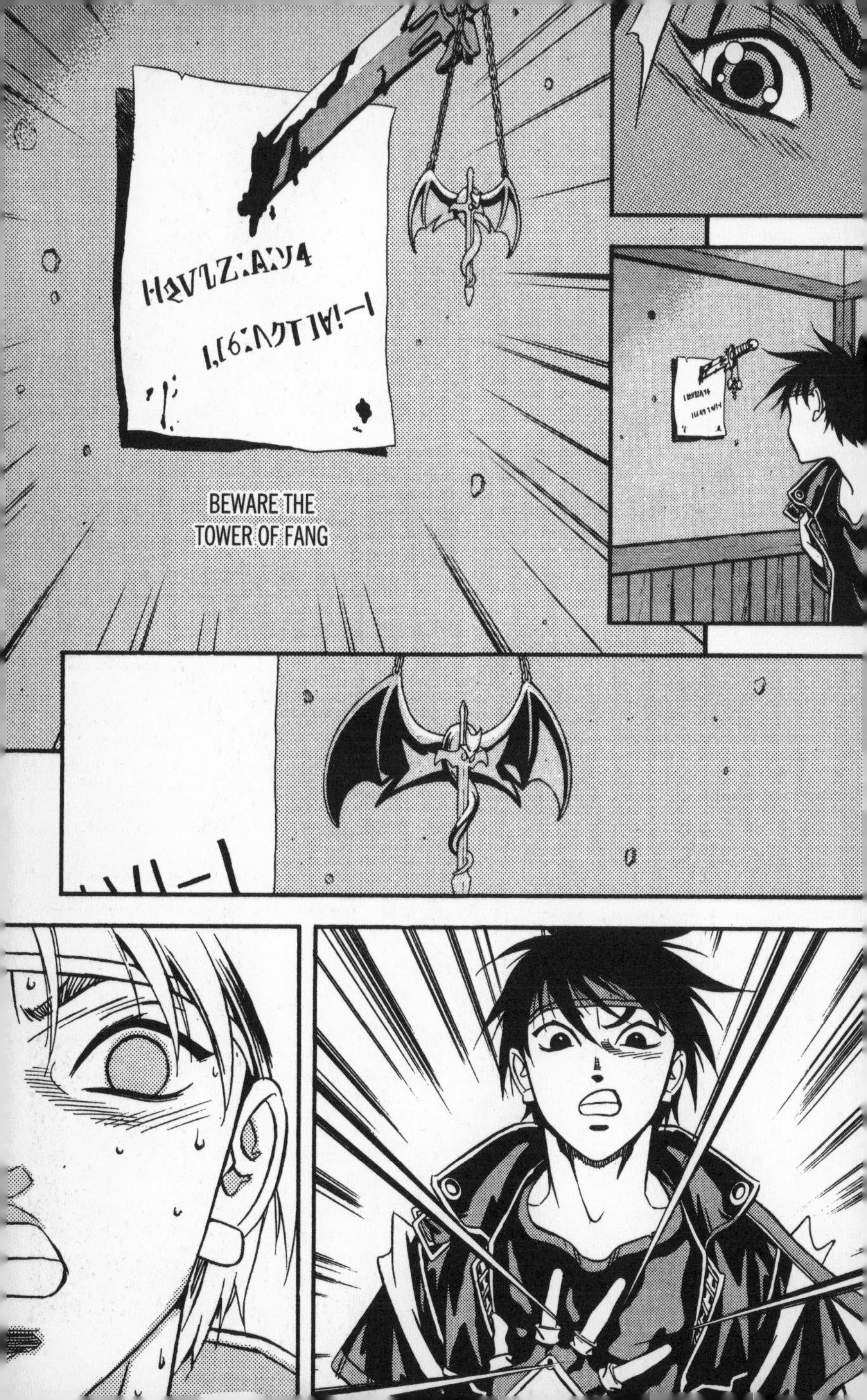

BEWARE THE TOWER OF FANG

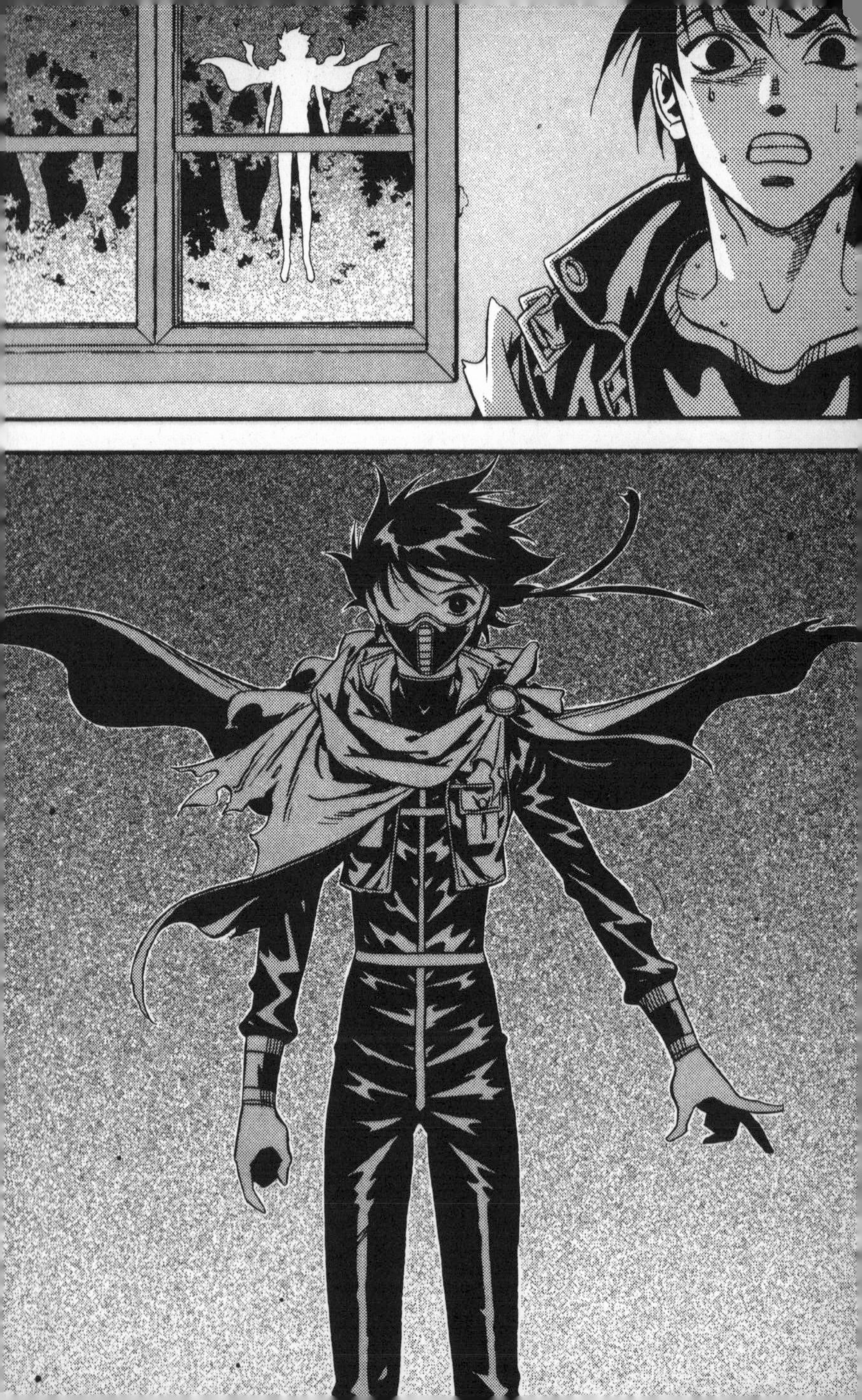

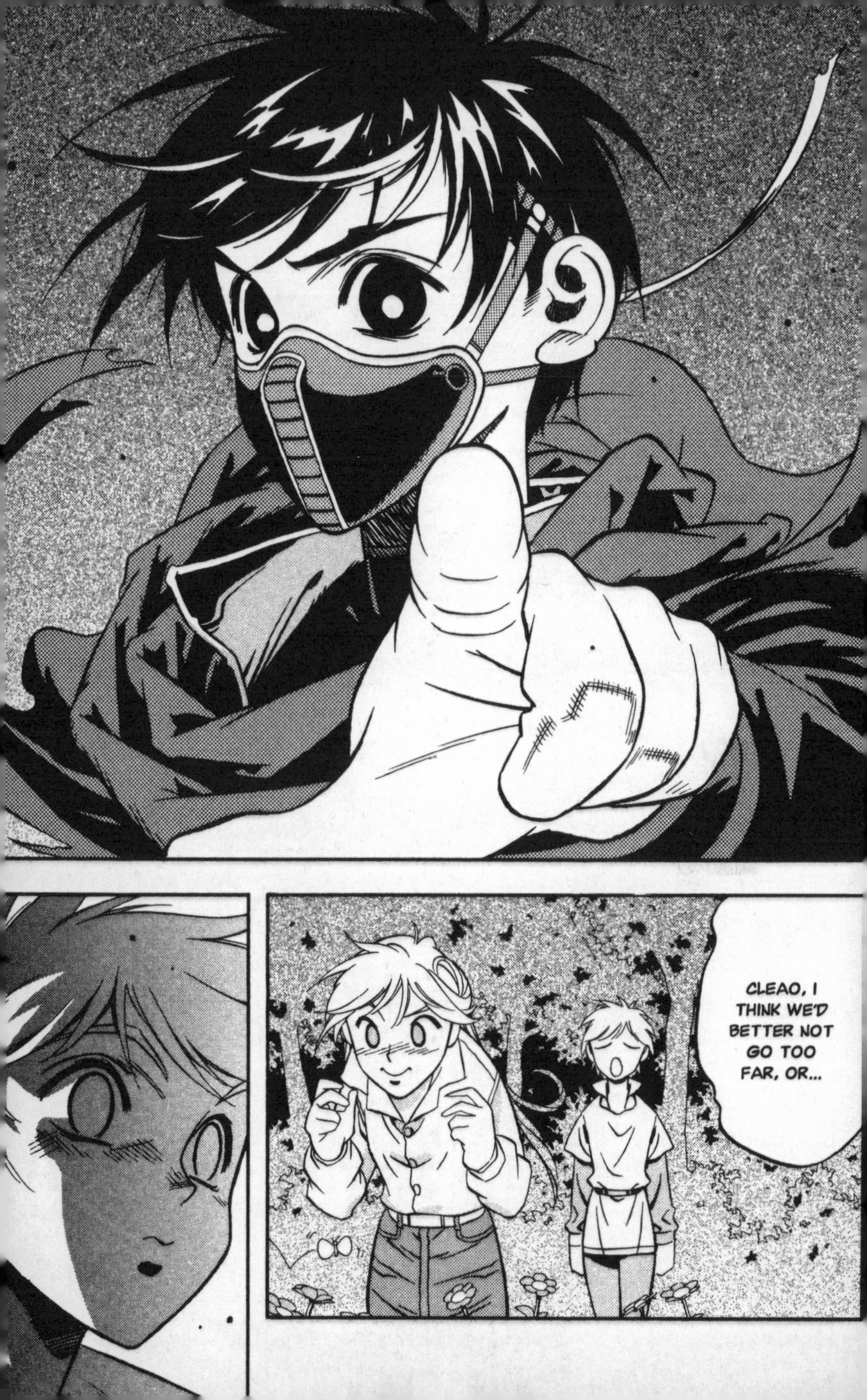
CLEAO, I THINK WE'D BETTER NOT GO TOO FAR, OR...

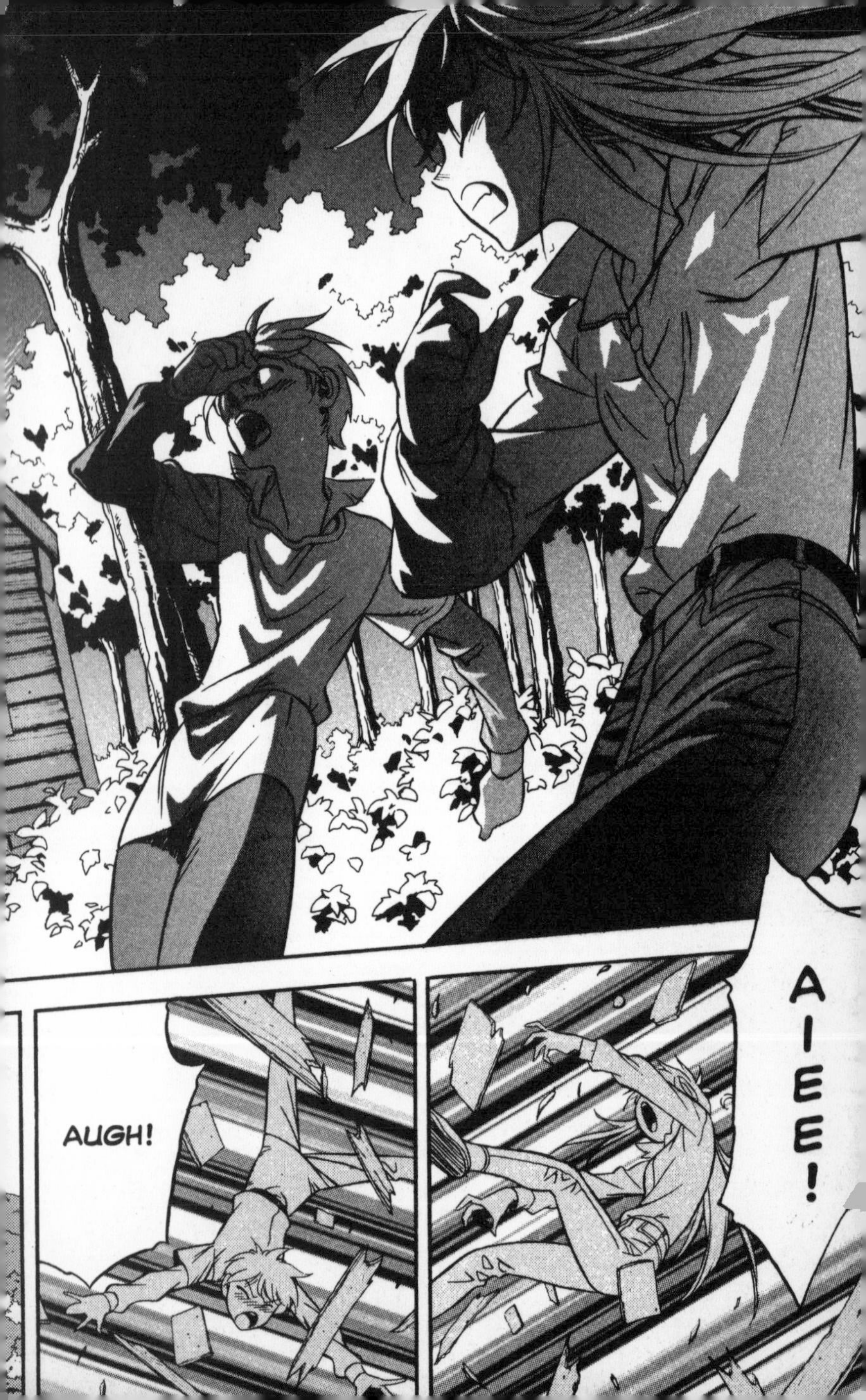
AIEE!
AUGH!

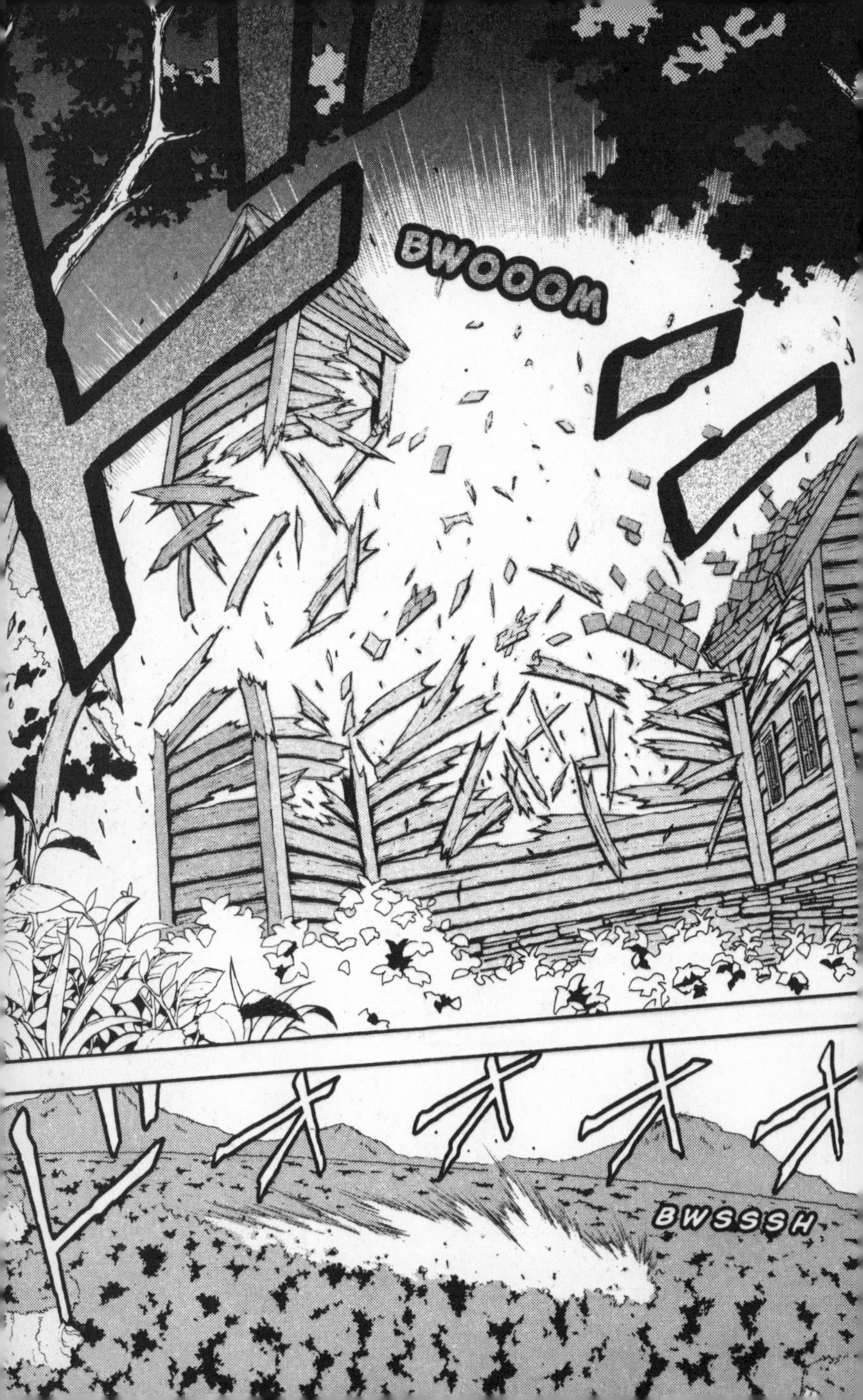
BWOOOM
BWSSSH

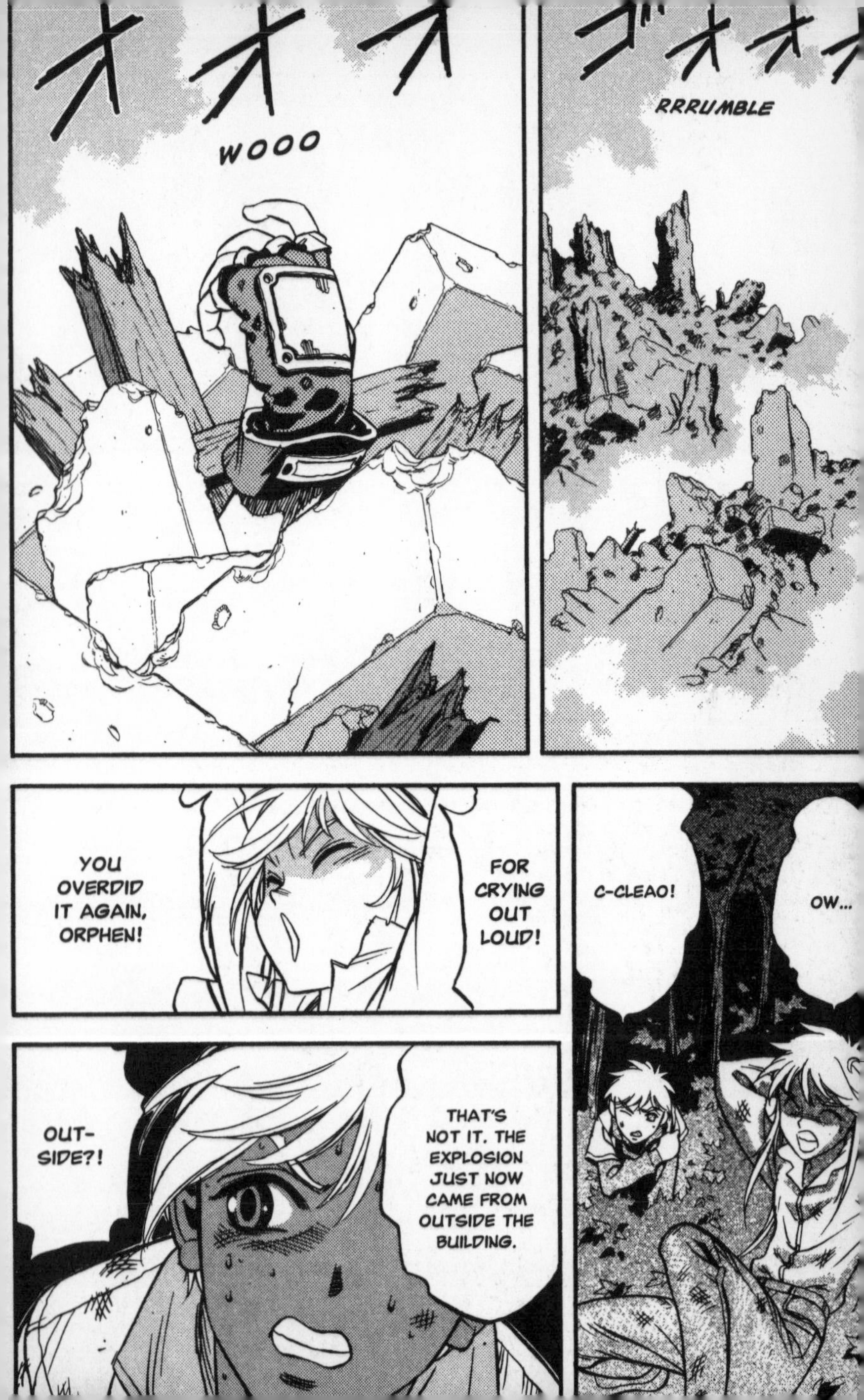
RRRUMBLE
WOOO
OW...
C-CLEAO!
FOR CRYING OUT LOUD!
YOU OVERDID IT AGAIN, ORPHEN!
THAT'S NOT IT. THE EXPLOSION JUST NOW CAME FROM OUTSIDE THE BUILDING.
OUT-SIDE?!

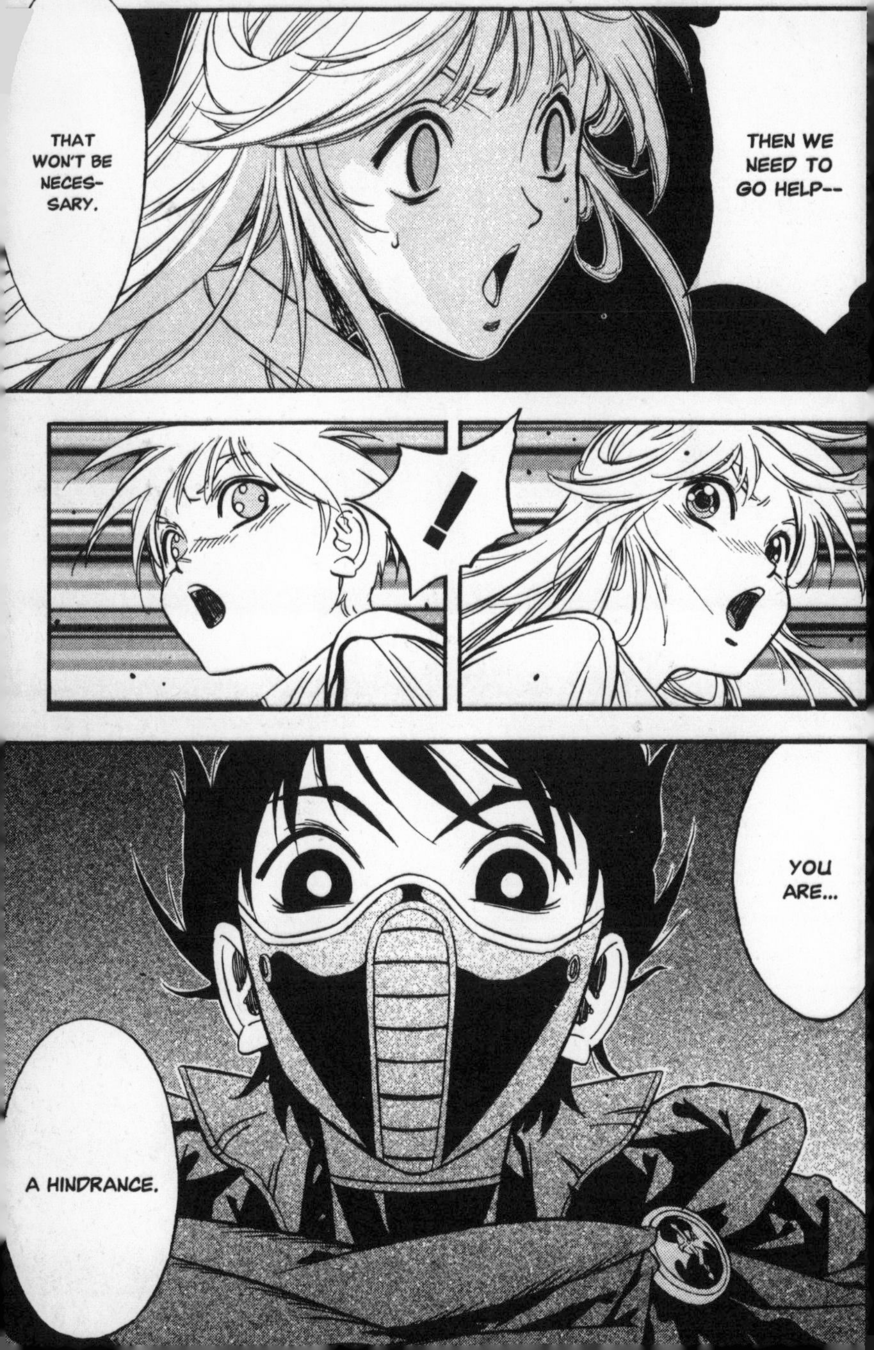
THEN WE NEED TO GO HELP--
THAT WON'T BE NECES-SARY.
!
YOU ARE...
A HINDRANCE.

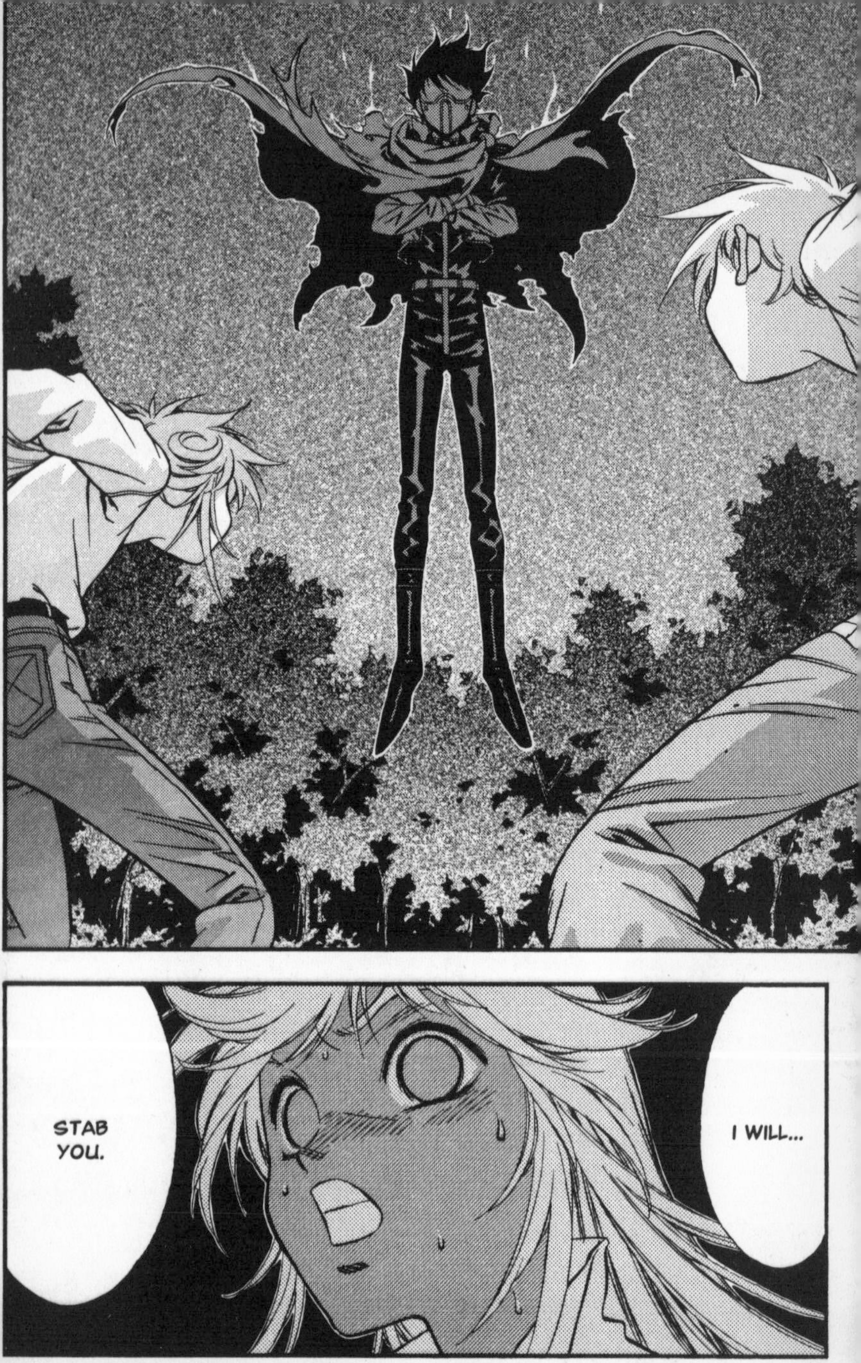
I WILL...
STAB YOU.

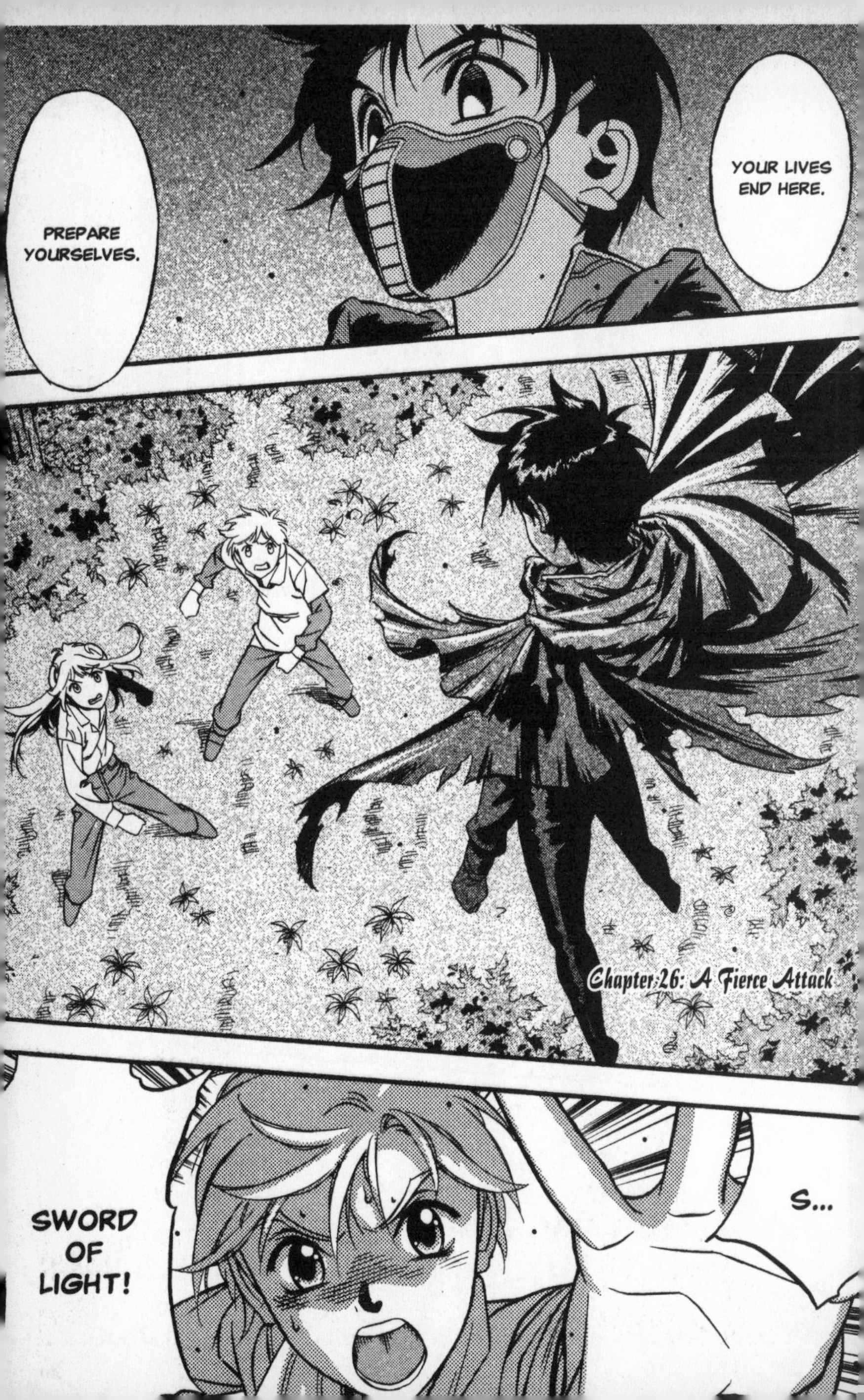
YOUR LIVES END HERE.
PREPARE YOURSELVES.
Chapter 26: A Fierce Attack
S...
SWORD OF LIGHT!

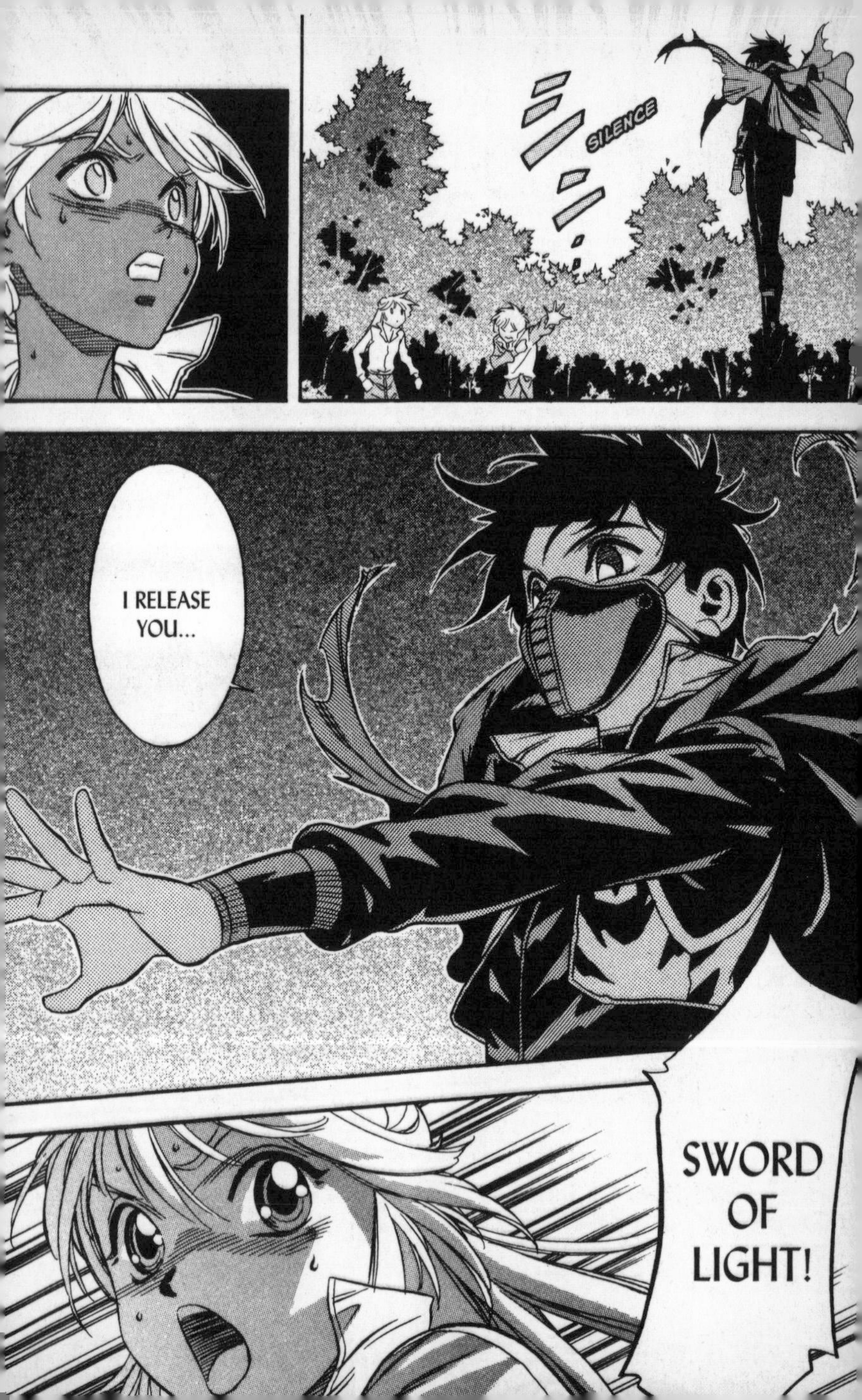
SILENCE
I RELEASE YOU...
SWORD OF LIGHT!

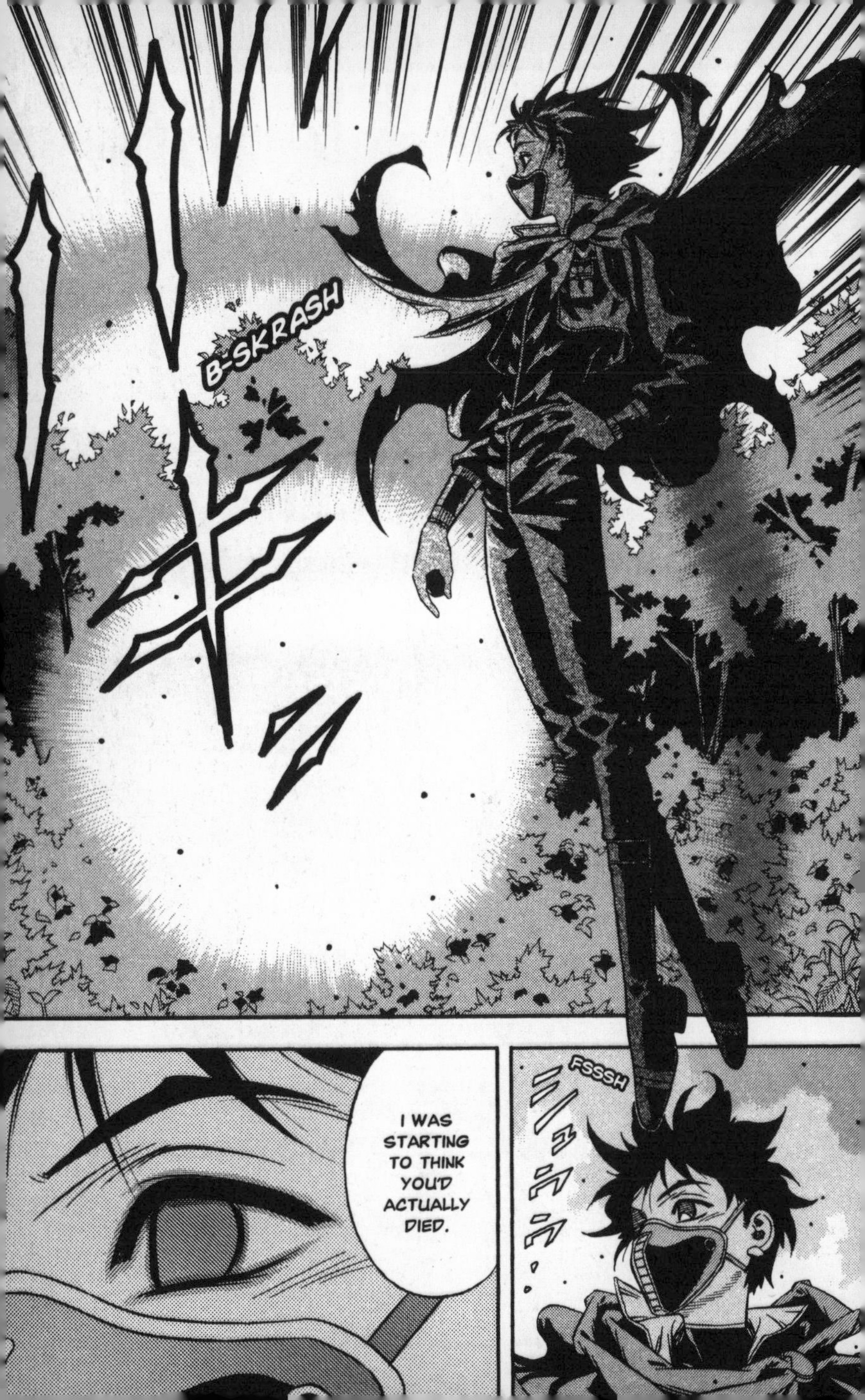
B-SKRASH
FSSSH
I WAS STARTING TO THINK YOU'D ACTUALLY DIED.

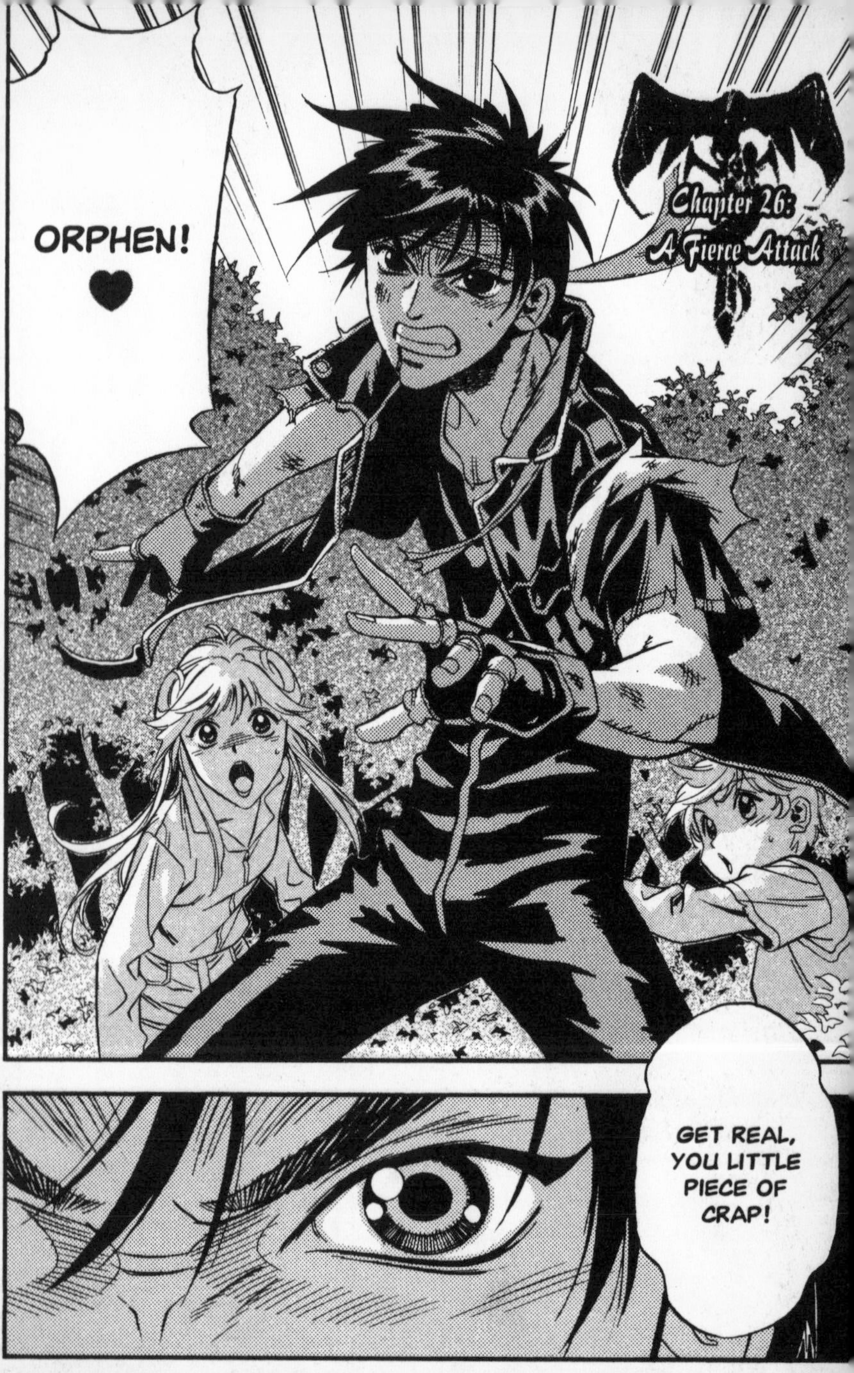

ORPHEN! ♥
Chapter 26:
A Fierce Attack
GET REAL, YOU LITTLE PIECE OF CRAP!

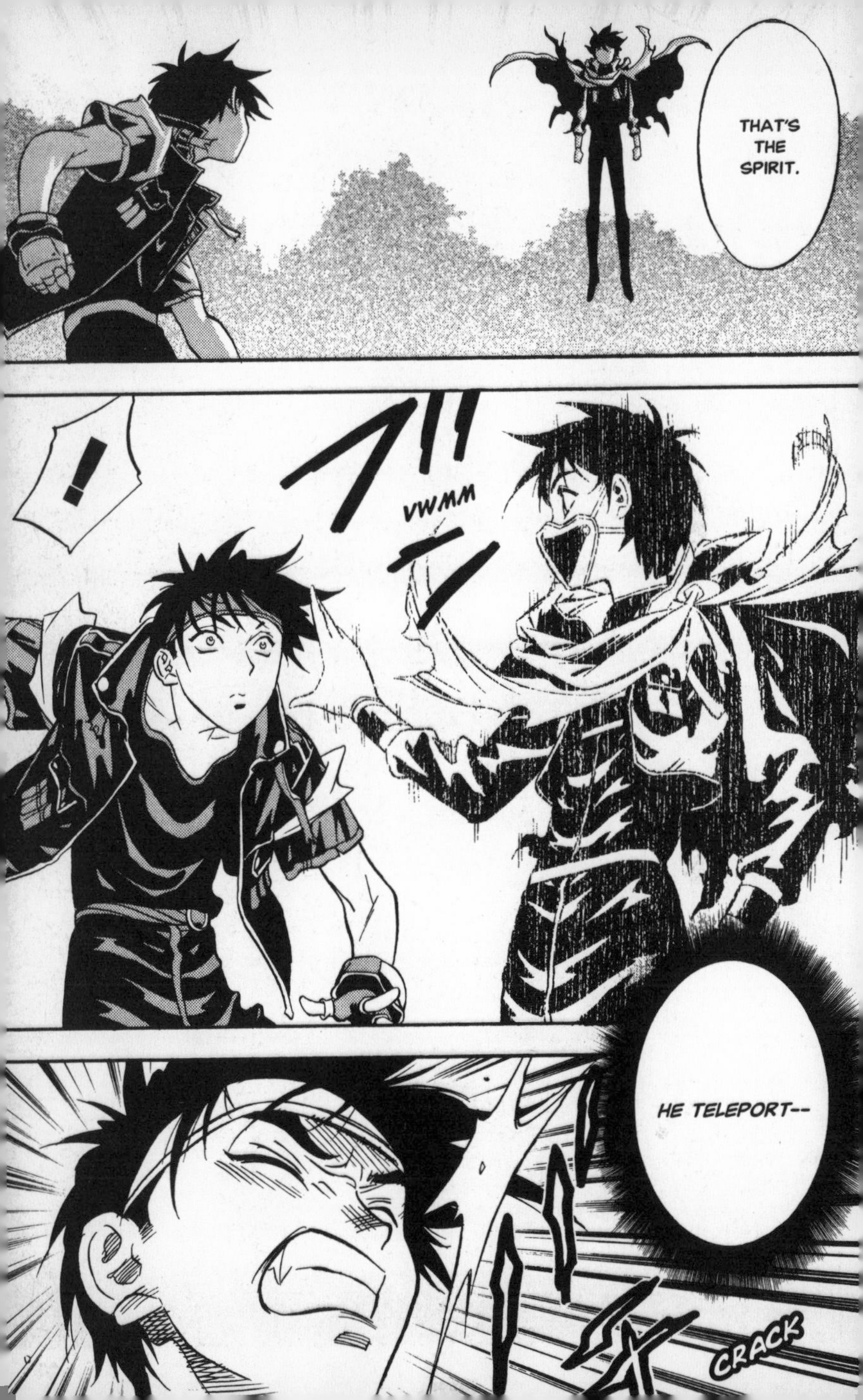
THAT'S THE SPIRIT.
!
VWMM
HE TELEPORT--
CRACK

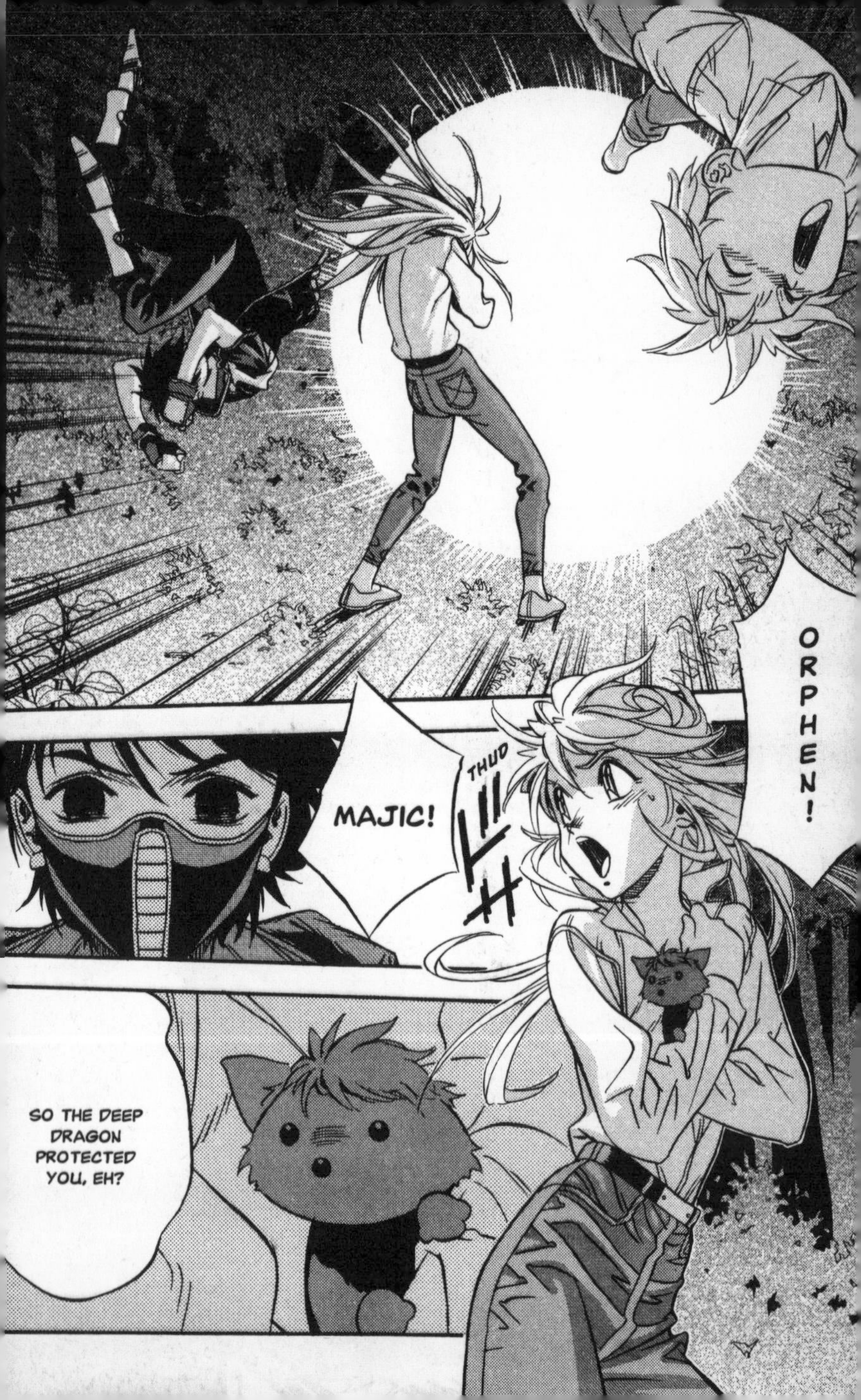
ORPHEN!
THUD
MAJIC!
SO THE DEEP DRAGON PROTECTED YOU, EH?

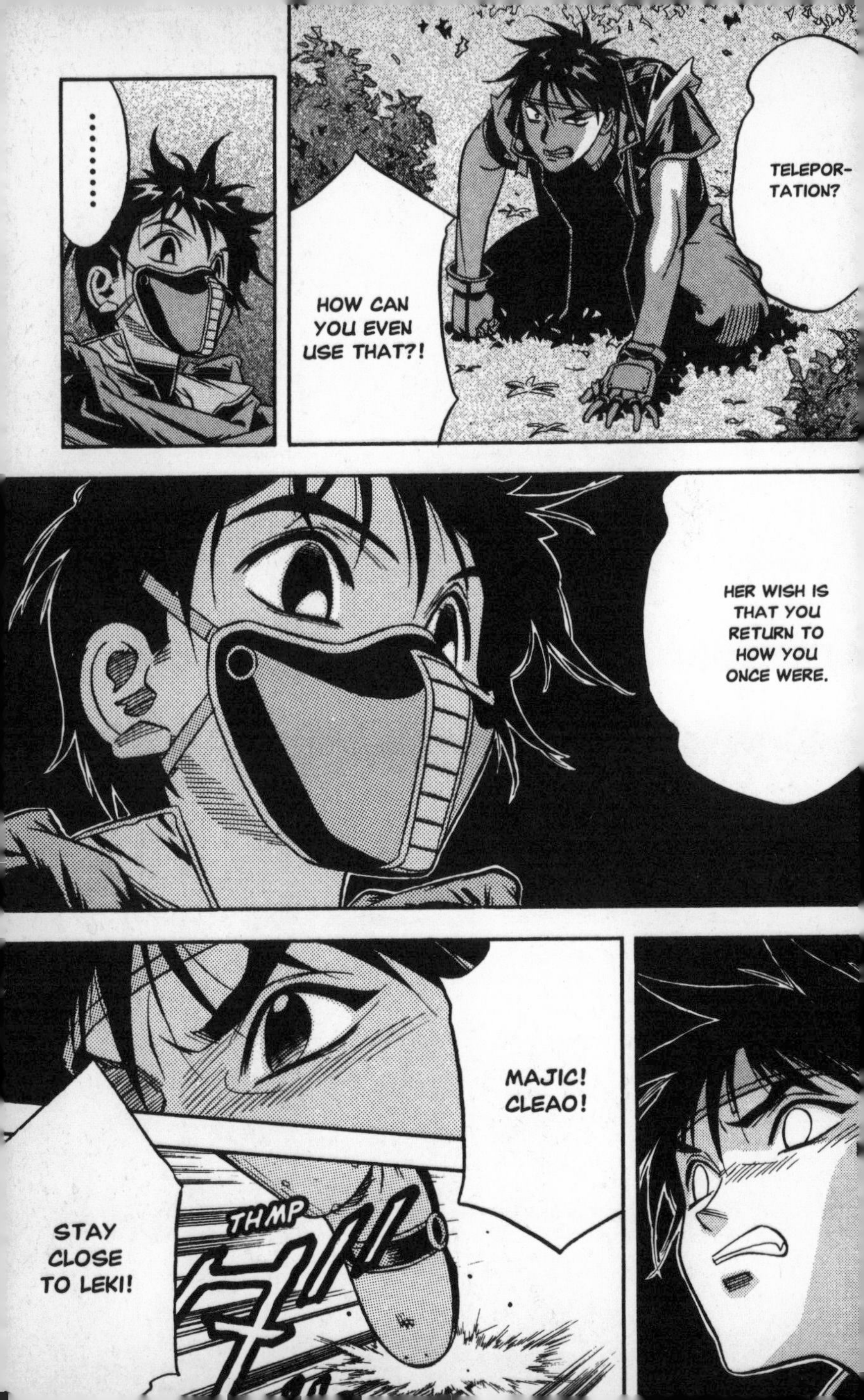
TELEPOR-TATION?
HOW CAN YOU EVEN USE THAT?!
......
HER WISH IS THAT YOU RETURN TO HOW YOU ONCE WERE.
MAJIC! CLEAO!
THMP
STAY CLOSE TO LEKI!

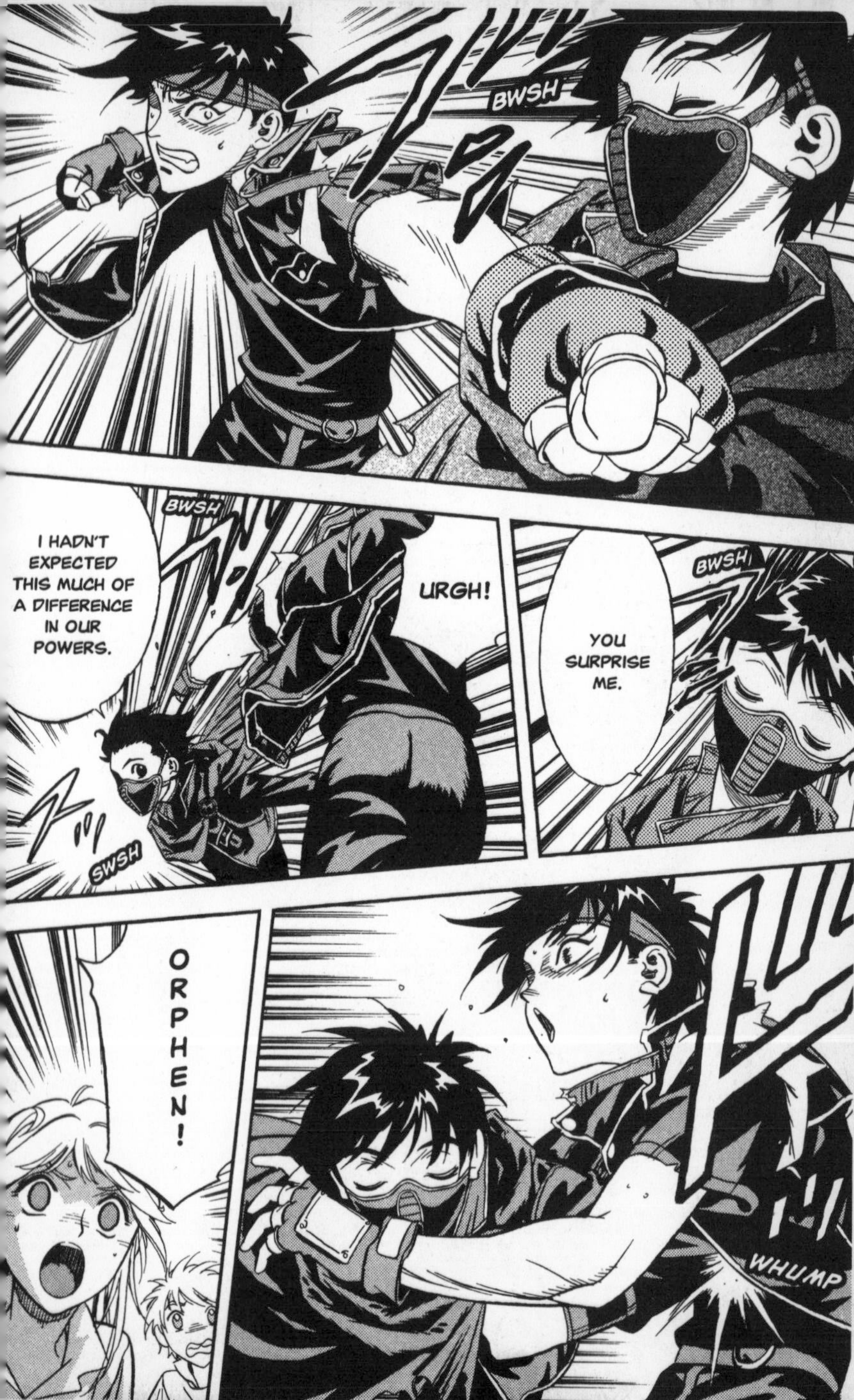
BWSH
BWSH
YOU SURPRISE ME.
URGH!
BWSH
I HADN'T EXPECTED THIS MUCH OF A DIFFERENCE IN OUR POWERS.
SWSH
WHUMP
ORPHEN!

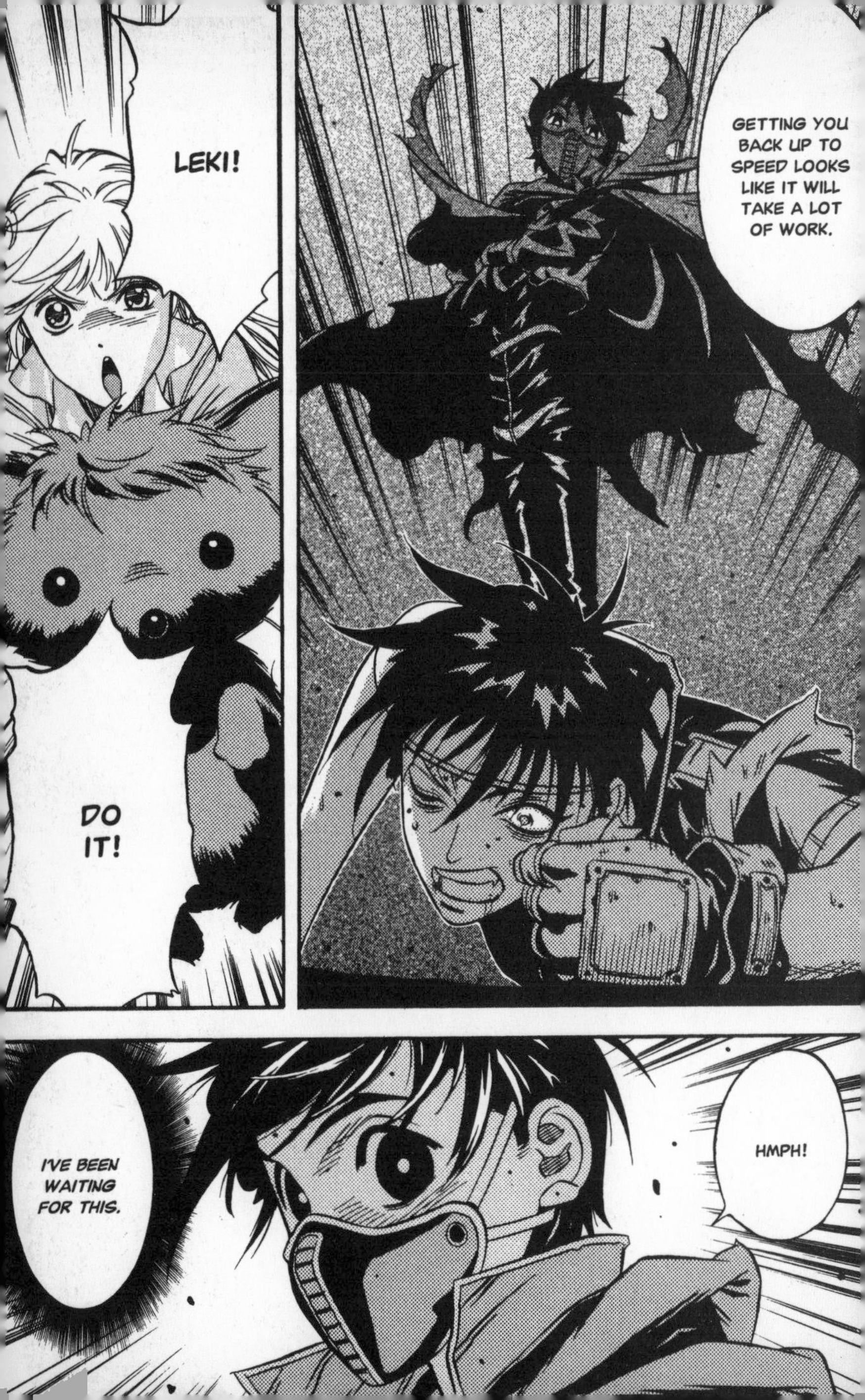
GETTING YOU BACK UP TO SPEED LOOKS LIKE IT WILL TAKE A LOT OF WORK.
LEKI!
DO IT!
HMPH!
I'VE BEEN WAITING FOR THIS.

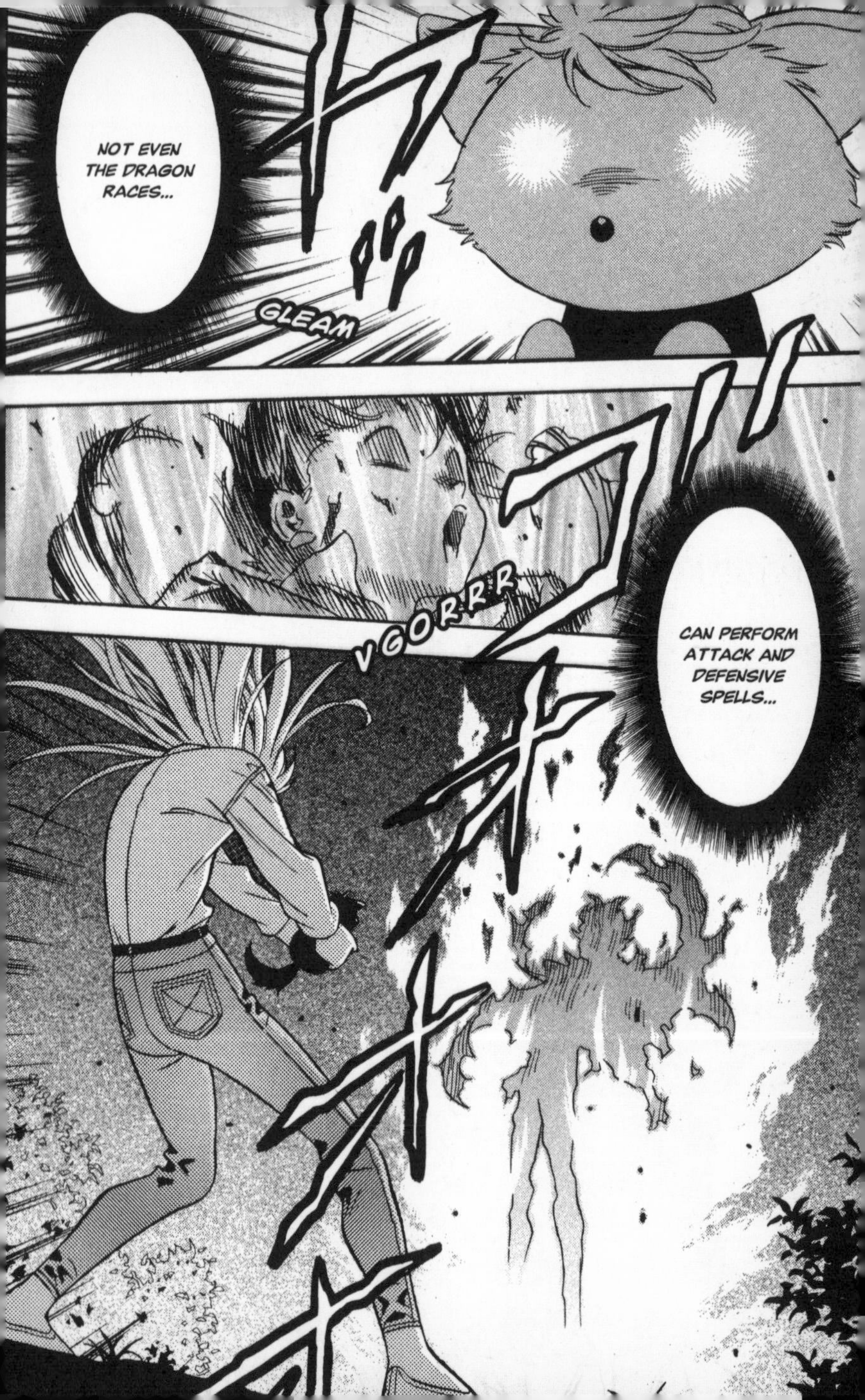

NOT EVEN THE DRAGON RACES...
GLEAM
CAN PERFORM ATTACK AND DEFENSIVE SPELLS...
VGORRRR

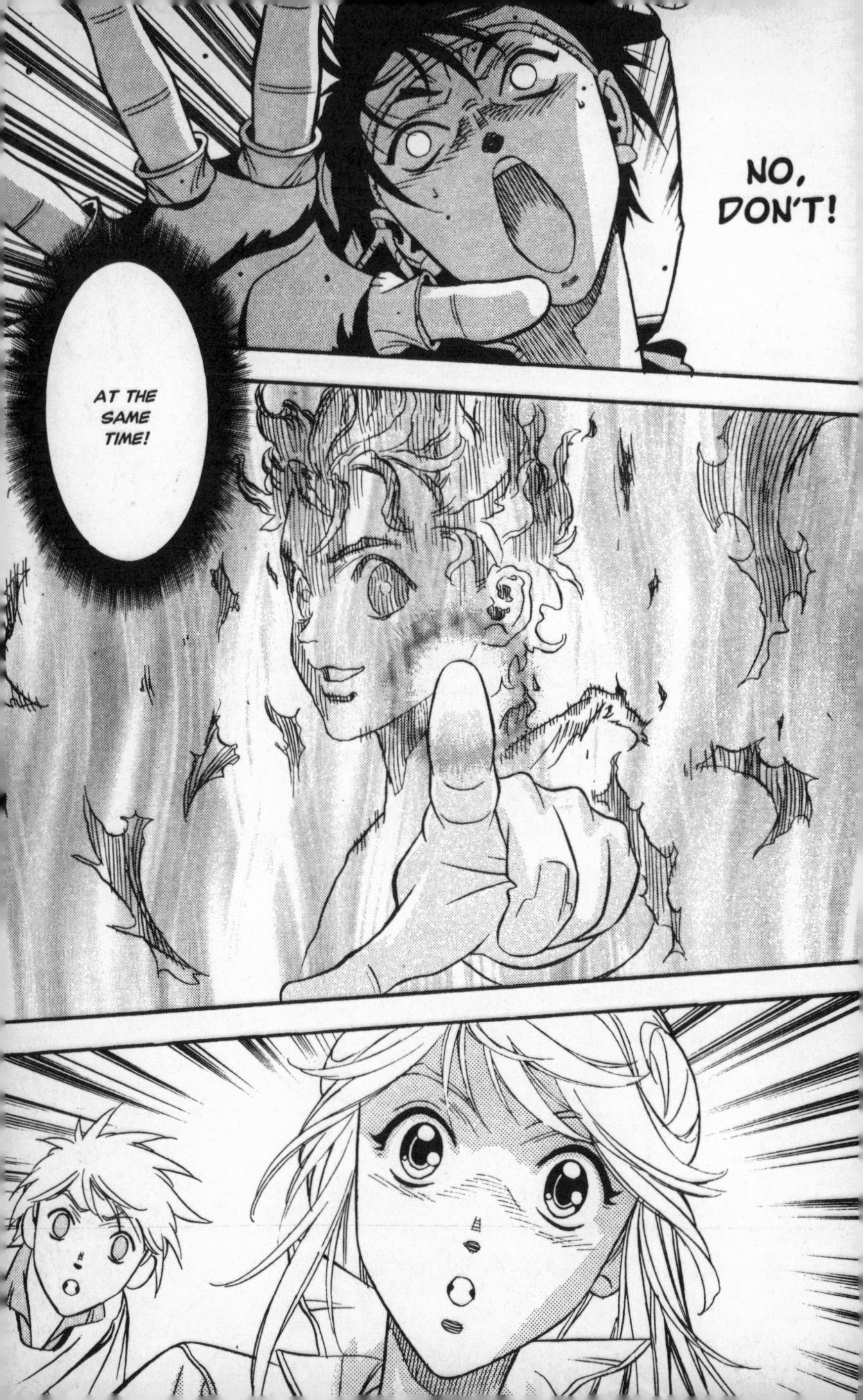
NO, DON'T!
AT THE SAME TIME!

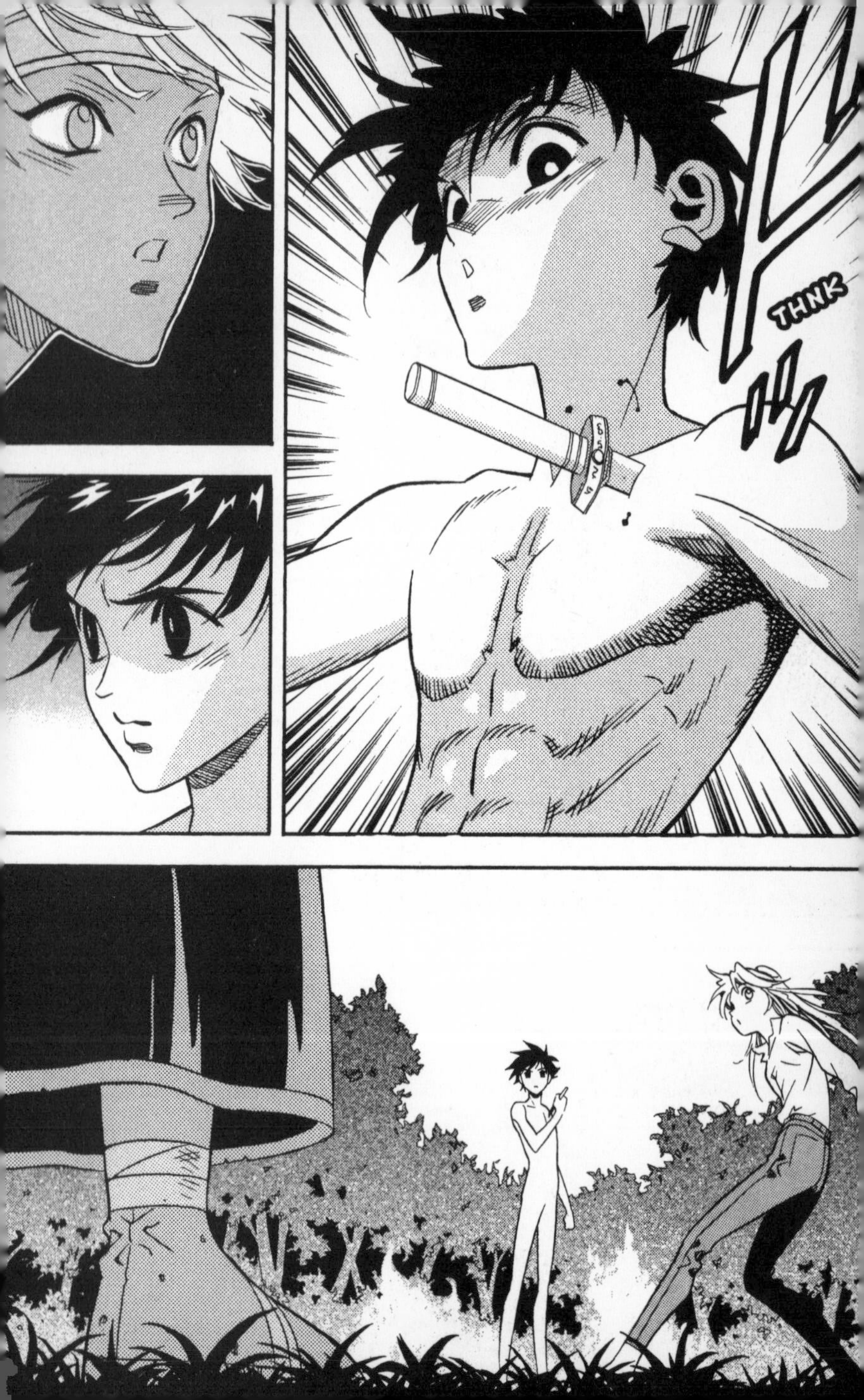
THNK

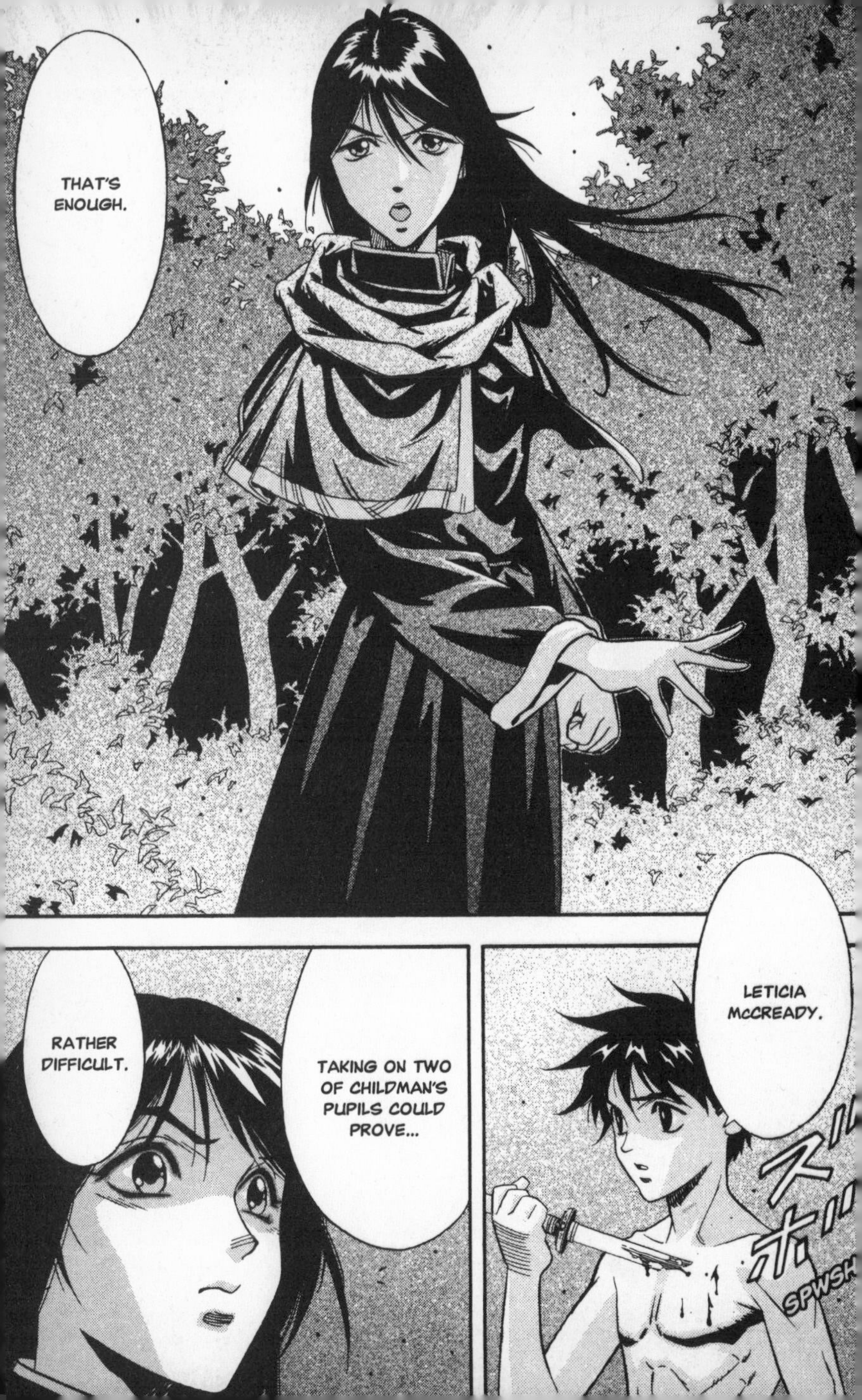
THAT'S ENOUGH.
LETICIA McCREADY.
SPWSH
TAKING ON TWO OF CHILDMAN'S PUPILS COULD PROVE...
RATHER DIFFICULT.

FWOOOO

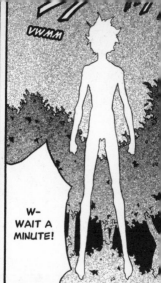
W-WAIT A MINUTE!

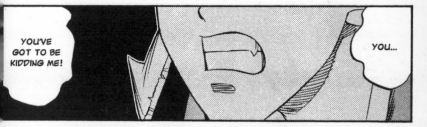
YOU'VE GOT TO BE KIDDING ME!

YOU...

IT WAS...

THAT KID'S FACE!

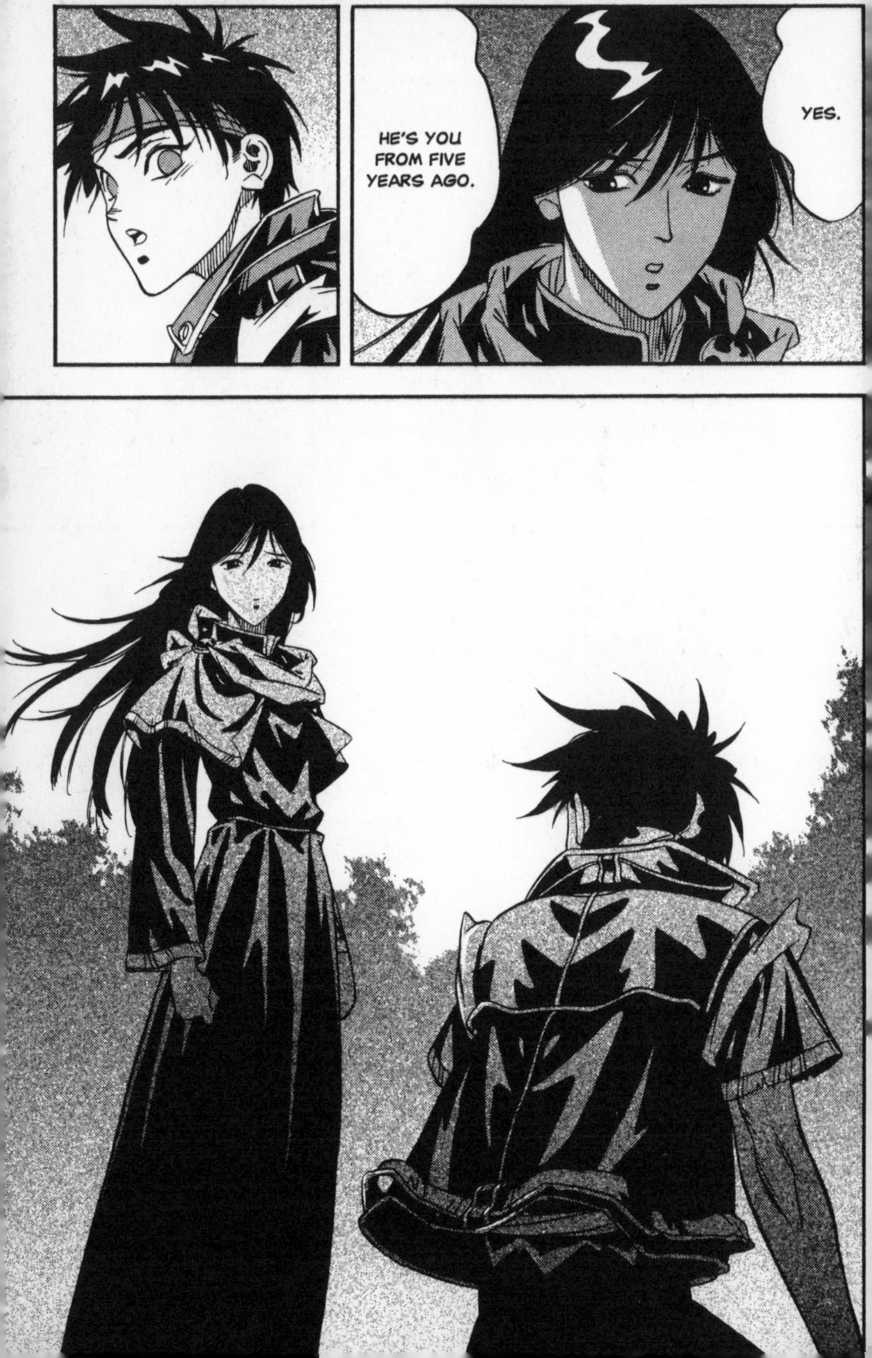
YES.
HE'S YOU FROM FIVE YEARS AGO.

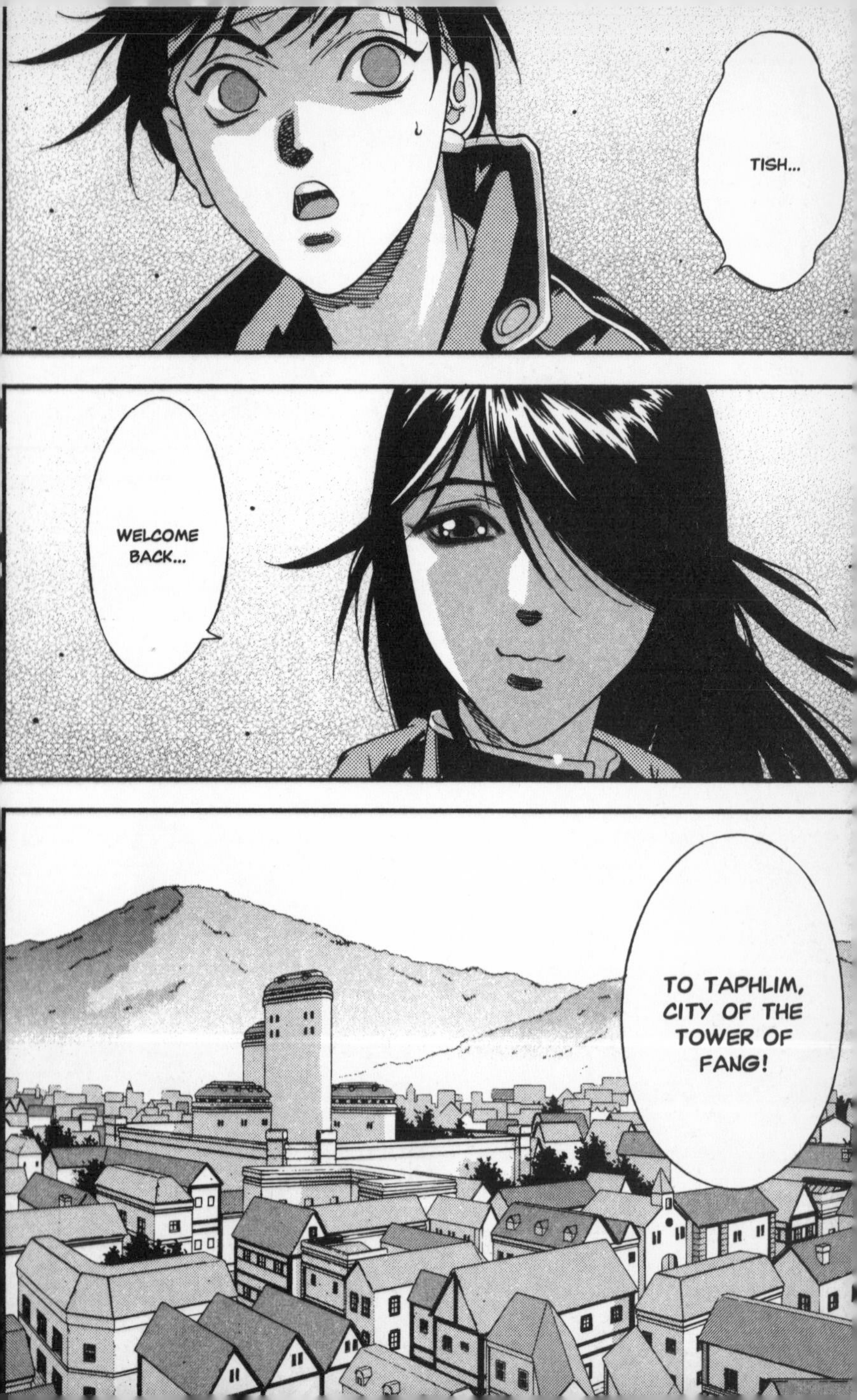
TISH...
WELCOME BACK...
TO TAPHLIM, CITY OF THE TOWER OF FANG!

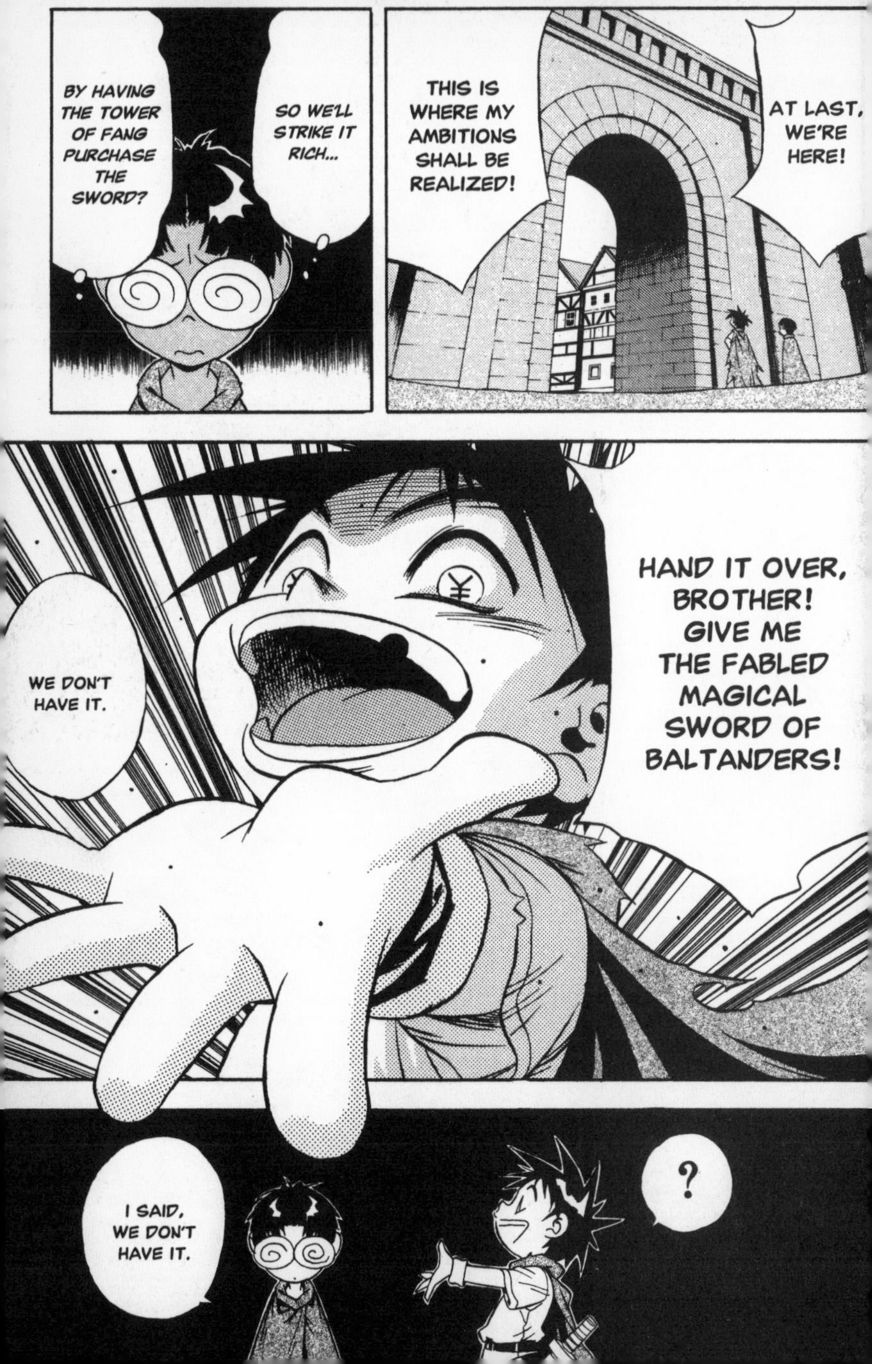
AT LAST, WE'RE HERE!
THIS IS WHERE MY AMBITIONS SHALL BE REALIZED!
SO WE'LL STRIKE IT RICH...
BY HAVING THE TOWER OF FANG PURCHASE THE SWORD?
HAND IT OVER, BROTHER! GIVE ME THE FABLED MAGICAL SWORD OF BALTANDERS!
WE DON'T HAVE IT.
?
I SAID, WE DON'T HAVE IT.

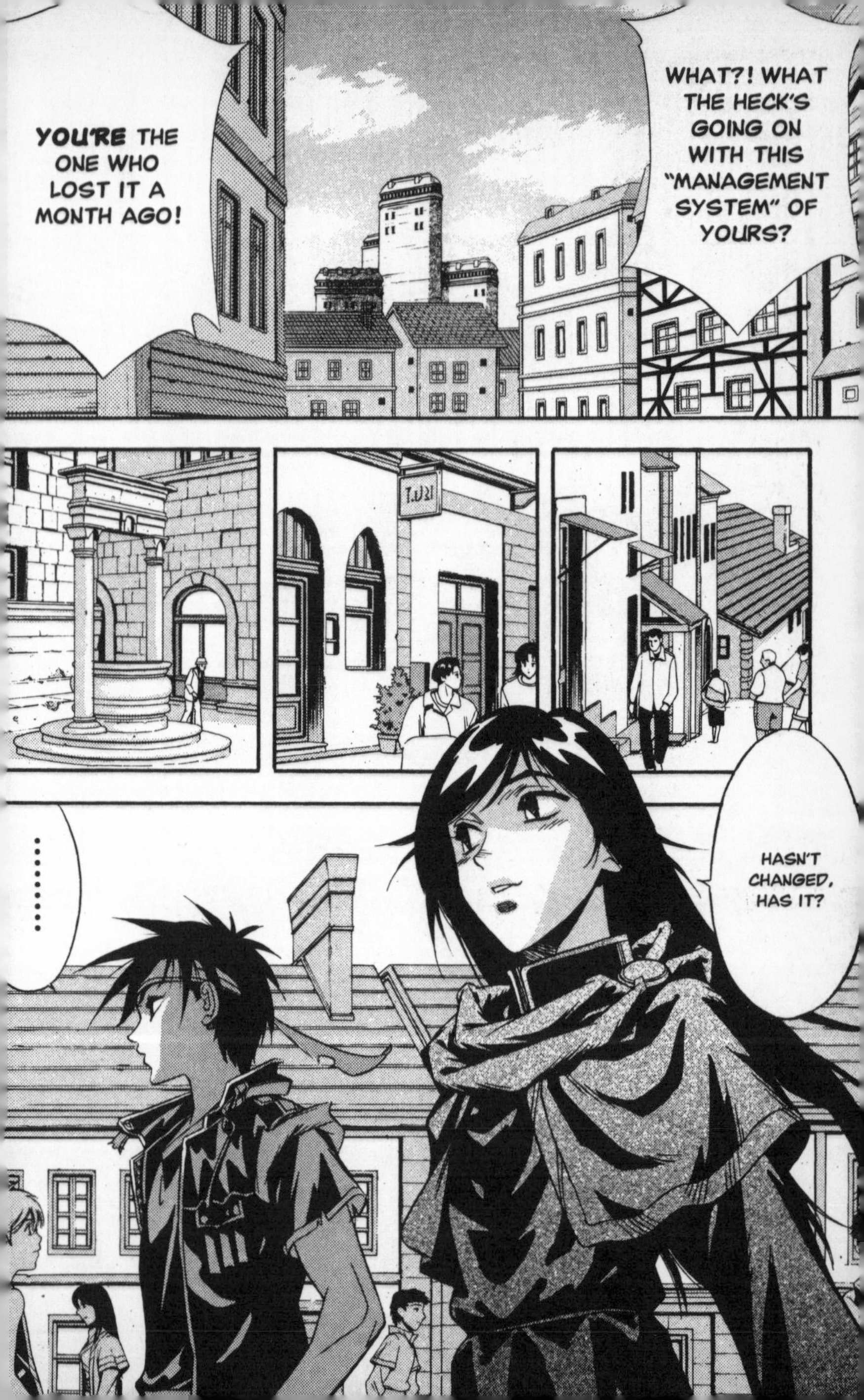
WHAT?! WHAT THE HECK'S GOING ON WITH THIS "MANAGEMENT SYSTEM" OF YOURS?
YOU'RE THE ONE WHO LOST IT A MONTH AGO!
HASN'T CHANGED, HAS IT?
....

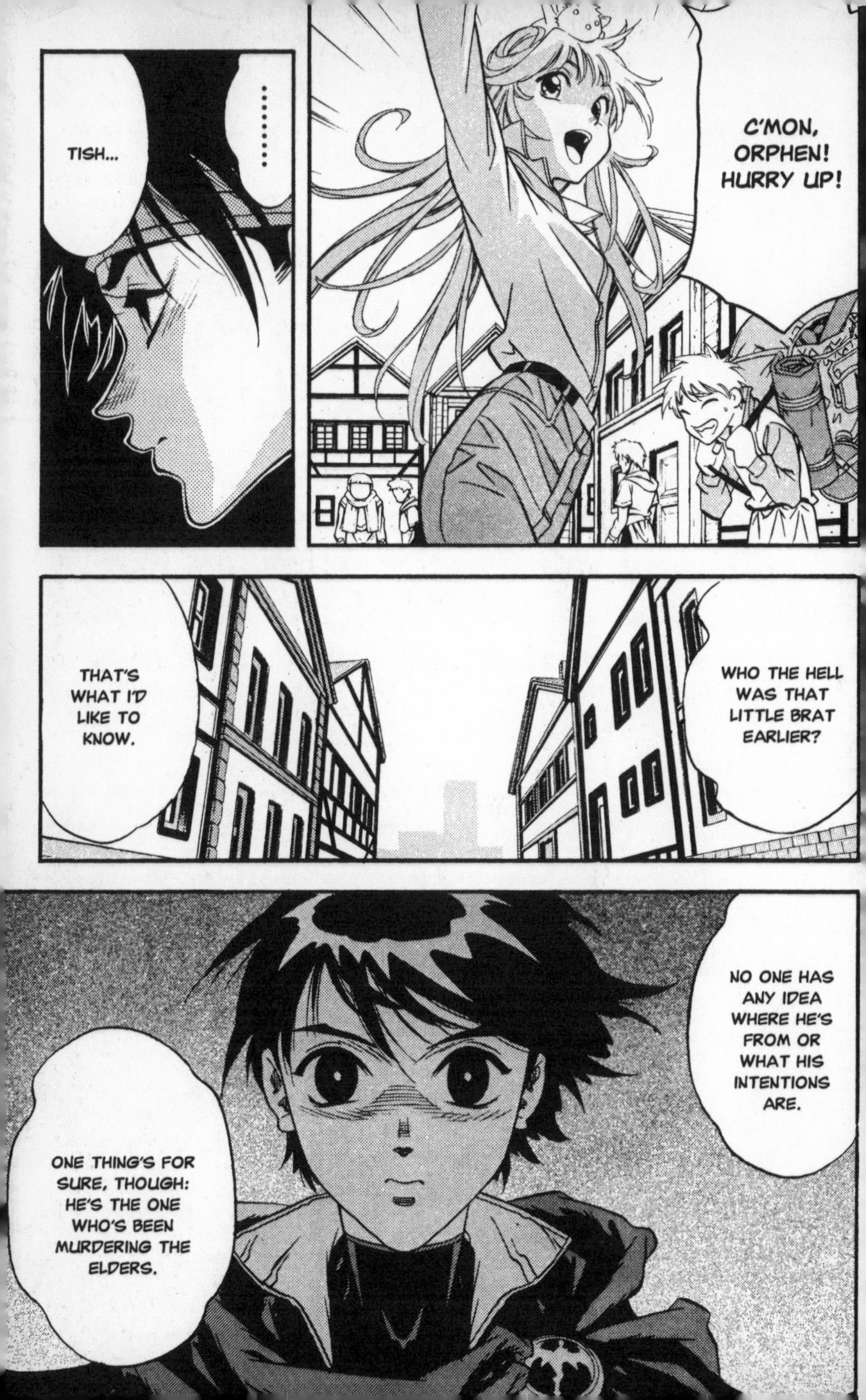
C'MON, ORPHEN! HURRY UP!
......
TISH...
WHO THE HELL WAS THAT LITTLE BRAT EARLIER?
THAT'S WHAT I'D LIKE TO KNOW.
NO ONE HAS ANY IDEA WHERE HE'S FROM OR WHAT HIS INTENTIONS ARE.
ONE THING'S FOR SURE, THOUGH: HE'S THE ONE WHO'S BEEN MURDERING THE ELDERS.

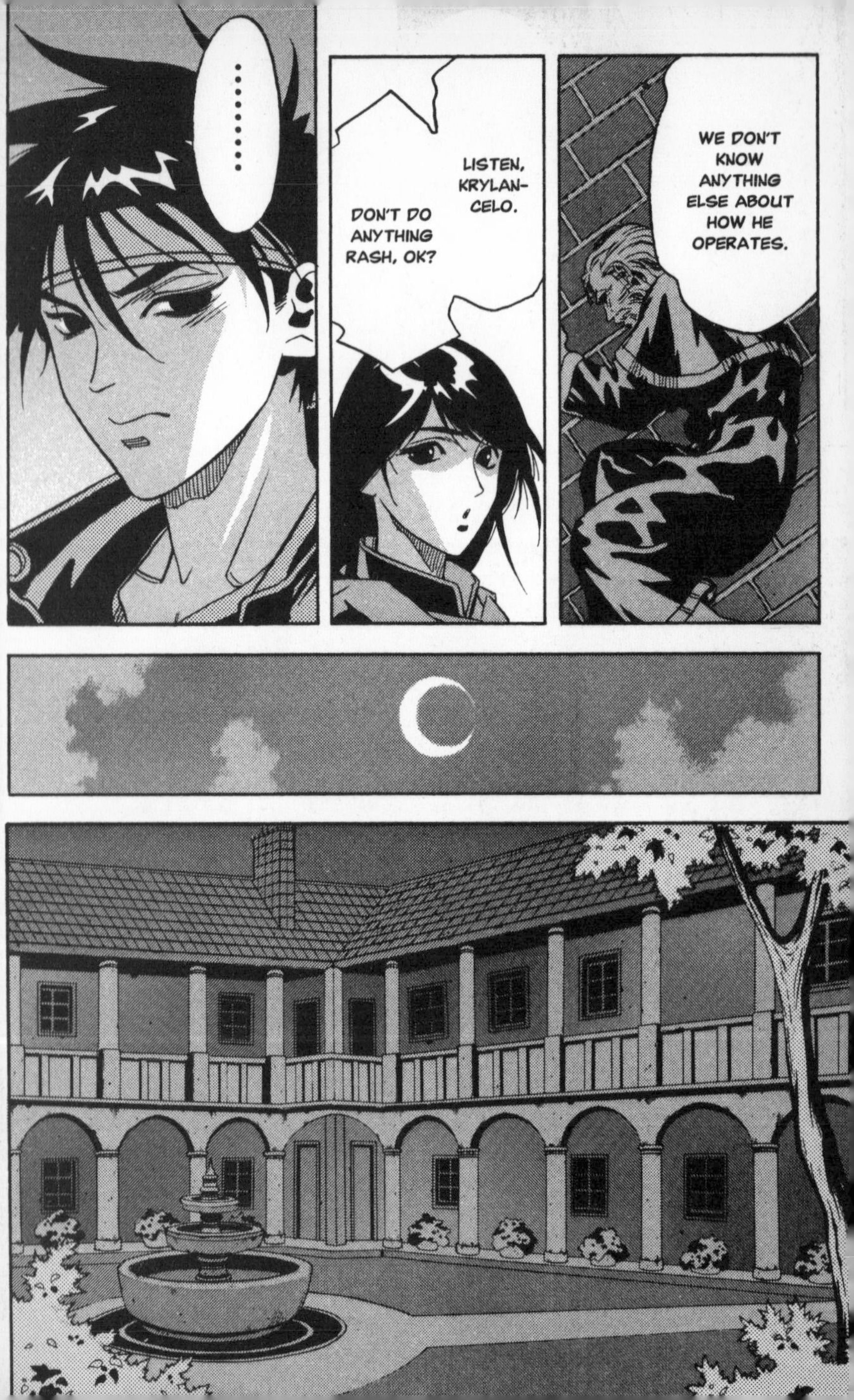
WE DON'T KNOW ANYTHING ELSE ABOUT HOW HE OPERATES.
LISTEN, KRYLAN-CELO.
DON'T DO ANYTHING RASH, OK?
......

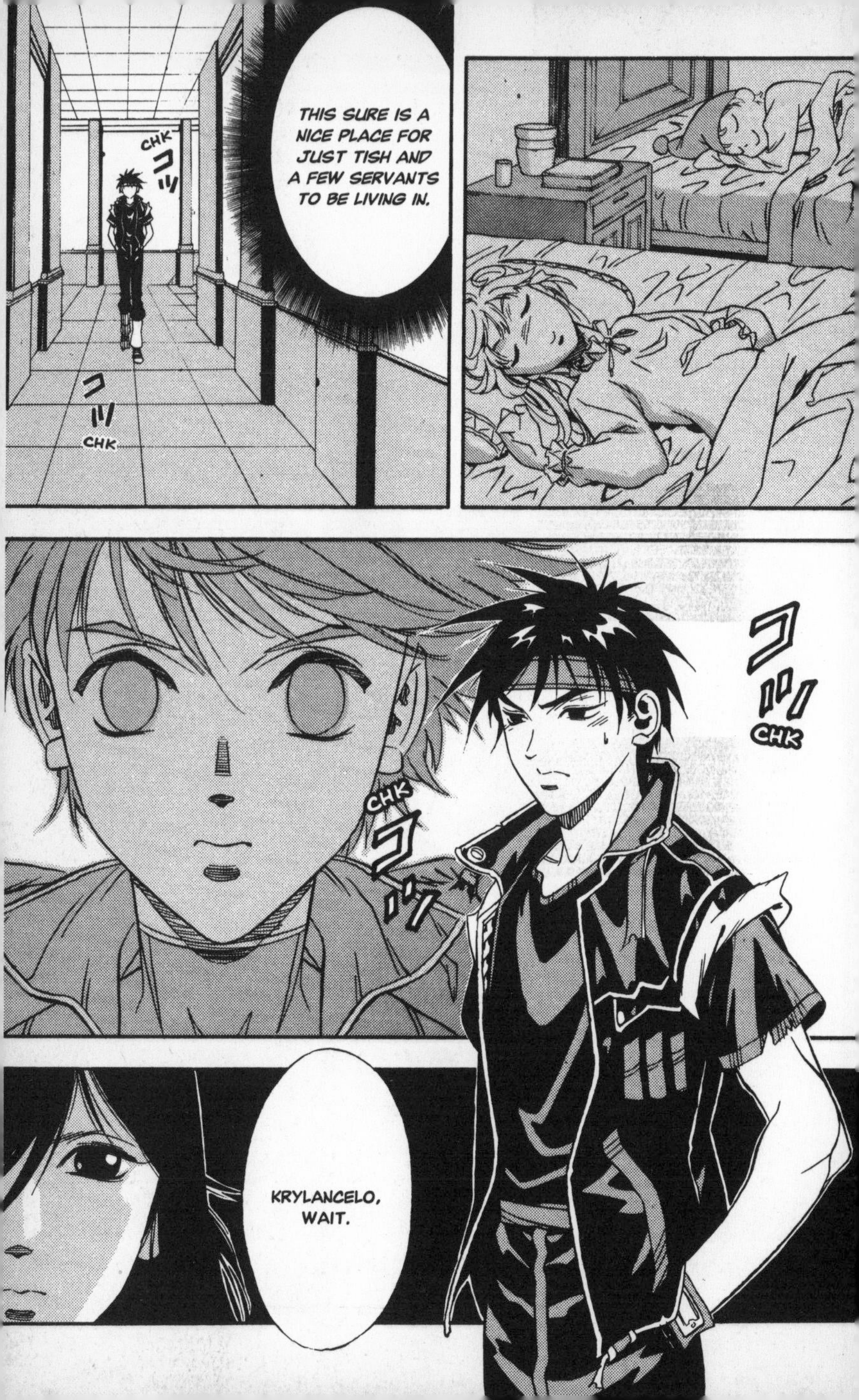
THIS SURE IS A NICE PLACE FOR JUST TISH AND A FEW SERVANTS TO BE LIVING IN.
コツ CHK
コツ CHK
コツ CHK
コツ CHK
KRYLANCELO, WAIT.

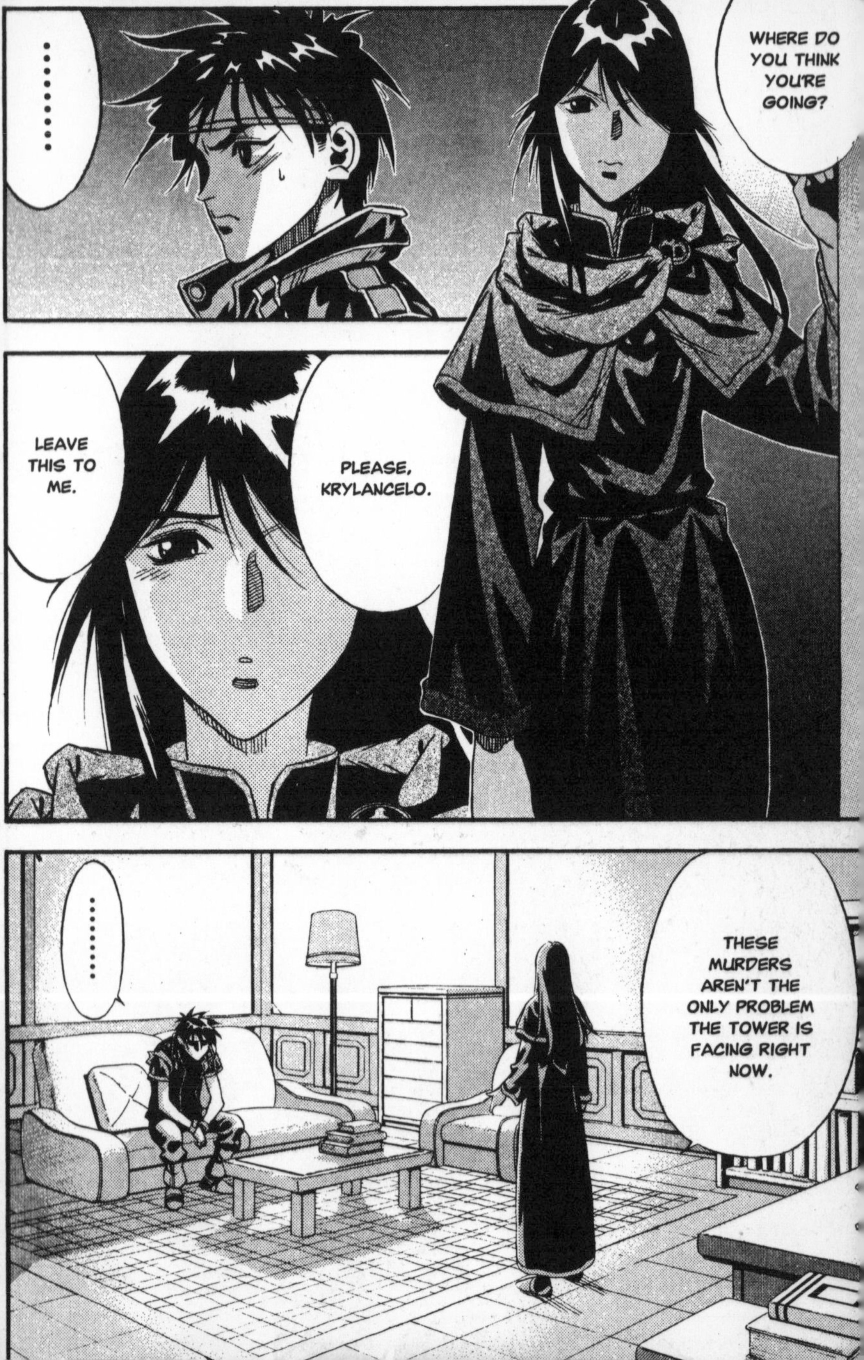
WHERE DO YOU THINK YOU'RE GOING?
....
PLEASE, KRYLANCELO.
LEAVE THIS TO ME.
THESE MURDERS AREN'T THE ONLY PROBLEM THE TOWER IS FACING RIGHT NOW.
....

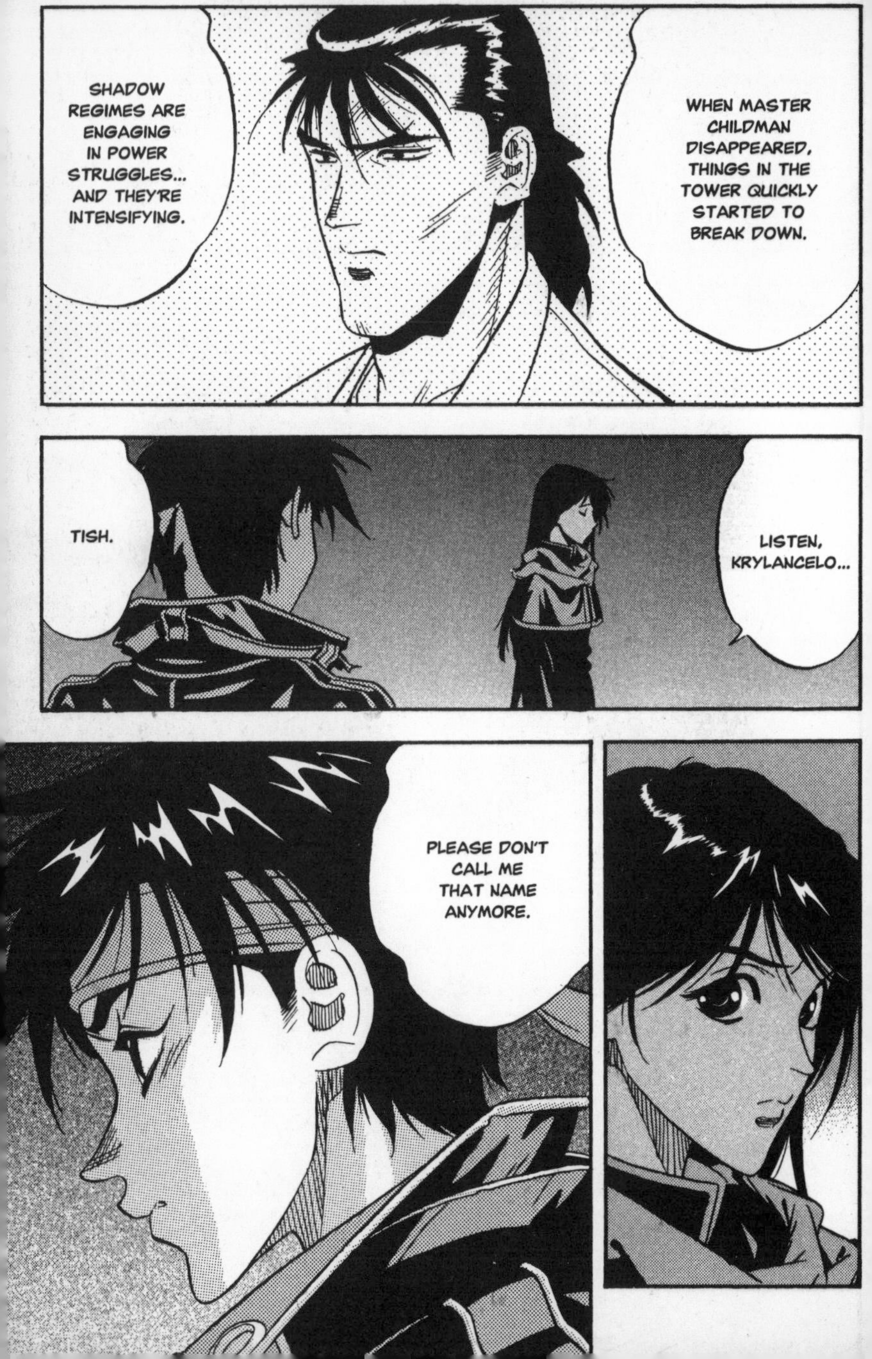
WHEN MASTER CHILDMAN DISAPPEARED, THINGS IN THE TOWER QUICKLY STARTED TO BREAK DOWN.
SHADOW REGIMES ARE ENGAGING IN POWER STRUGGLES... AND THEY'RE INTENSIFYING.
LISTEN, KRYLANCELO...
TISH.
PLEASE DON'T CALL ME THAT NAME ANYMORE.

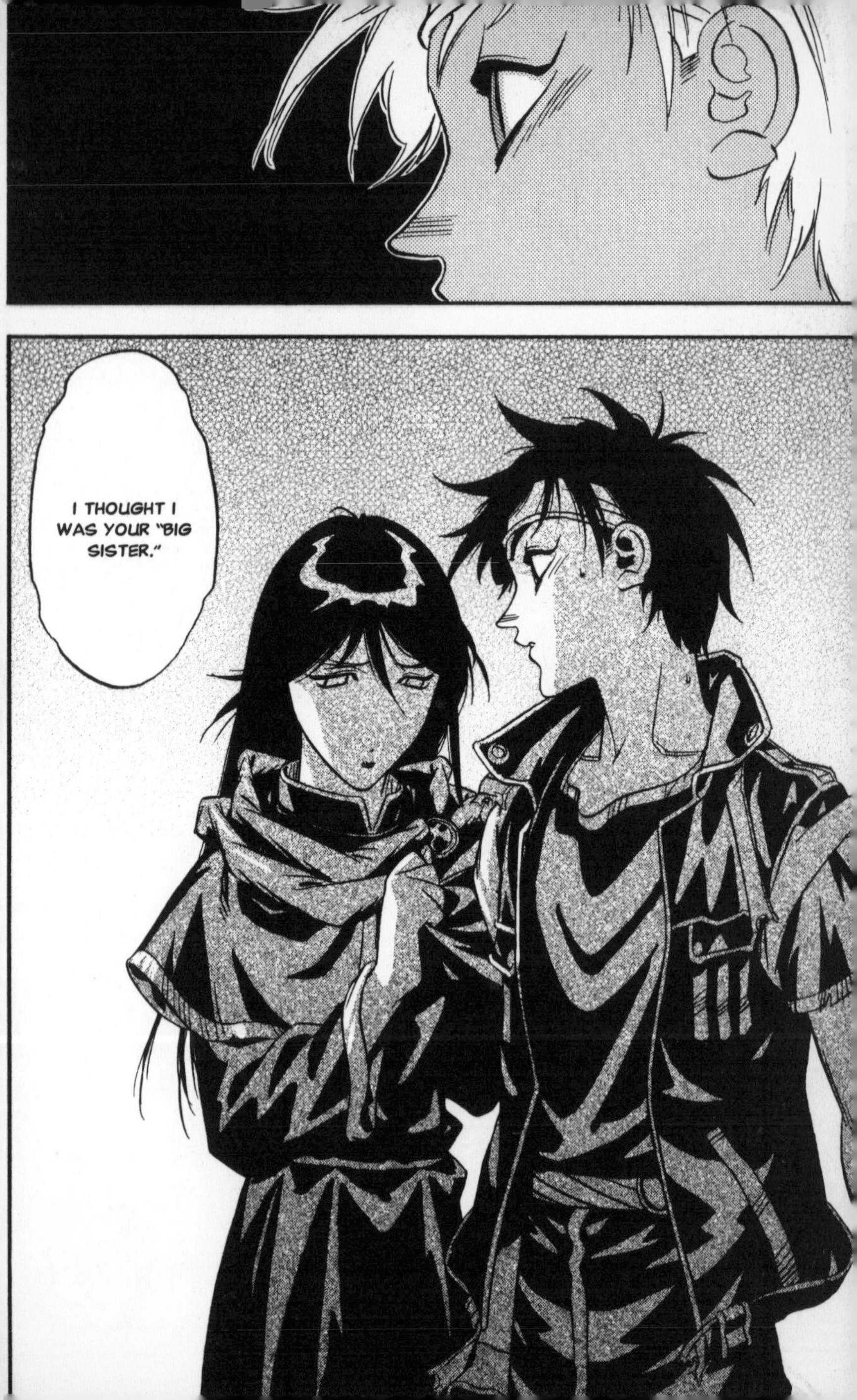
I THOUGHT I WAS YOUR "BIG SISTER."

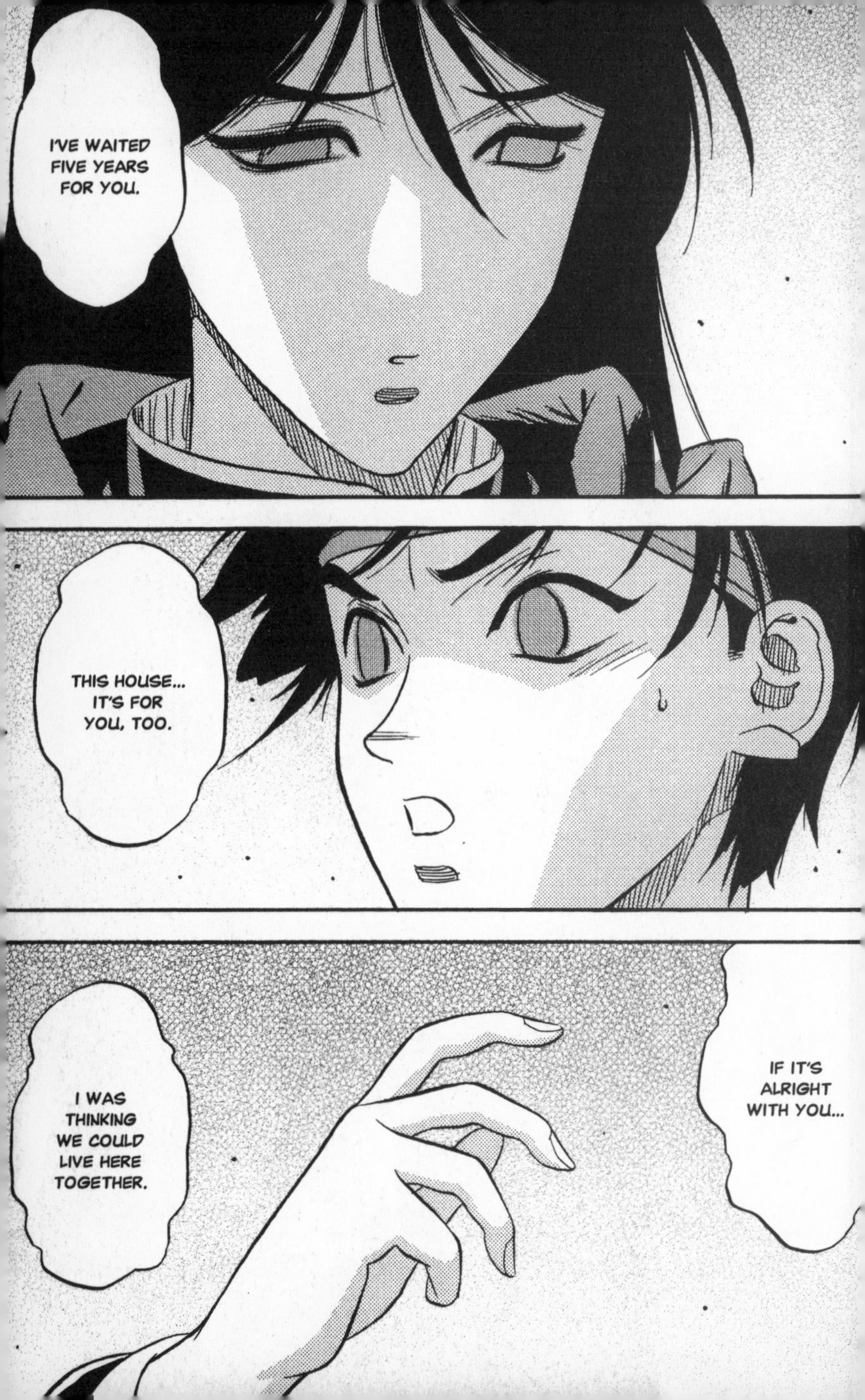
I'VE WAITED FIVE YEARS FOR YOU.
THIS HOUSE... IT'S FOR YOU, TOO.
IF IT'S ALRIGHT WITH YOU...
I WAS THINKING WE COULD LIVE HERE TOGETHER.

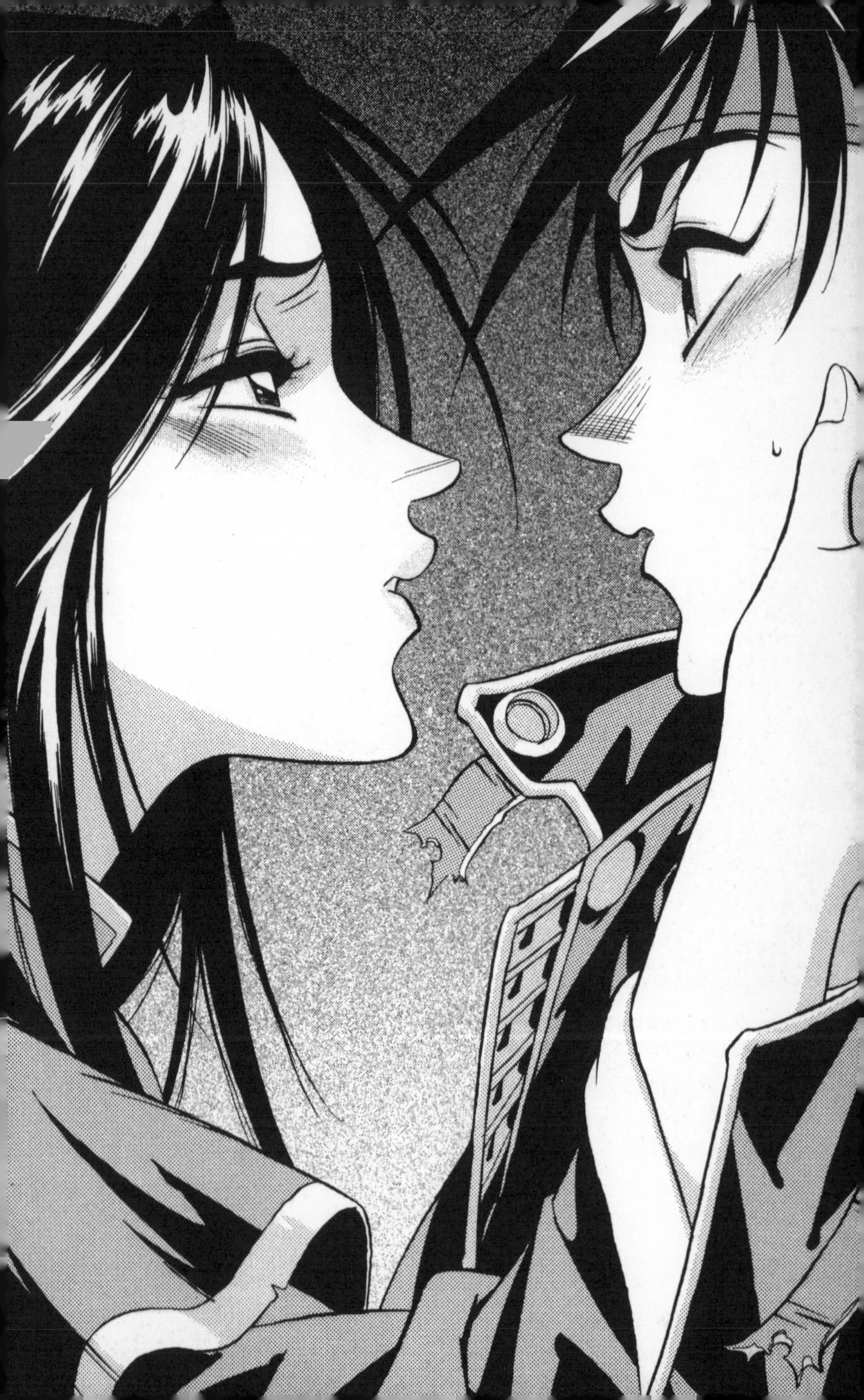

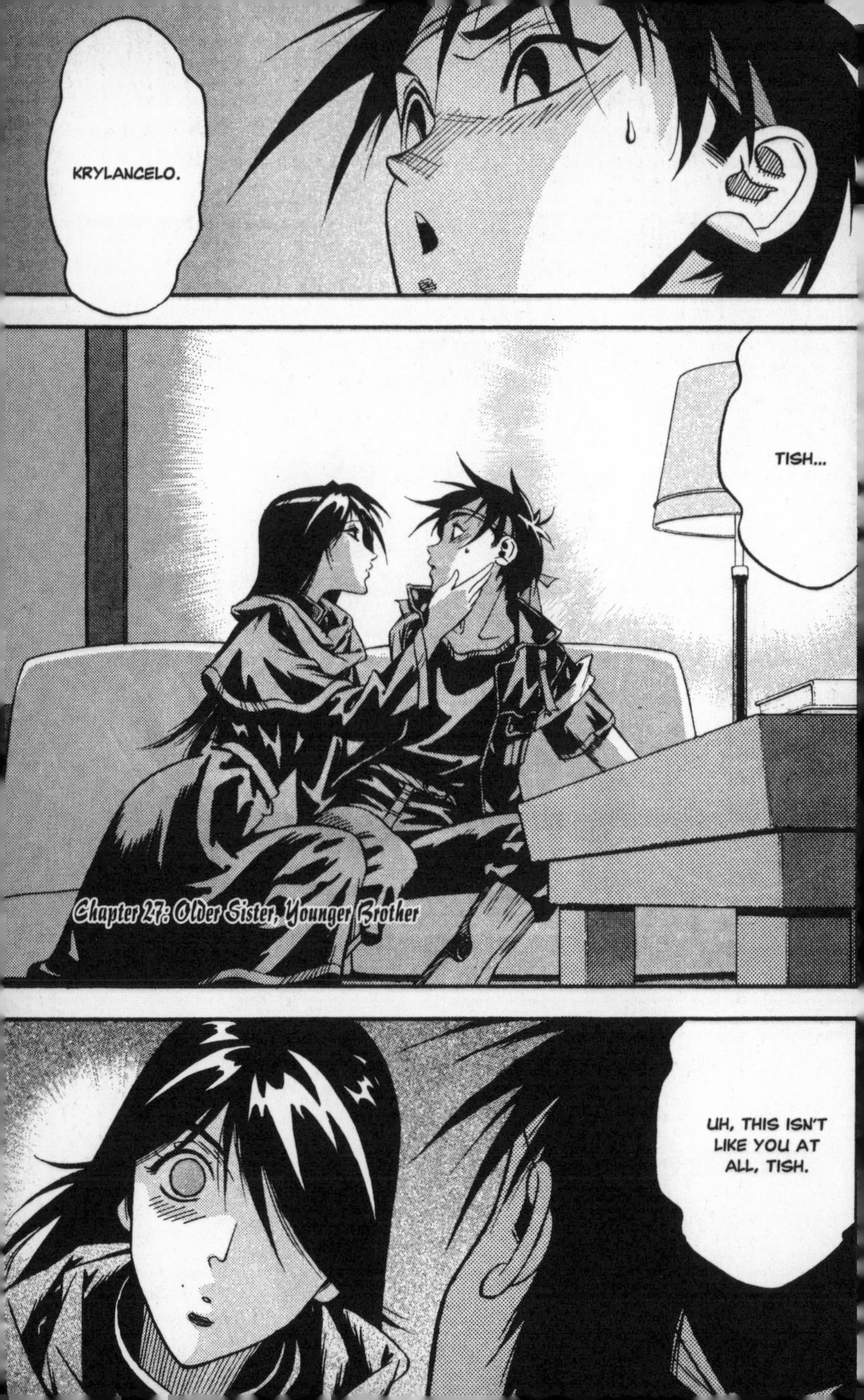
KRYLANCELO.
TISH...
Chapter 27: Older Sister, Younger Brother
UH, THIS ISN'T LIKE YOU AT ALL, TISH.

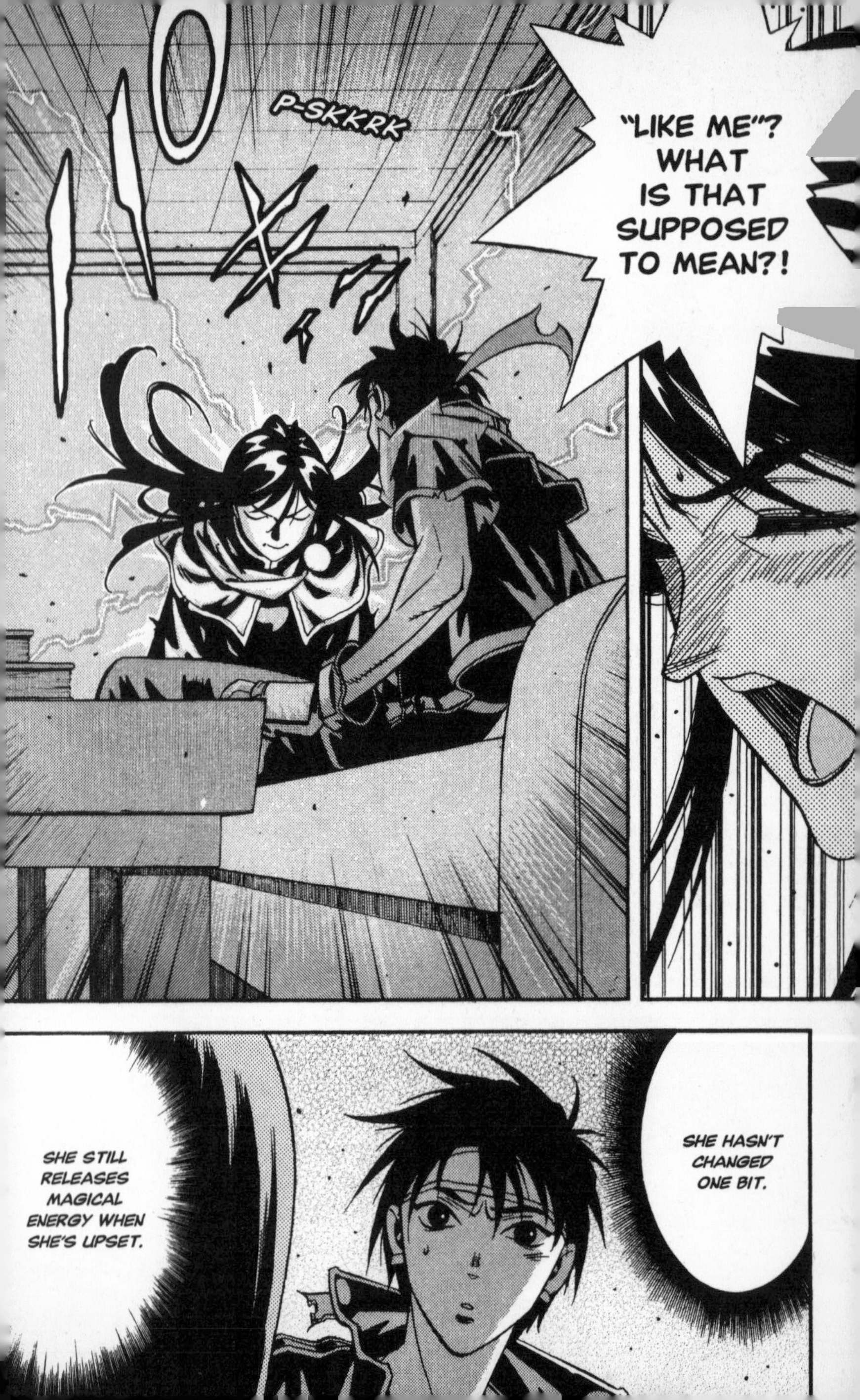
"LIKE ME"? WHAT IS THAT SUPPOSED TO MEAN?!
P-SKKRK
SHE HASN'T CHANGED ONE BIT.
SHE STILL RELEASES MAGICAL ENERGY WHEN SHE'S UPSET.

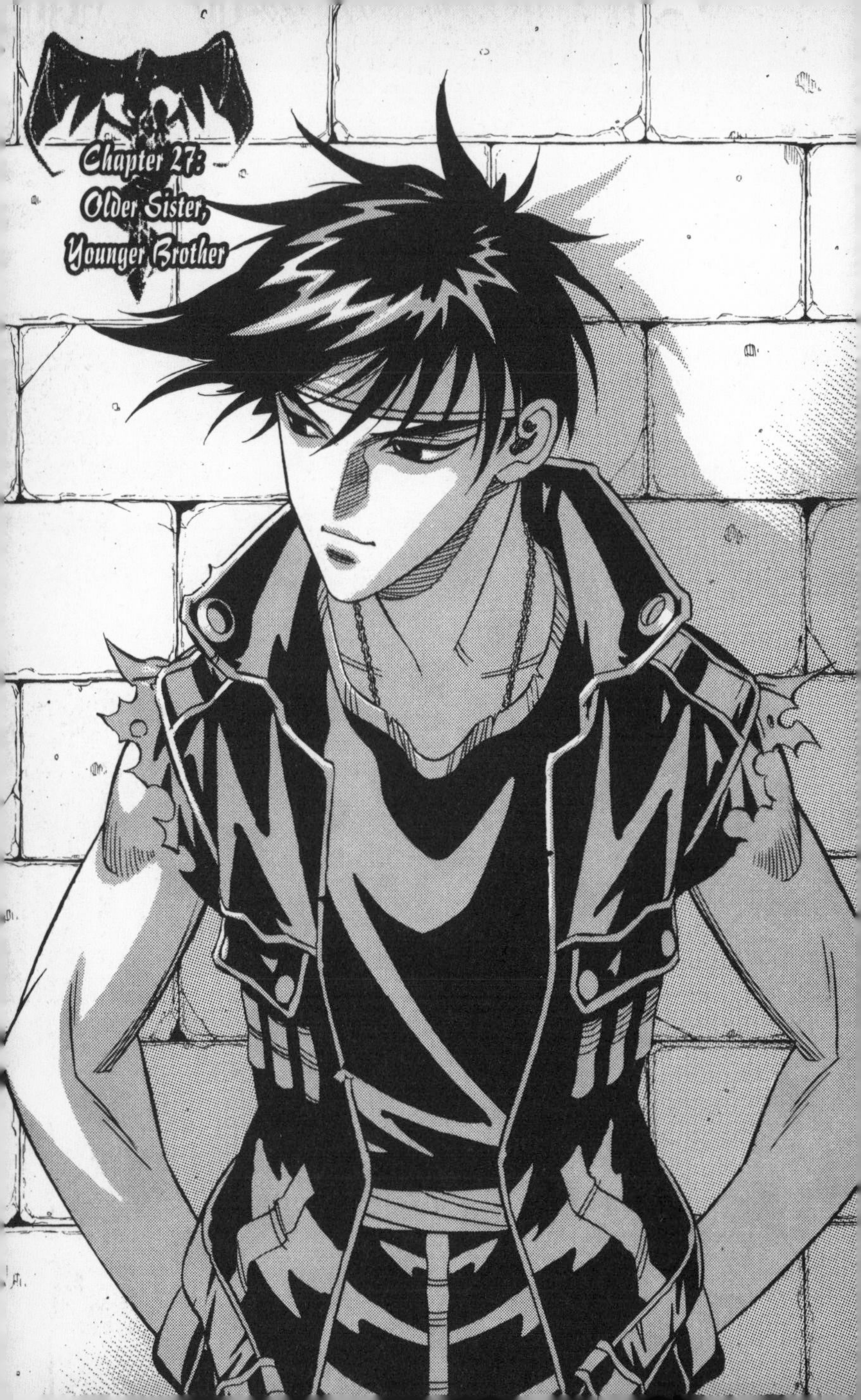
Chapter 27:
Older Sister,
Younger Brother

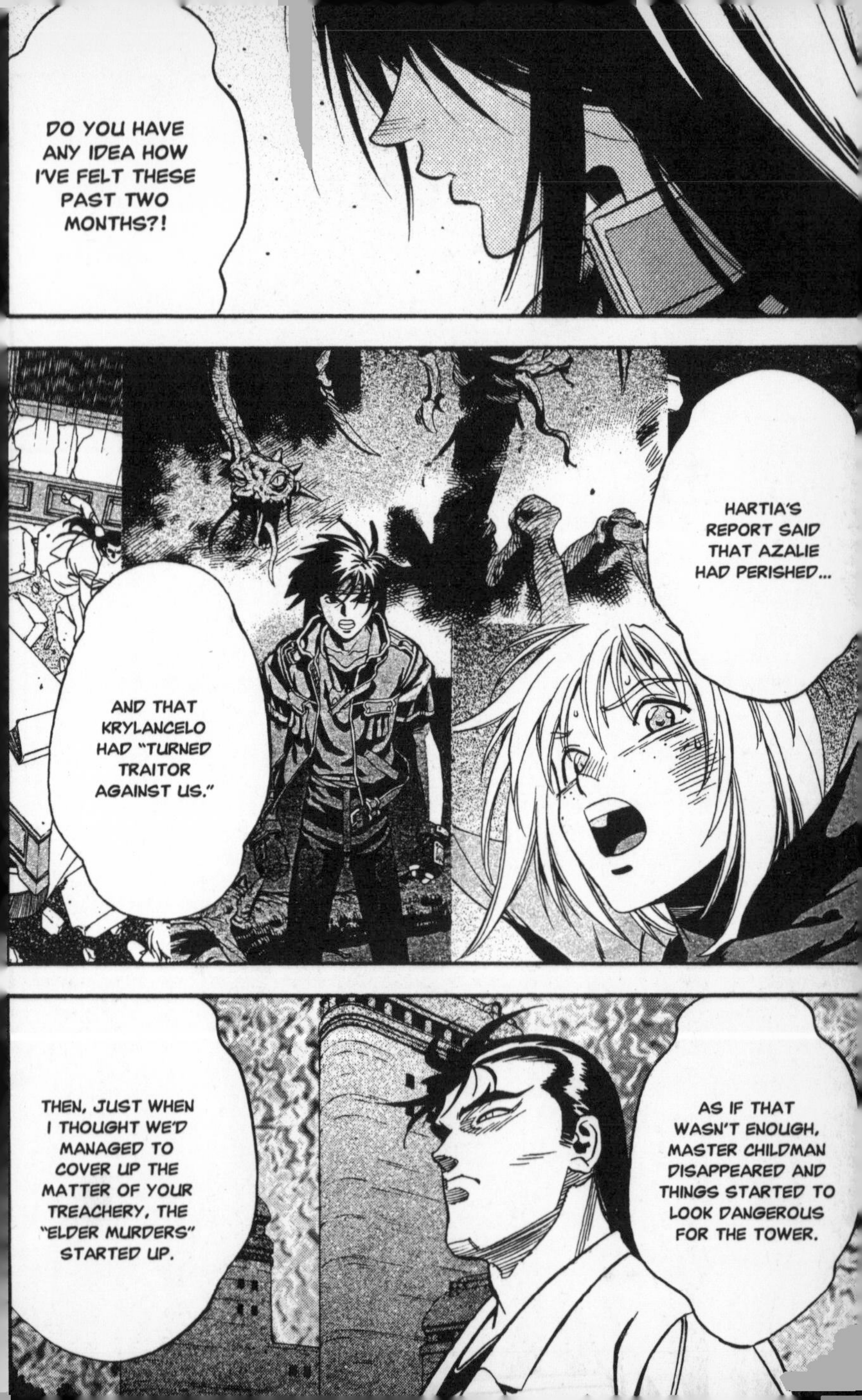
DO YOU HAVE ANY IDEA HOW I'VE FELT THESE PAST TWO MONTHS?!
HARTIA'S REPORT SAID THAT AZALIE HAD PERISHED...
AND THAT KRYLANCELO HAD "TURNED TRAITOR AGAINST US."
THEN, JUST WHEN I THOUGHT WE'D MANAGED TO COVER UP THE MATTER OF YOUR TREACHERY, THE "ELDER MURDERS" STARTED UP.
AS IF THAT WASN'T ENOUGH, MASTER CHILDMAN DISAPPEARED AND THINGS STARTED TO LOOK DANGEROUS FOR THE TOWER.

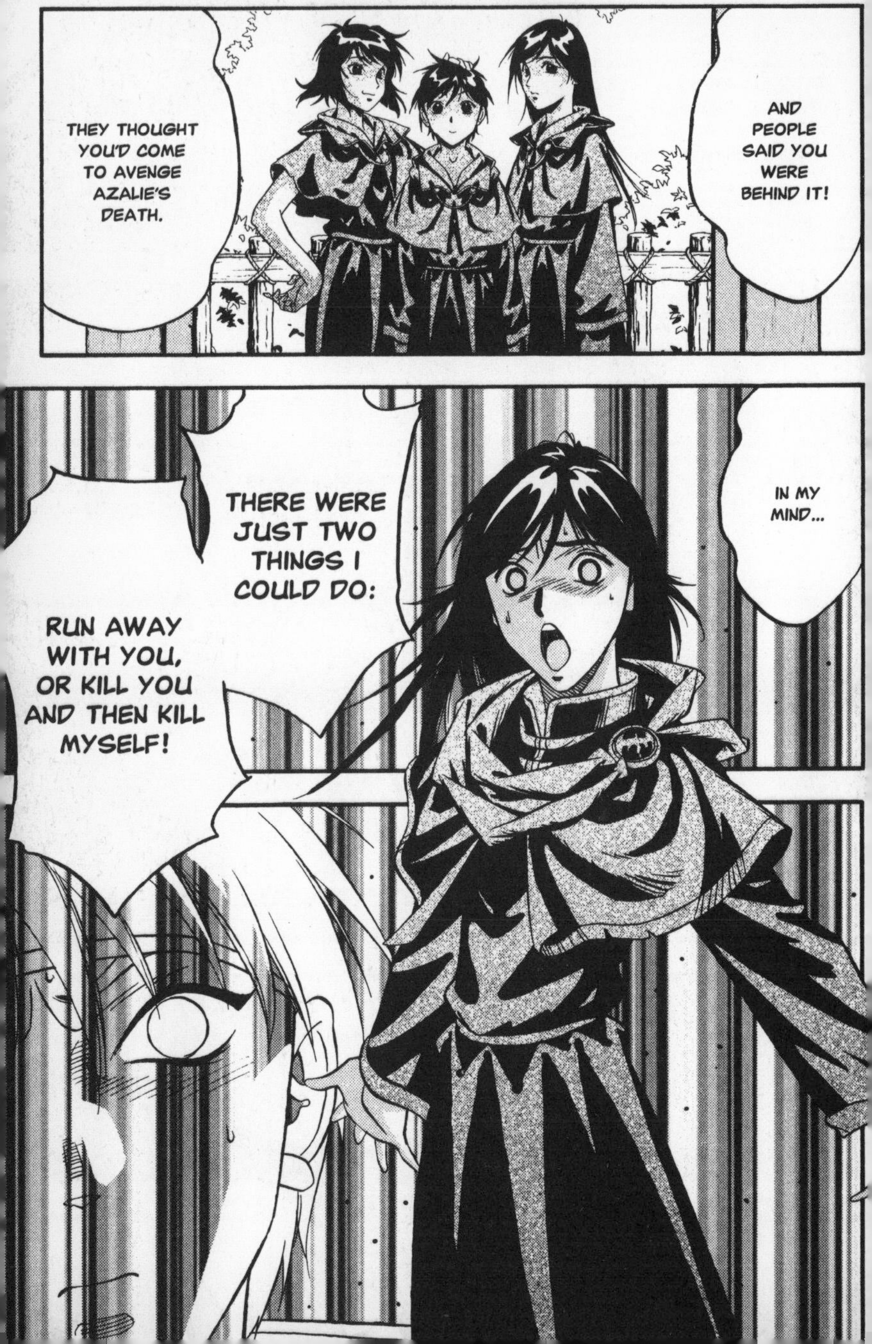
AND PEOPLE SAID YOU WERE BEHIND IT!
THEY THOUGHT YOU'D COME TO AVENGE AZALIE'S DEATH.
IN MY MIND...
THERE WERE JUST TWO THINGS I COULD DO:
RUN AWAY WITH YOU, OR KILL YOU AND THEN KILL MYSELF!

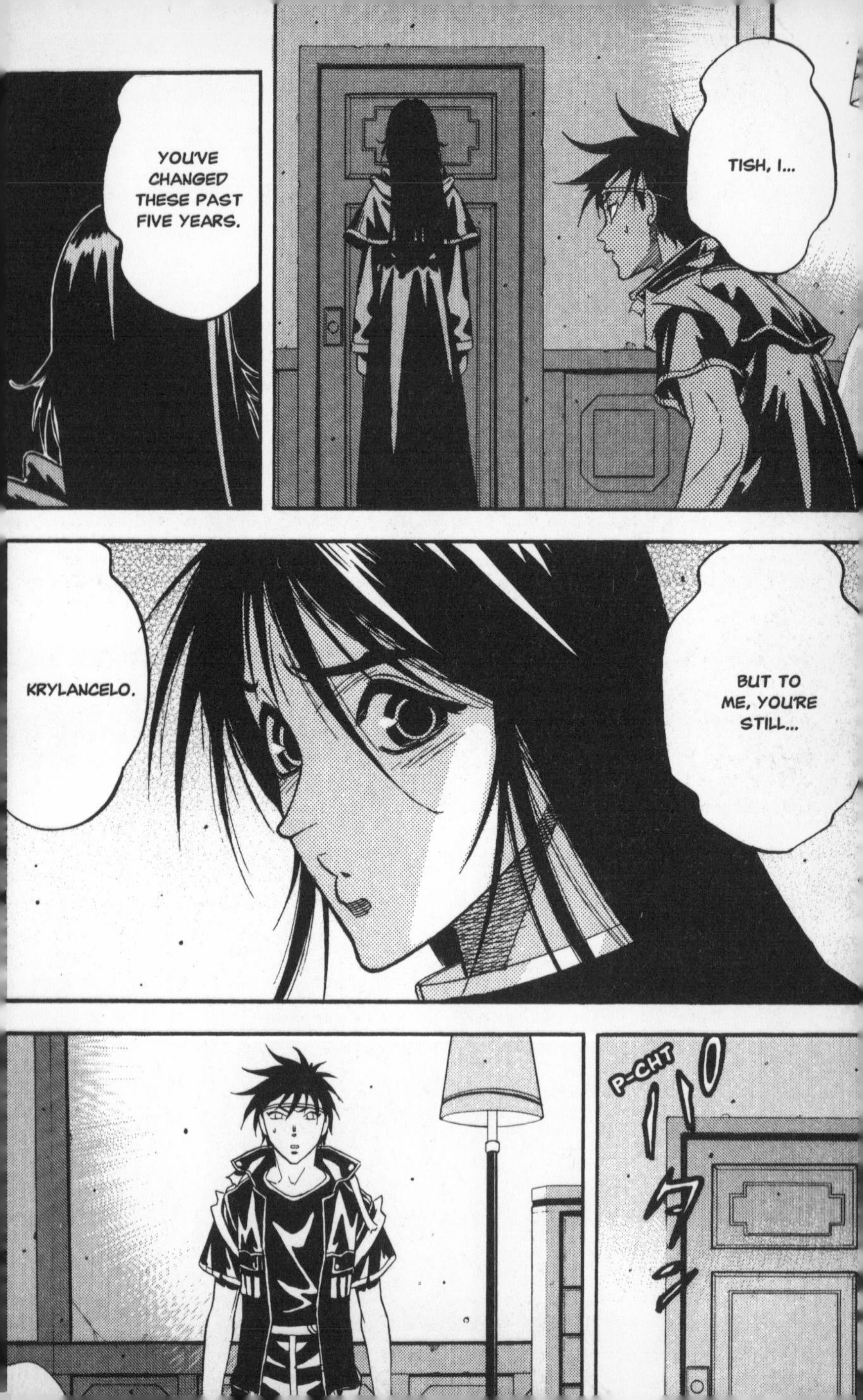
TISH, I...
YOU'VE CHANGED THESE PAST FIVE YEARS.
BUT TO ME, YOU'RE STILL...
KRYLANCELO.
P-CHT

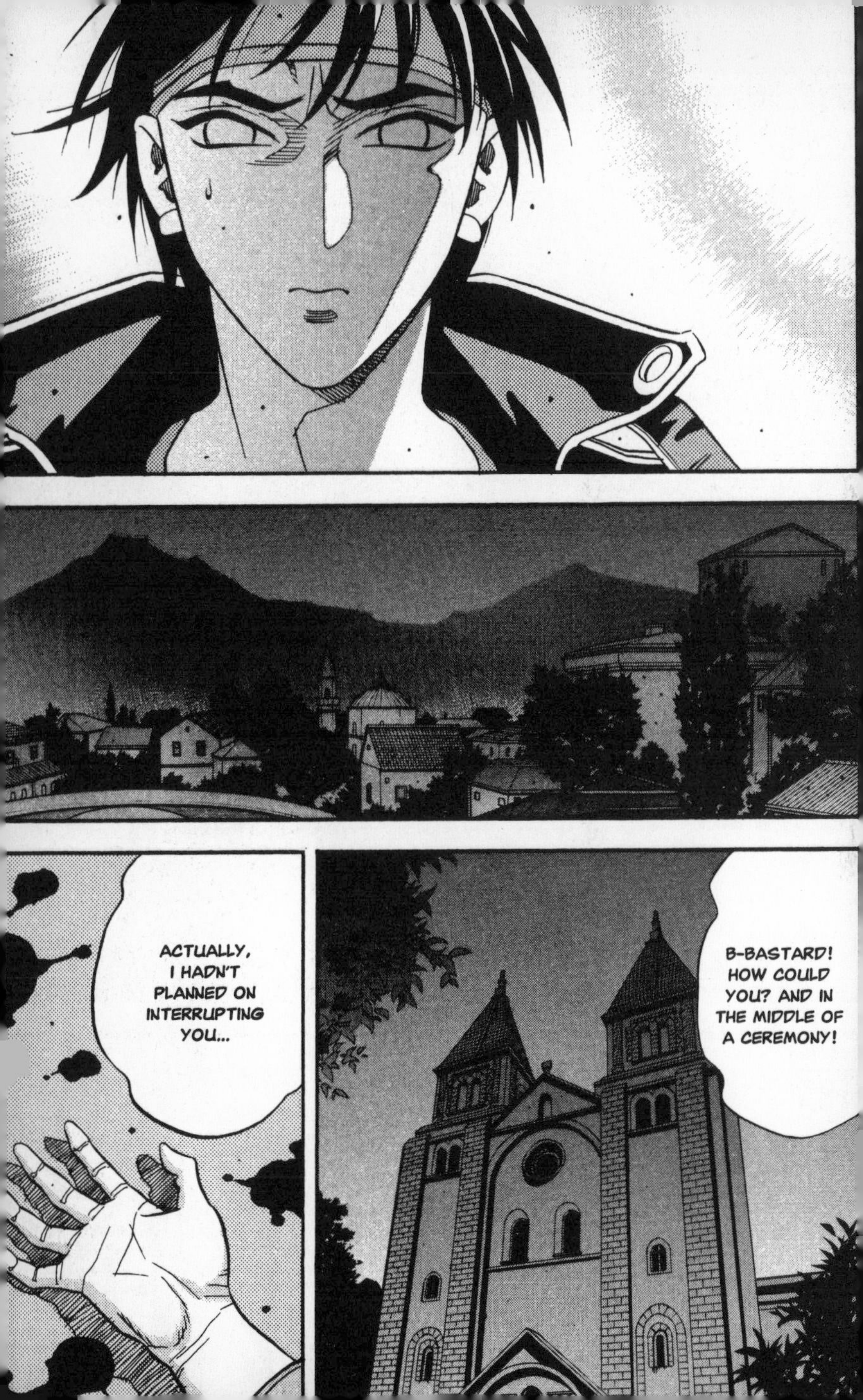
B-BASTARD! HOW COULD YOU? AND IN THE MIDDLE OF A CEREMONY!
ACTUALLY, I HADN'T PLANNED ON INTERRUPTING YOU...

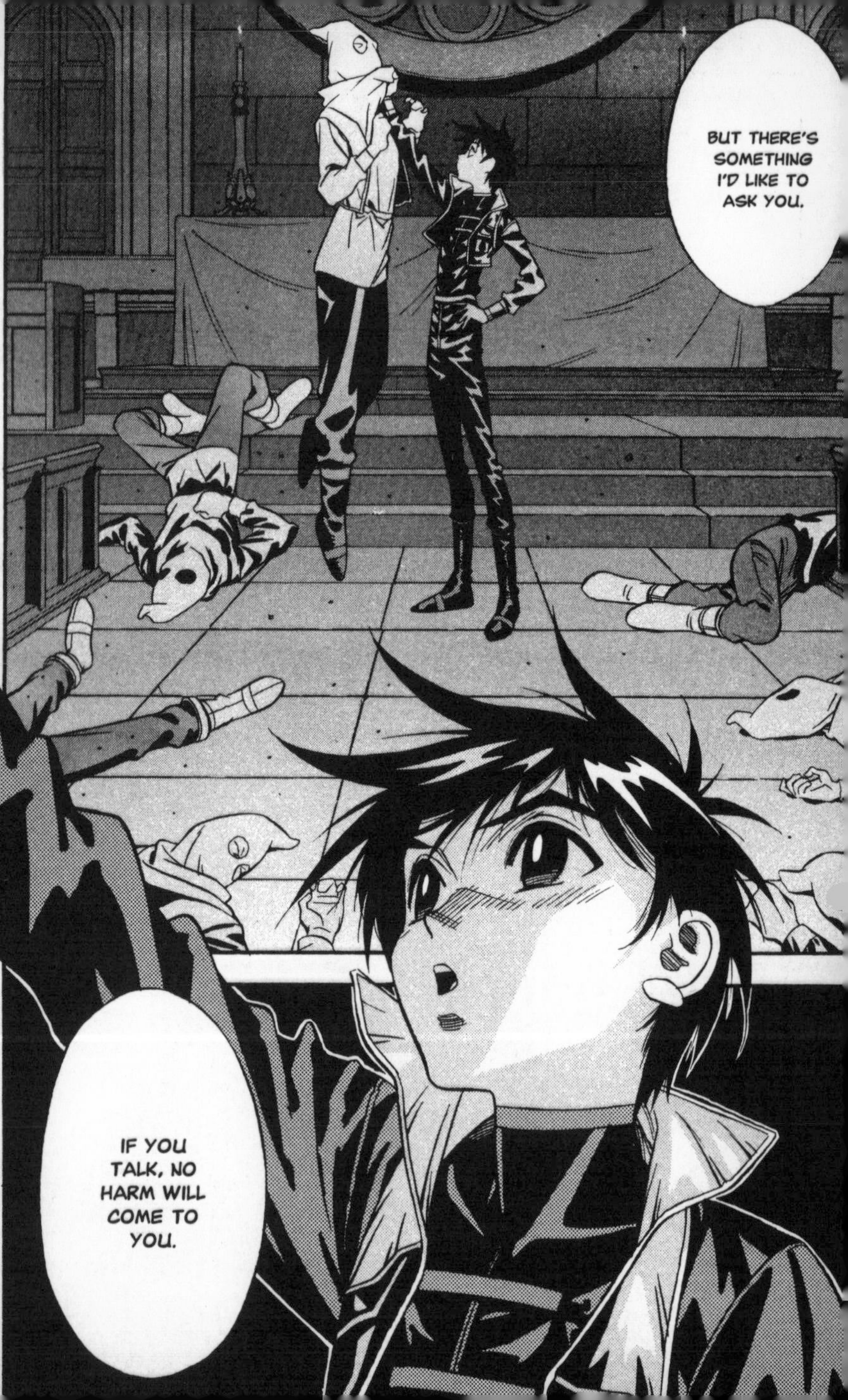
BUT THERE'S SOMETHING I'D LIKE TO ASK YOU.
IF YOU TALK, NO HARM WILL COME TO YOU.

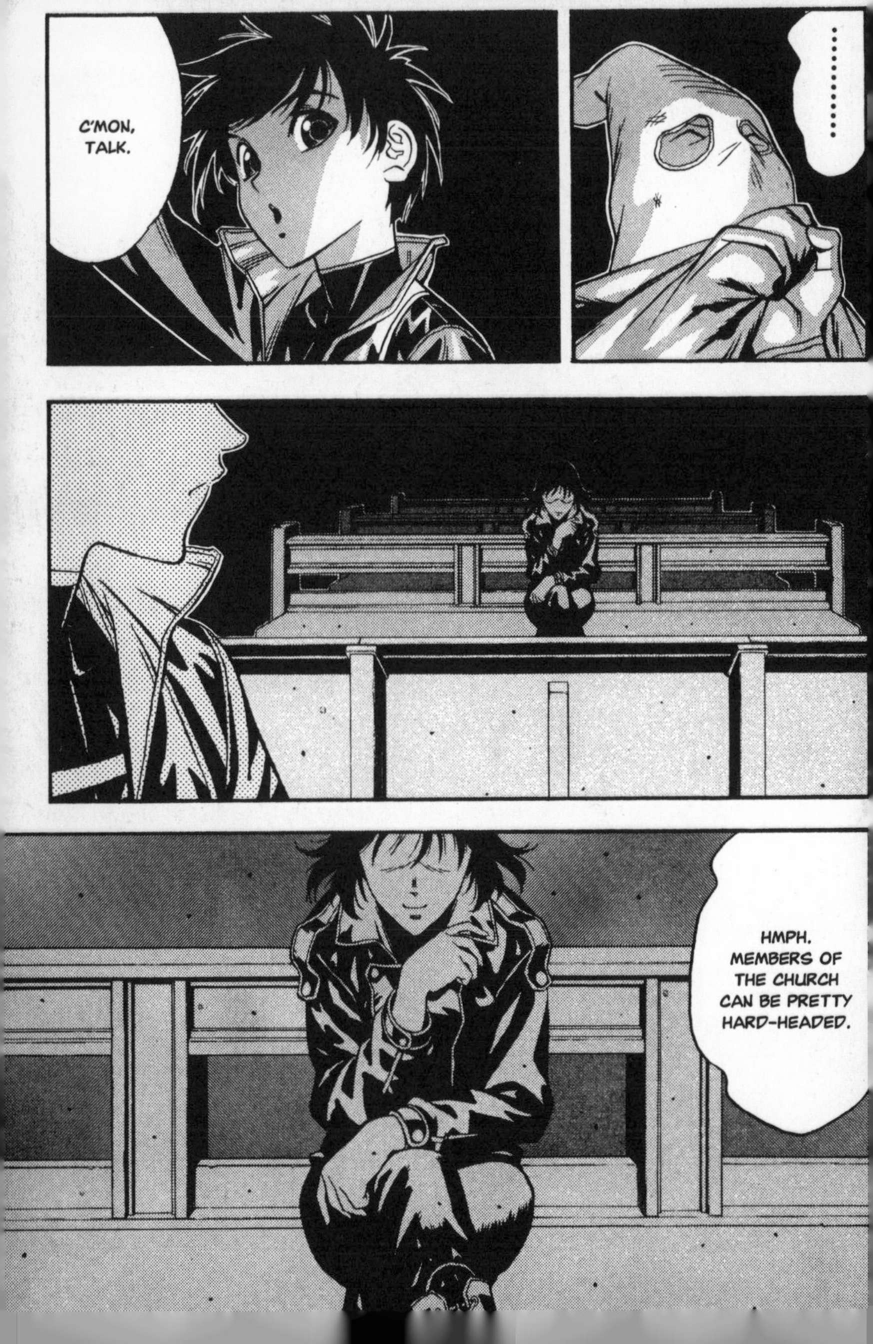

C'MON, TALK.
......
HMPH. MEMBERS OF THE CHURCH CAN BE PRETTY HARD-HEADED.

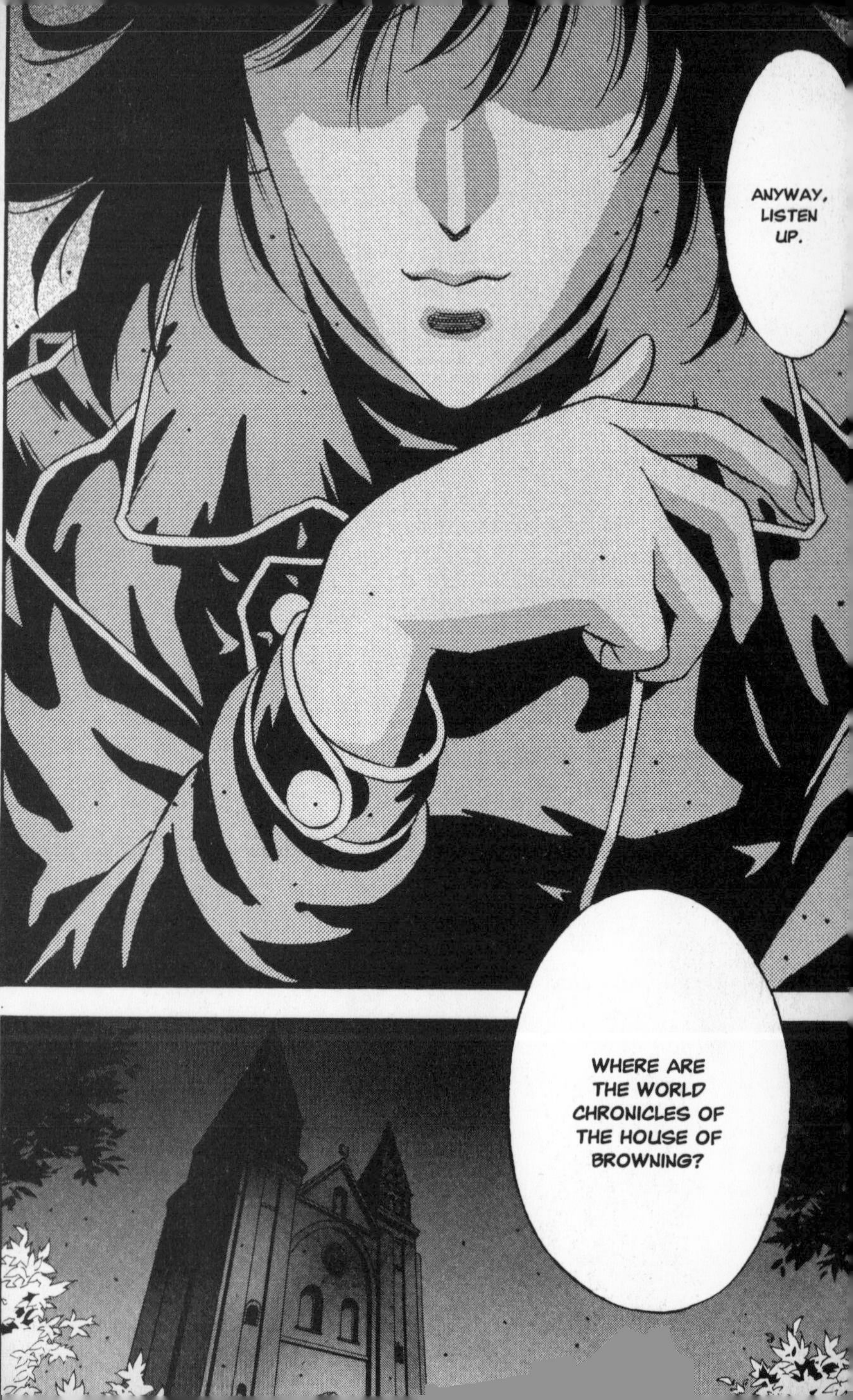
ANYWAY, LISTEN UP.
WHERE ARE THE WORLD CHRONICLES OF THE HOUSE OF BROWNING?

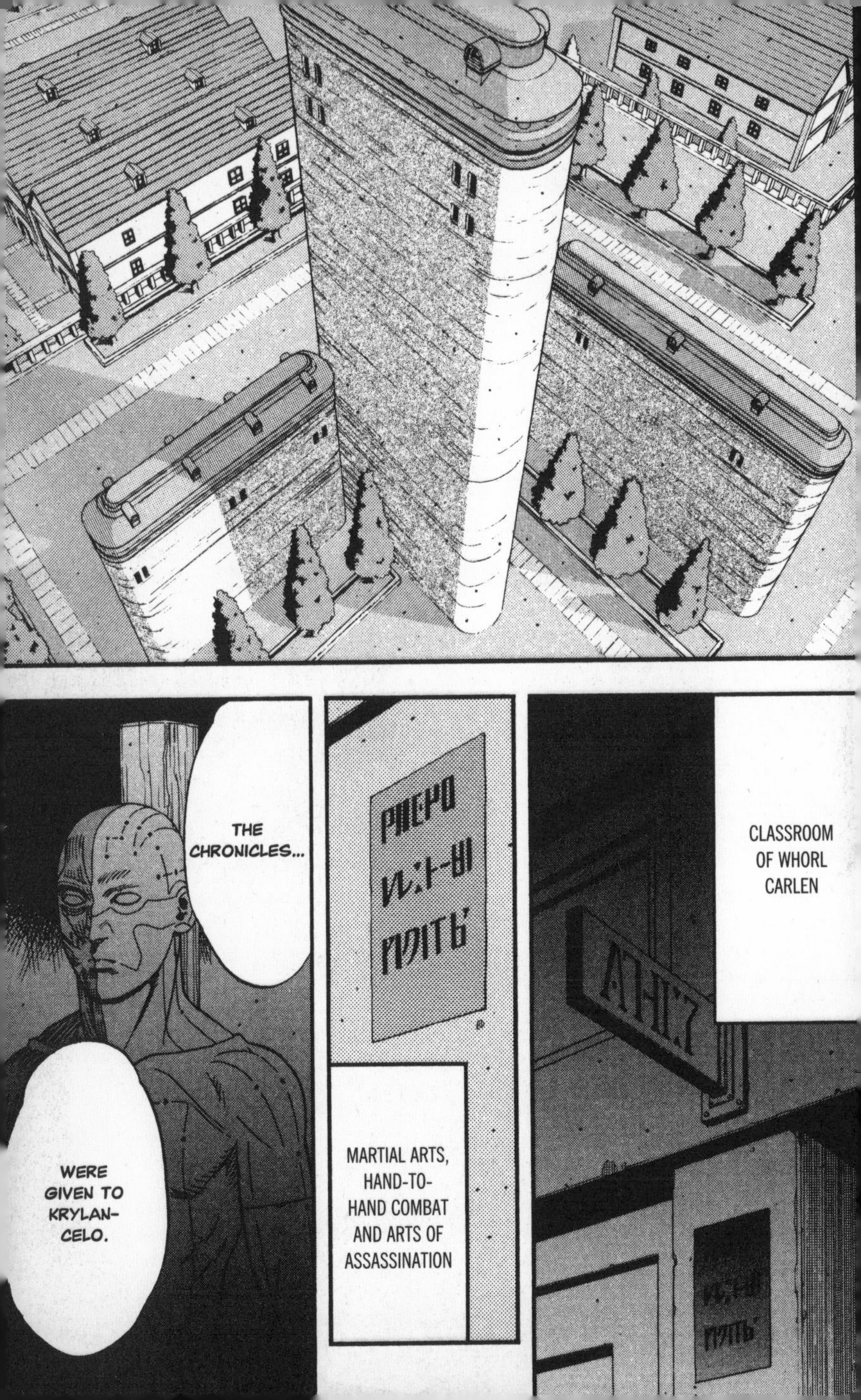
THE CHRONICLES...
WERE GIVEN TO KRYLAN-CELO.
MARTIAL ARTS, HAND-TO-HAND COMBAT AND ARTS OF ASSASSINATION
CLASSROOM OF WHORL CARLEN

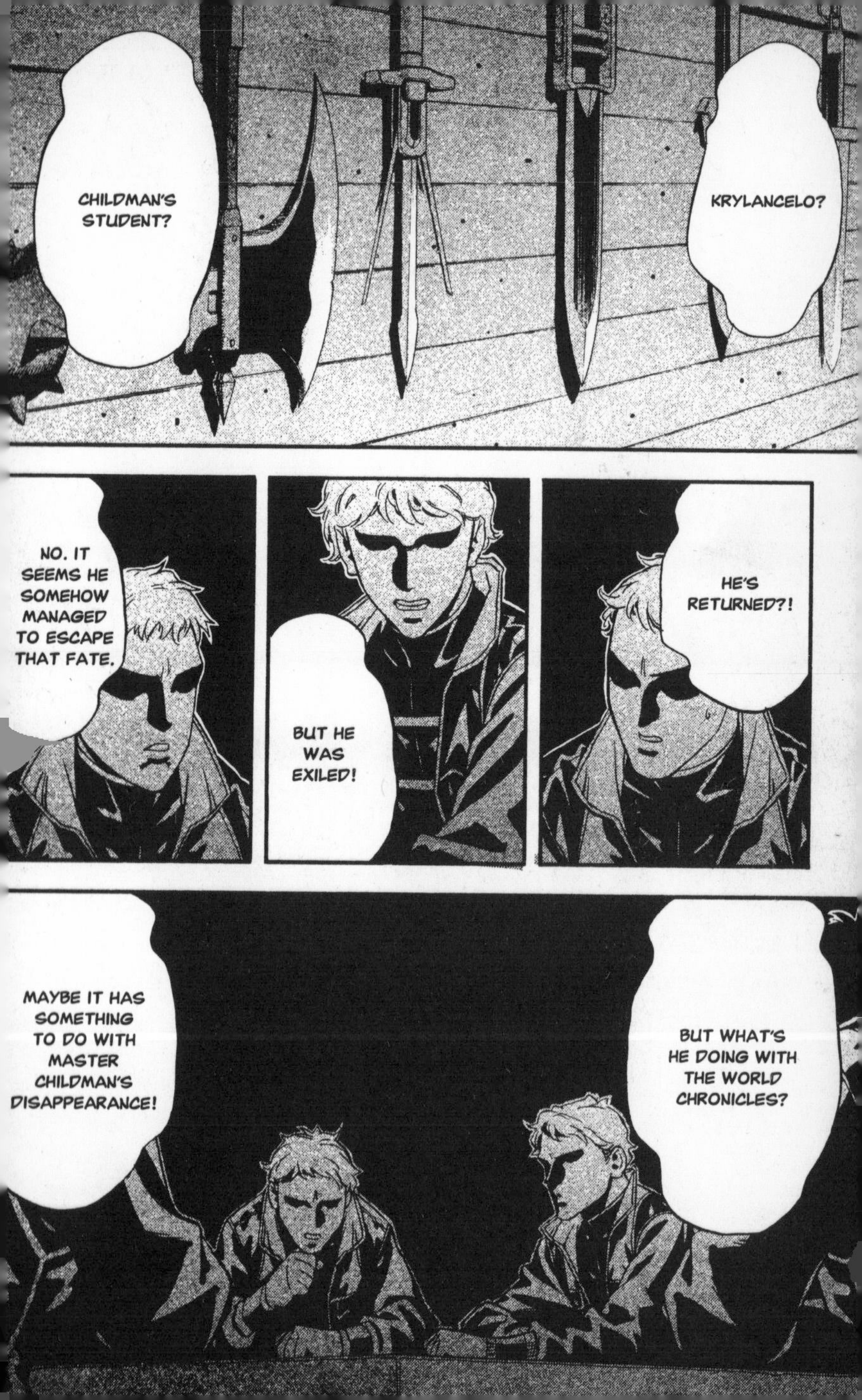
CHILDMAN'S STUDENT?
KRYLANCELO?
NO. IT SEEMS HE SOMEHOW MANAGED TO ESCAPE THAT FATE.
BUT HE WAS EXILED!
HE'S RETURNED?!
MAYBE IT HAS SOMETHING TO DO WITH MASTER CHILDMAN'S DISAPPEARANCE!
BUT WHAT'S HE DOING WITH THE WORLD CHRONICLES?

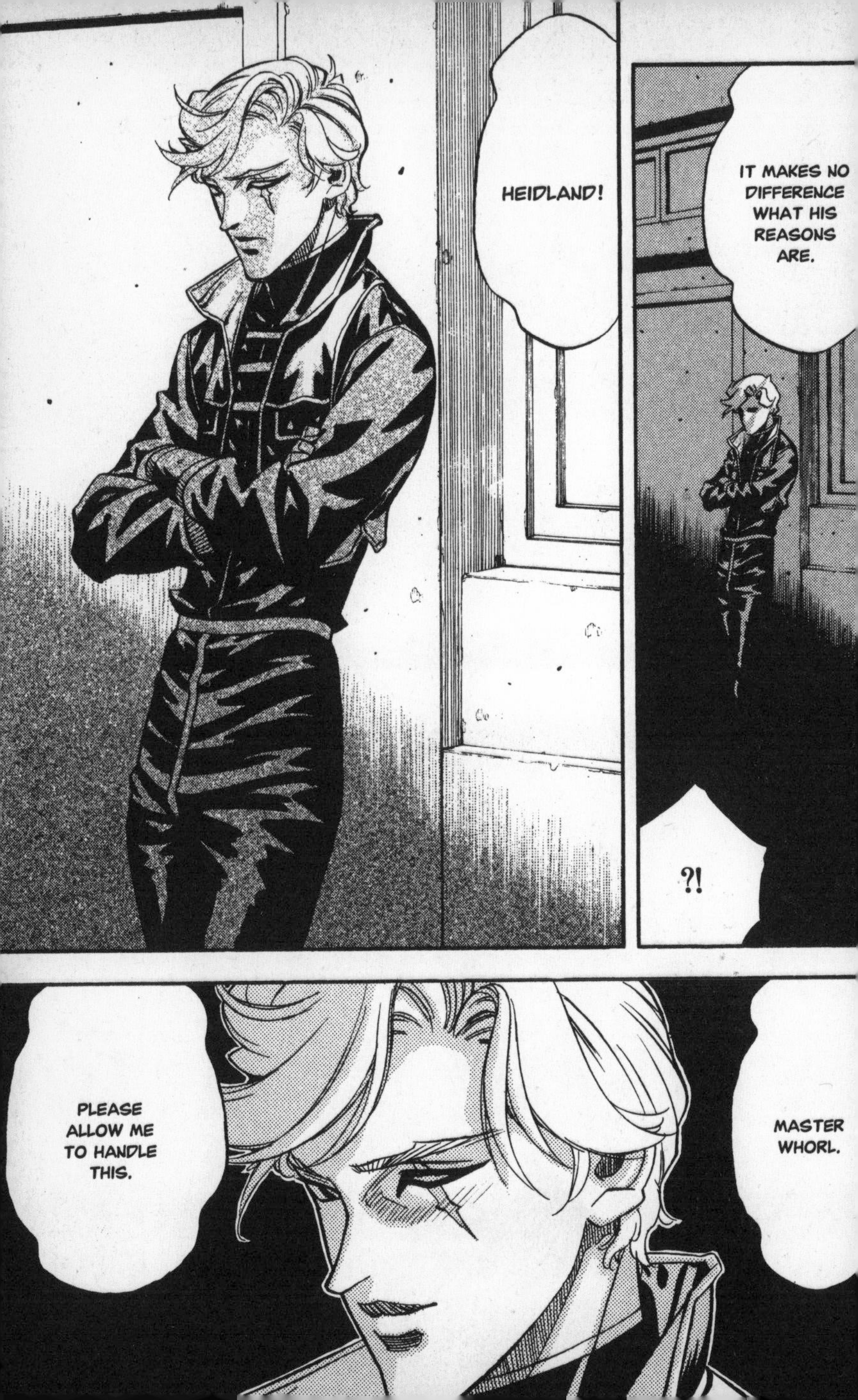
IT MAKES NO DIFFERENCE WHAT HIS REASONS ARE.
?!
HEIDLAND!
MASTER WHORL.
PLEASE ALLOW ME TO HANDLE THIS.

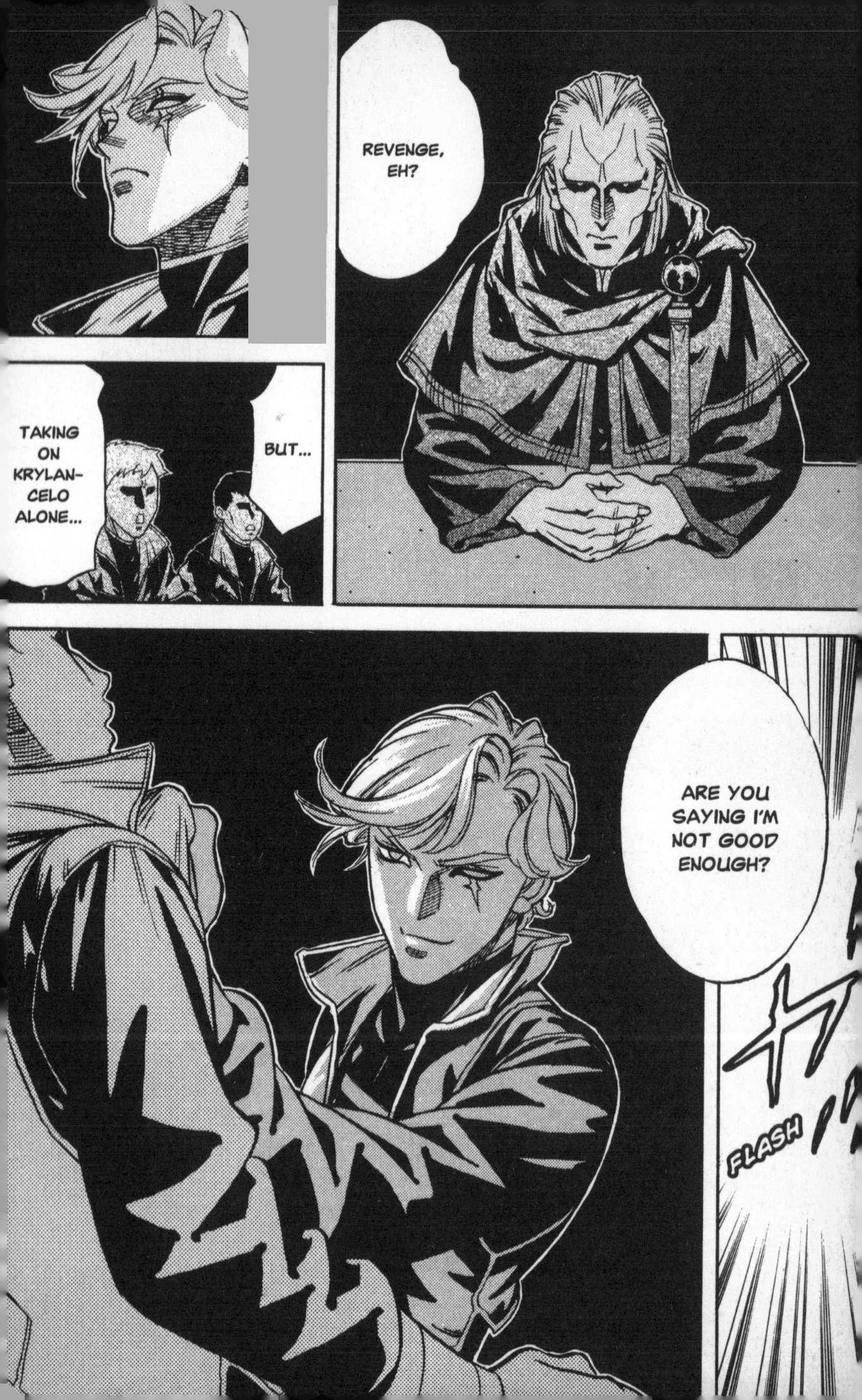
REVENGE, EH?
BUT...
TAKING ON KRYLAN-CELO ALONE...
ARE YOU SAYING I'M NOT GOOD ENOUGH?
FLASH

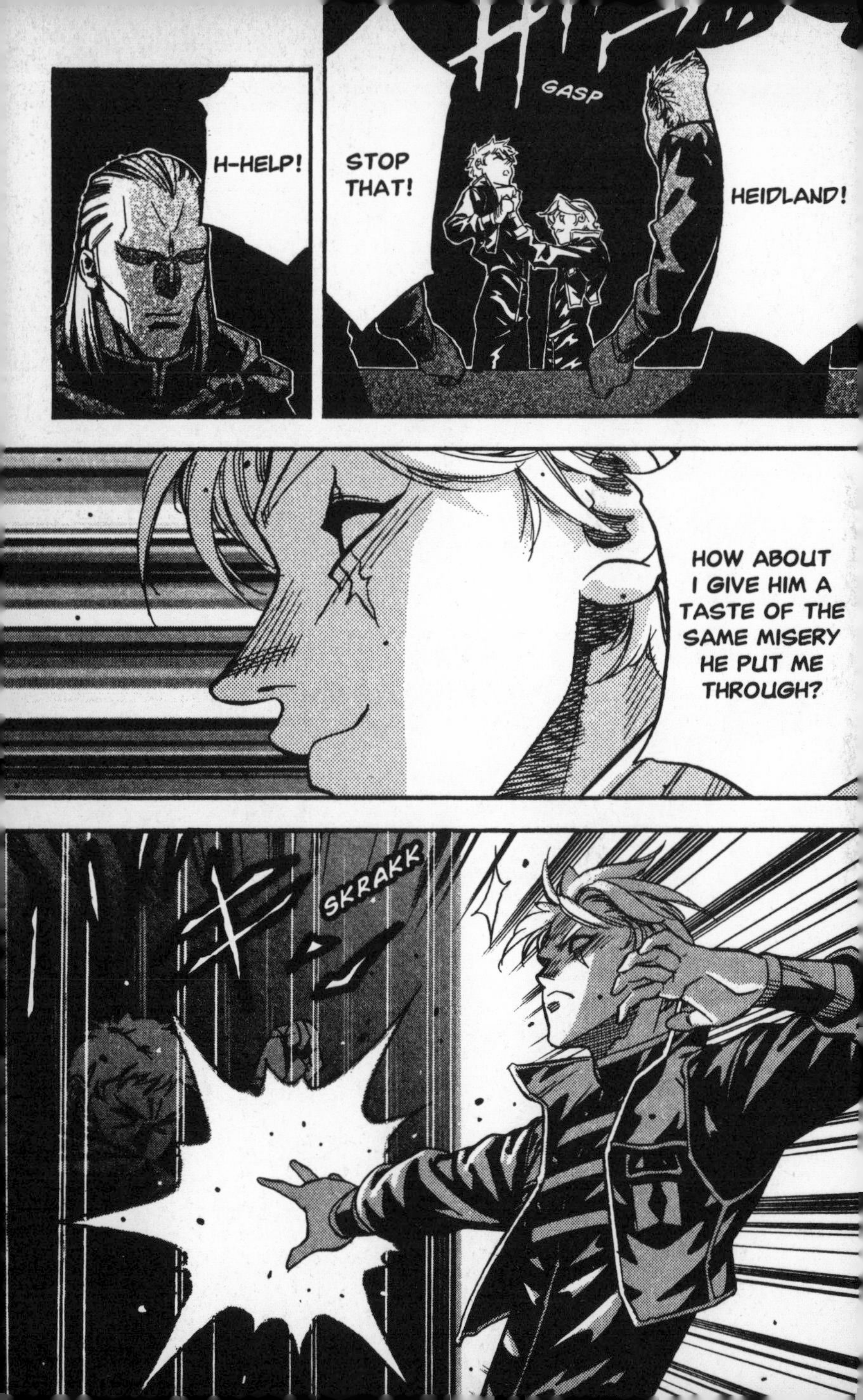
GASP
HEIDLAND!
STOP THAT!
H-HELP!
HOW ABOUT I GIVE HIM A TASTE OF THE SAME MISERY HE PUT ME THROUGH?
SKRAKK

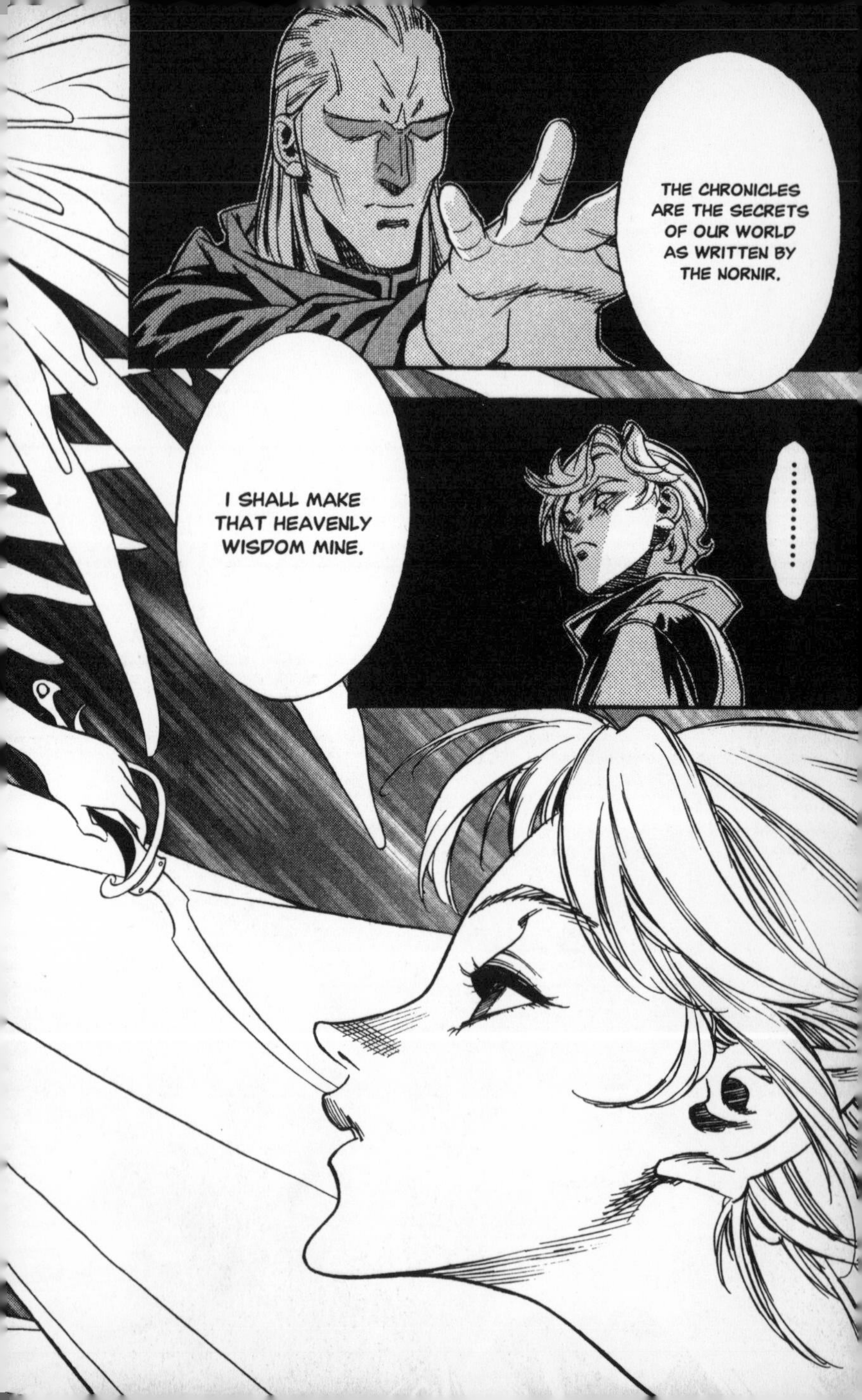
THE CHRONICLES ARE THE SECRETS OF OUR WORLD AS WRITTEN BY THE NORNIR.
......
I SHALL MAKE THAT HEAVENLY WISDOM MINE.

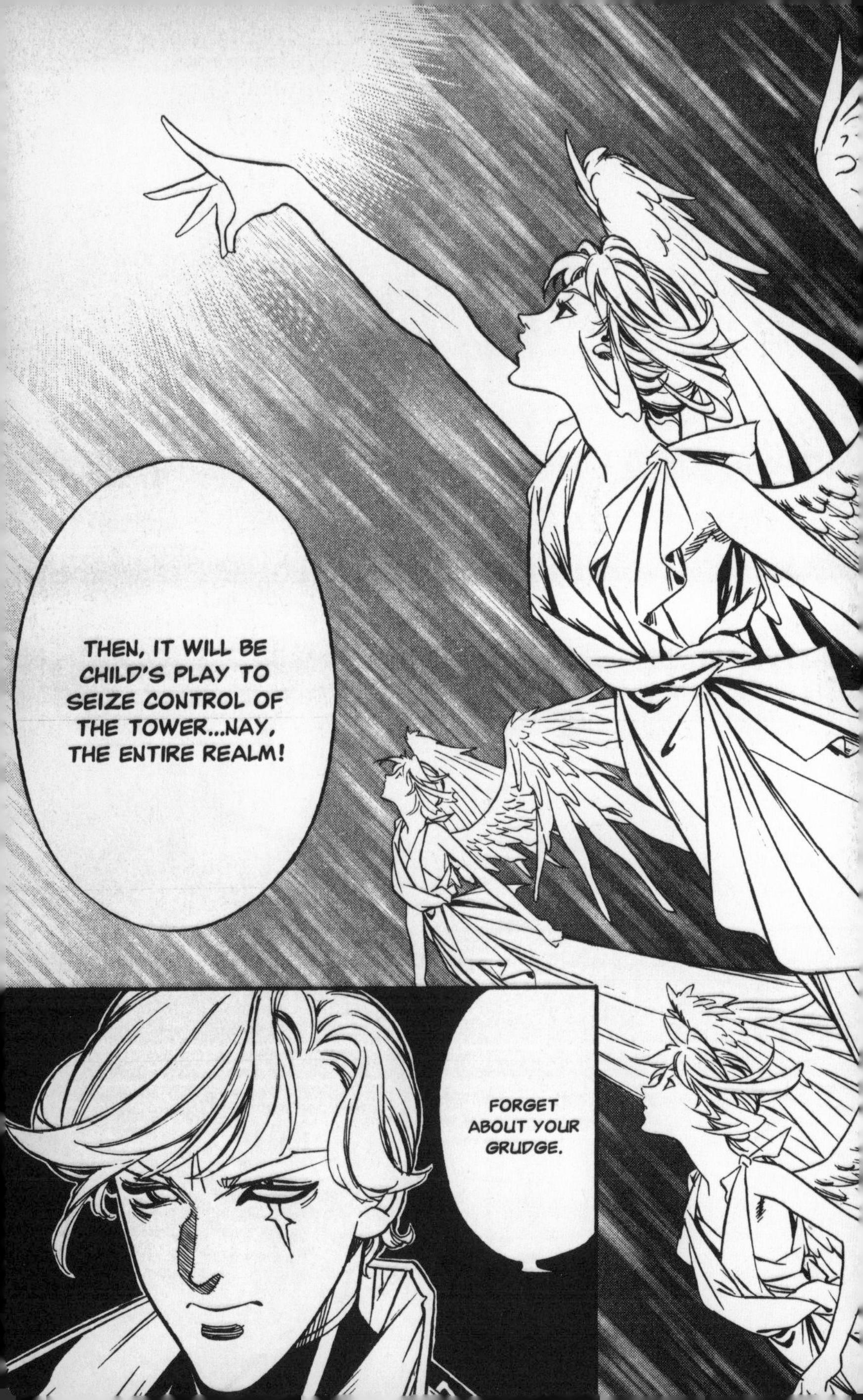
THEN, IT WILL BE CHILD'S PLAY TO SEIZE CONTROL OF THE TOWER...NAY, THE ENTIRE REALM!
FORGET ABOUT YOUR GRUDGE.

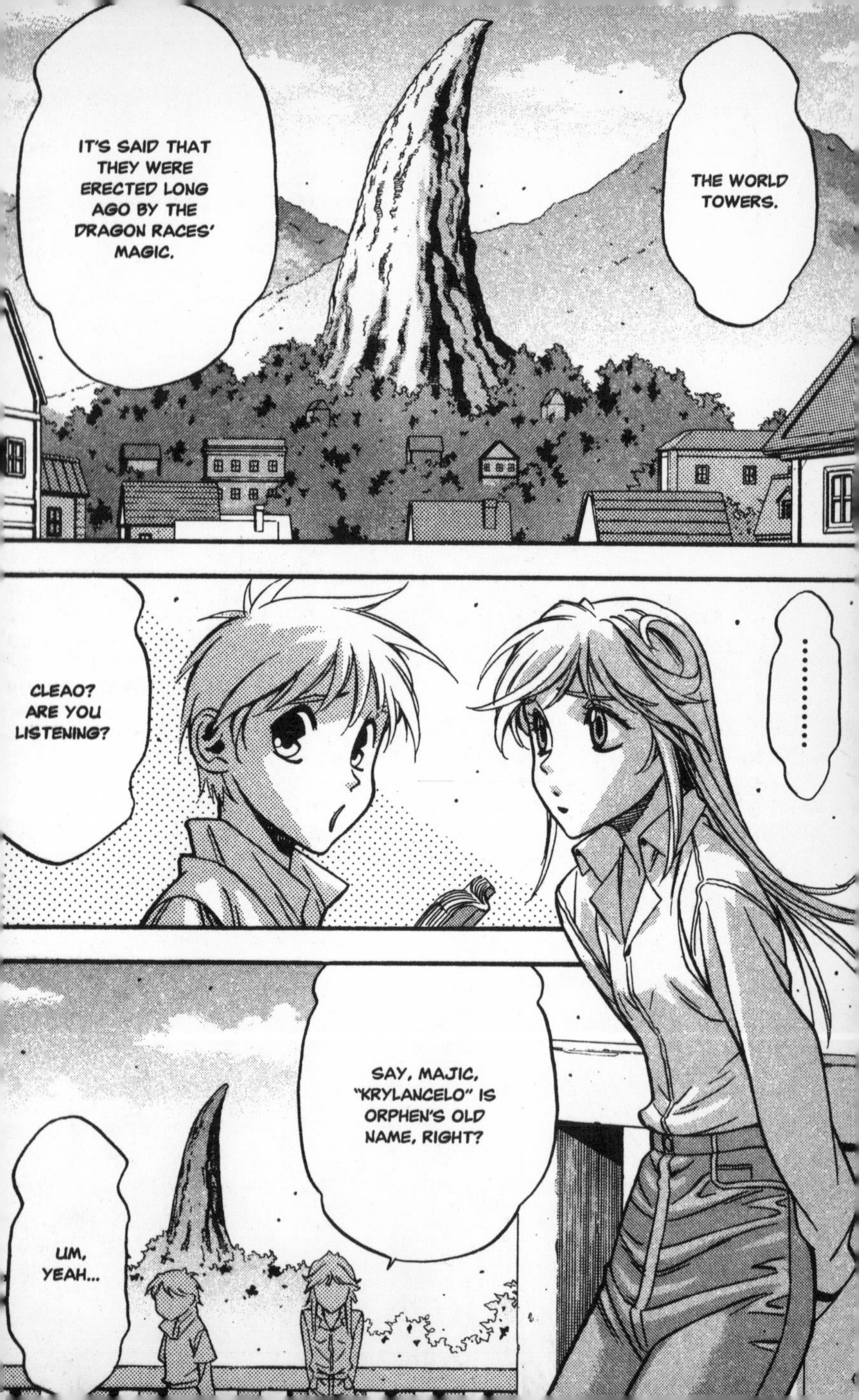
IT'S SAID THAT THEY WERE ERECTED LONG AGO BY THE DRAGON RACES' MAGIC.
THE WORLD TOWERS.
CLEAO? ARE YOU LISTENING?
......
SAY, MAJIC, "KRYLANCELO" IS ORPHEN'S OLD NAME, RIGHT?
UM, YEAH...

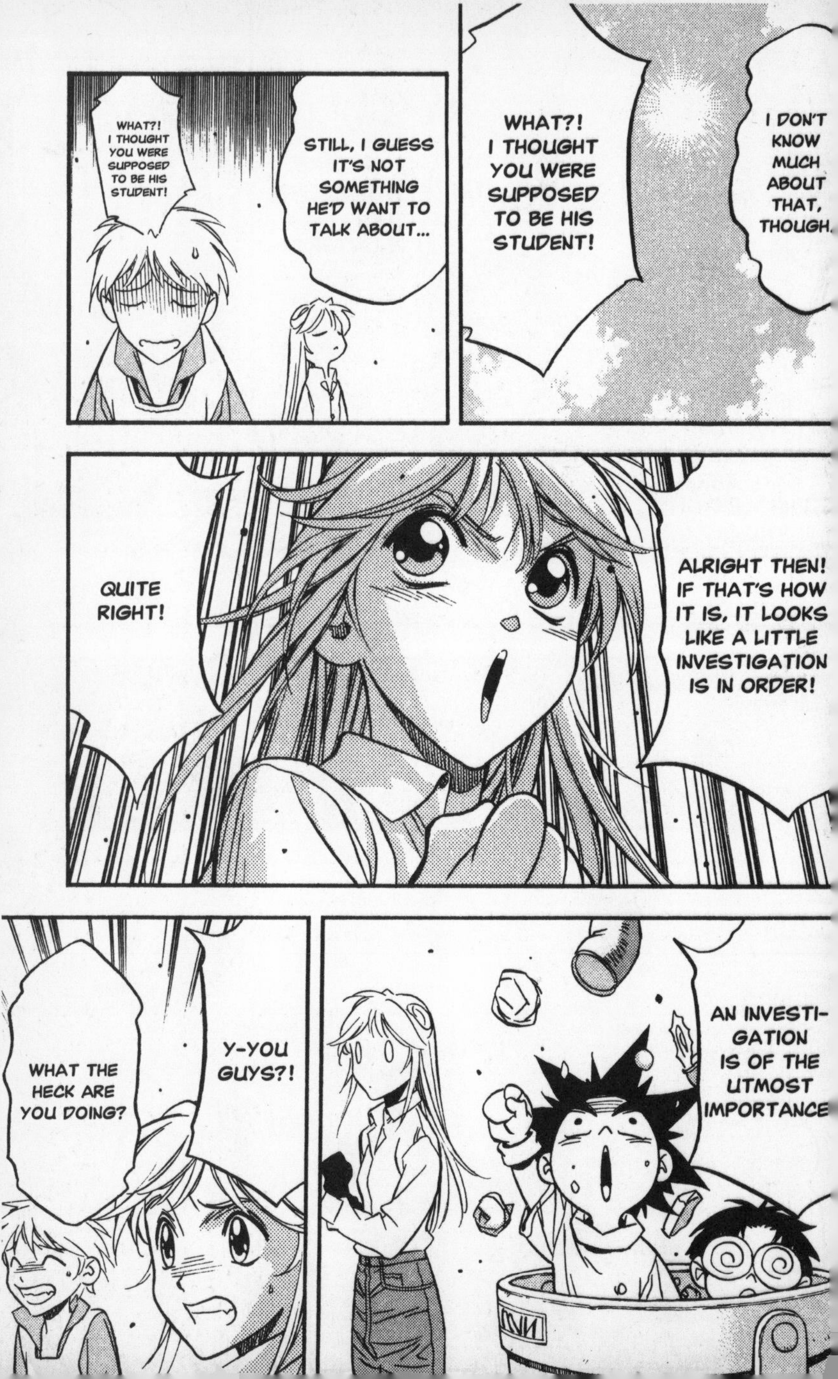
I DON'T KNOW MUCH ABOUT THAT, THOUGH.
WHAT?! I THOUGHT YOU WERE SUPPOSED TO BE HIS STUDENT!
STILL, I GUESS IT'S NOT SOMETHING HE'D WANT TO TALK ABOUT...
WHAT?! I THOUGHT YOU WERE SUPPOSED TO BE HIS STUDENT!
ALRIGHT THEN! IF THAT'S HOW IT IS, IT LOOKS LIKE A LITTLE INVESTIGATION IS IN ORDER!
QUITE RIGHT!
AN INVESTI-GATION IS OF THE UTMOST IMPORTANCE
Y-YOU GUYS?!
WHAT THE HECK ARE YOU DOING?

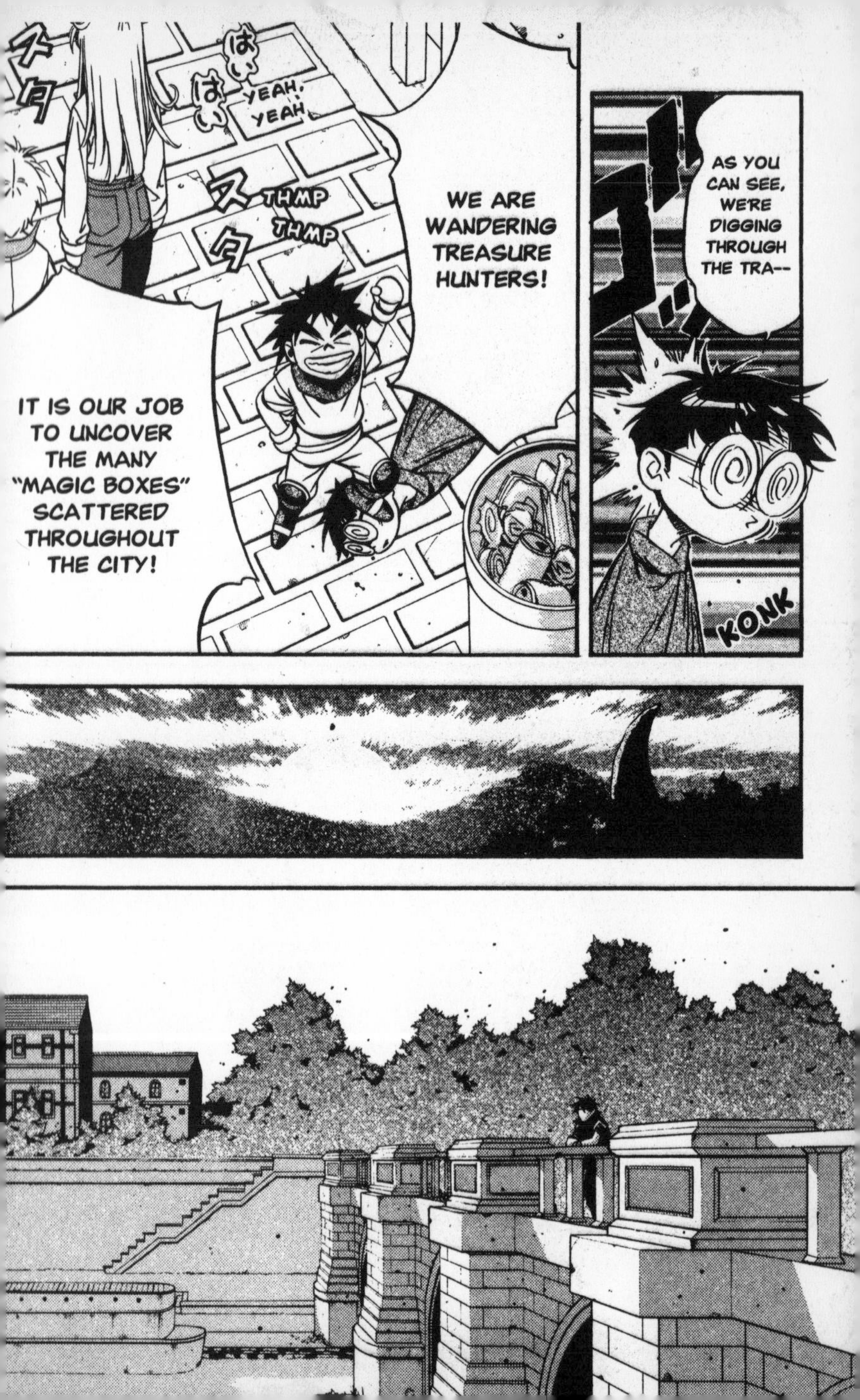
AS YOU CAN SEE, WE'RE DIGGING THROUGH THE TRA--
KONK
WE ARE WANDERING TREASURE HUNTERS!
IT IS OUR JOB TO UNCOVER THE MANY "MAGIC BOXES" SCATTERED THROUGHOUT THE CITY!
はいはい
YEAH, YEAH
スタスタ
THMP THMP

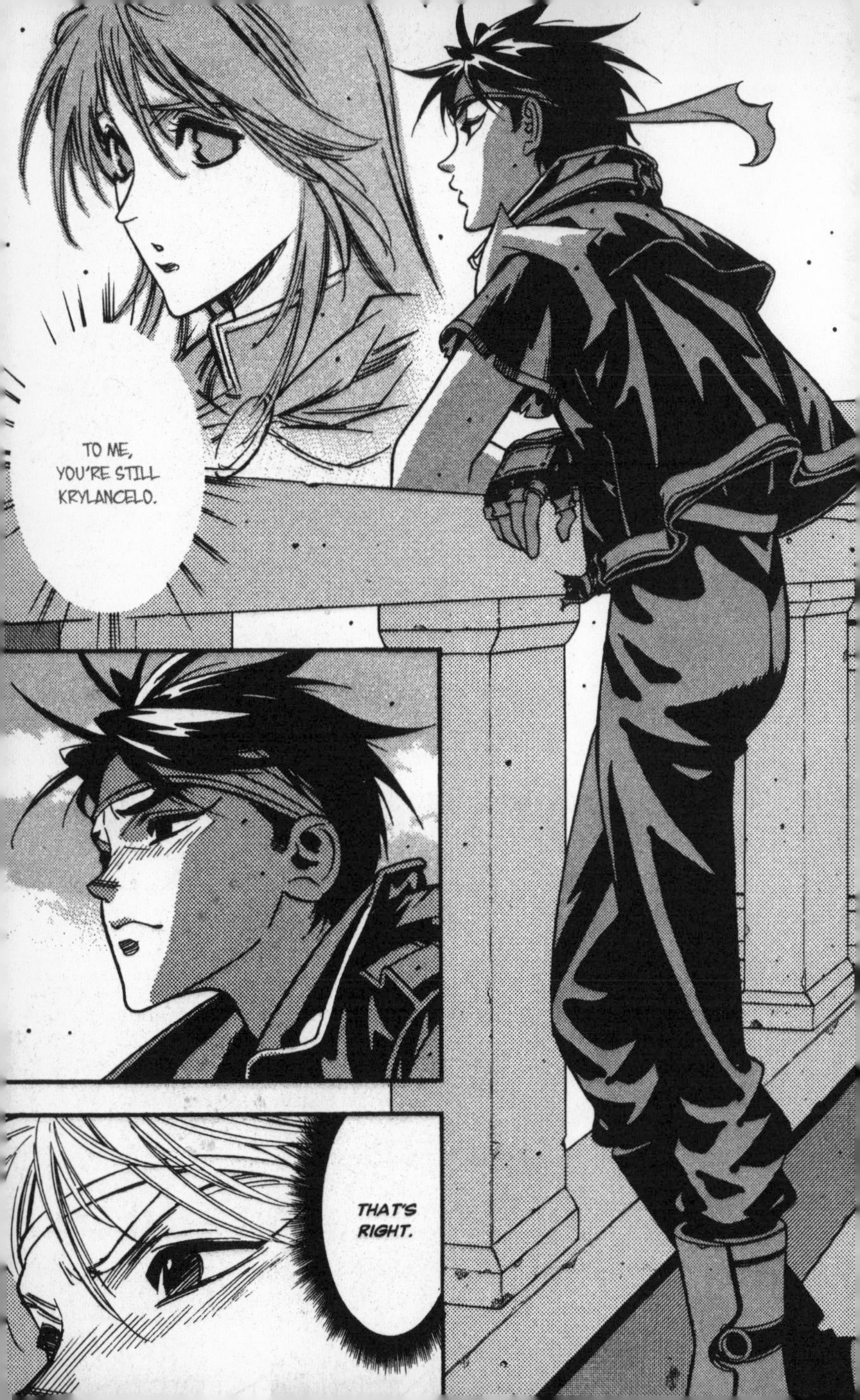
TO ME, YOU'RE STILL KRYLANCELO.
THAT'S RIGHT.

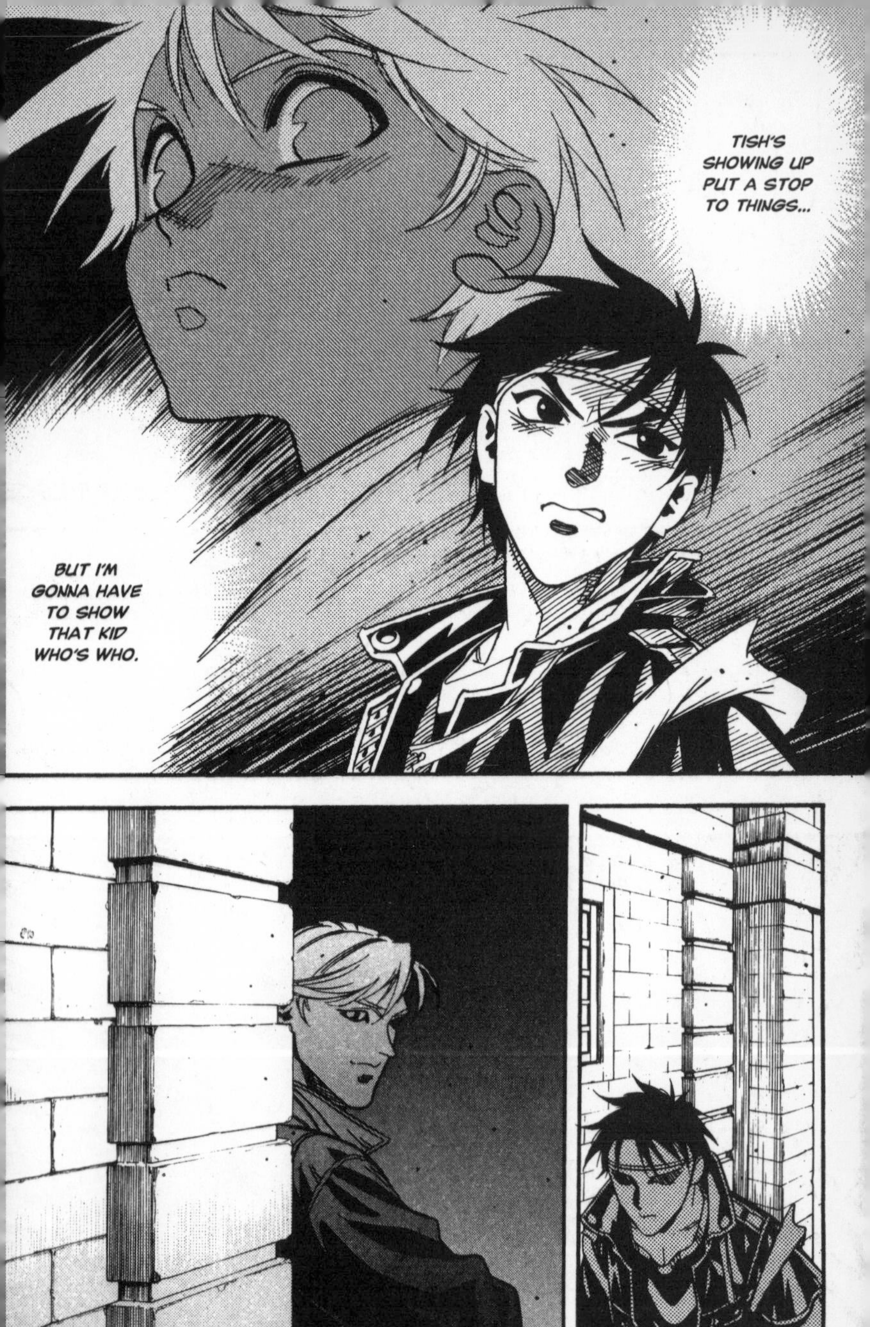
TISH'S SHOWING UP PUT A STOP TO THINGS...
BUT I'M GONNA HAVE TO SHOW THAT KID WHO'S WHO.

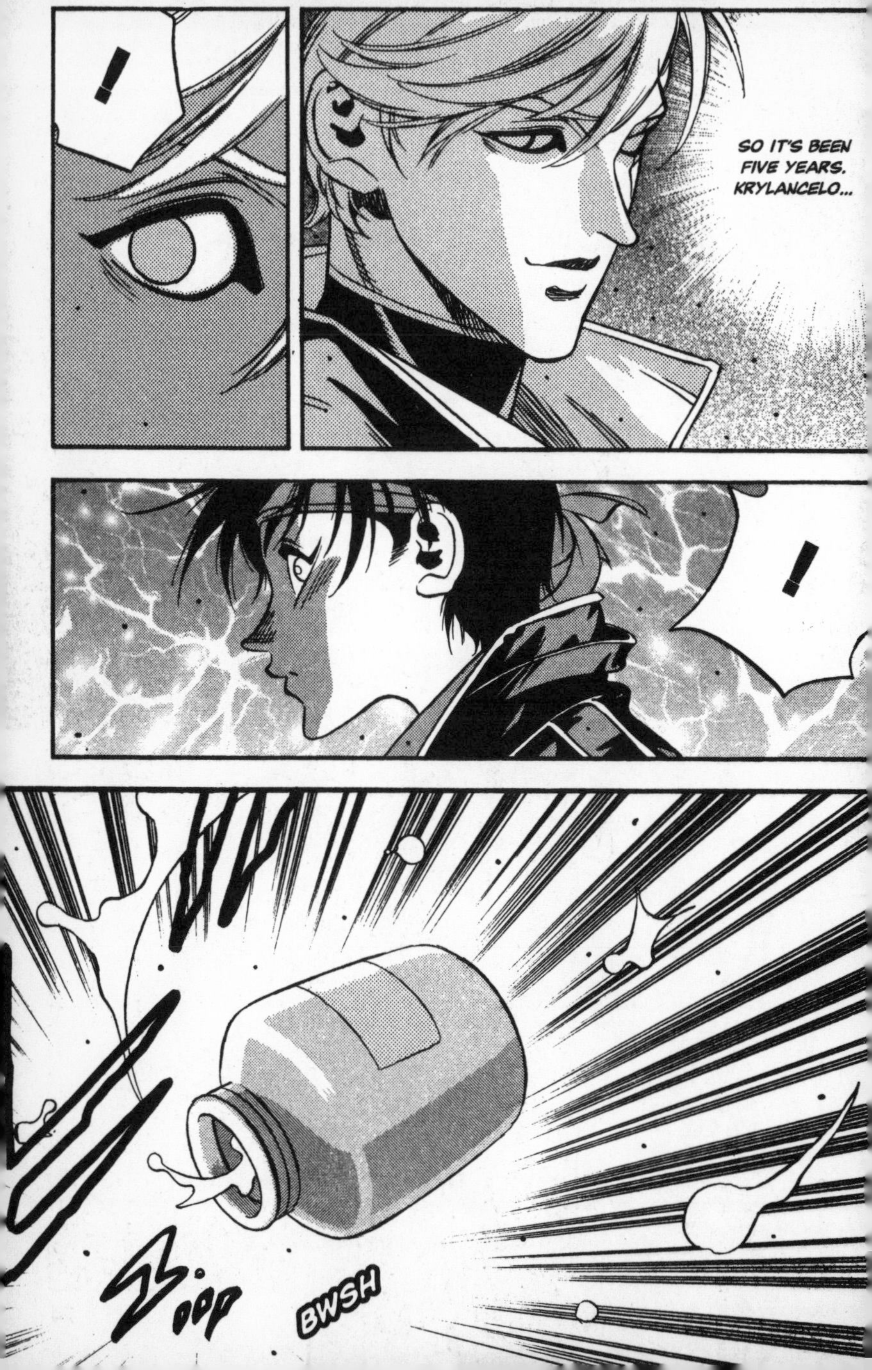
!
SO IT'S BEEN FIVE YEARS. KRYLANCELO...
!
BWSH
ZOOP

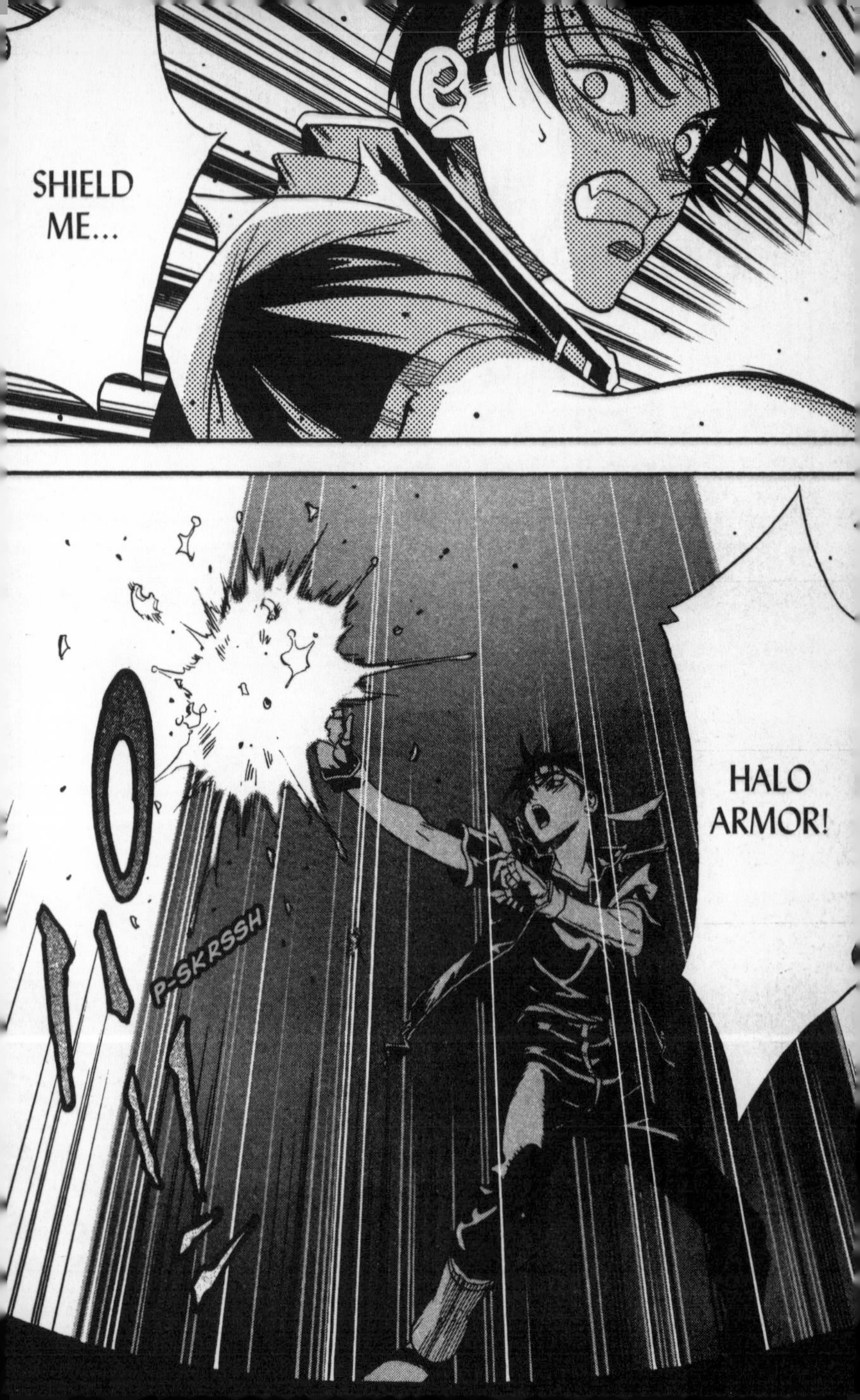
SHIELD ME...
HALO ARMOR!
P-SKRSSH

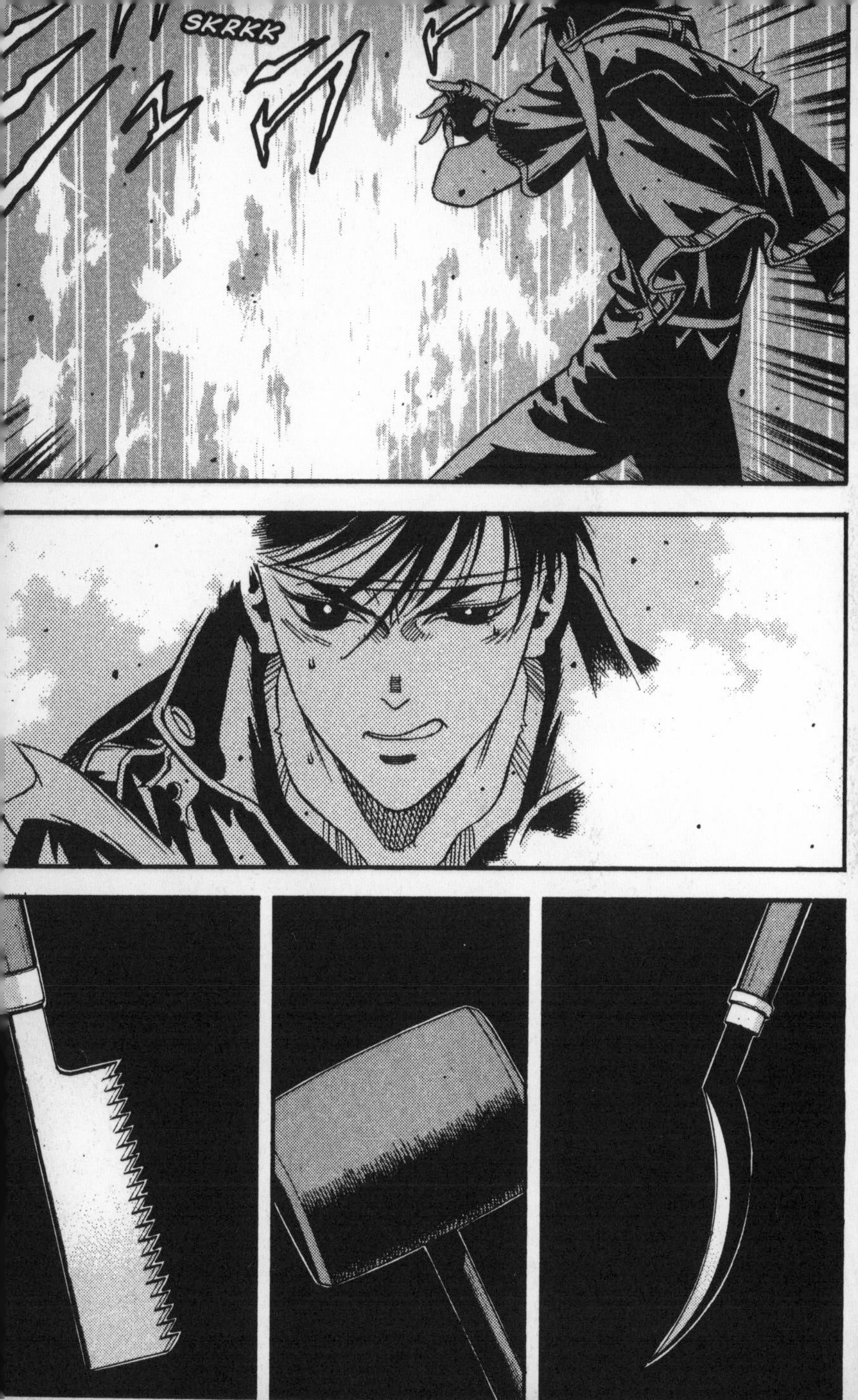
SKRKK

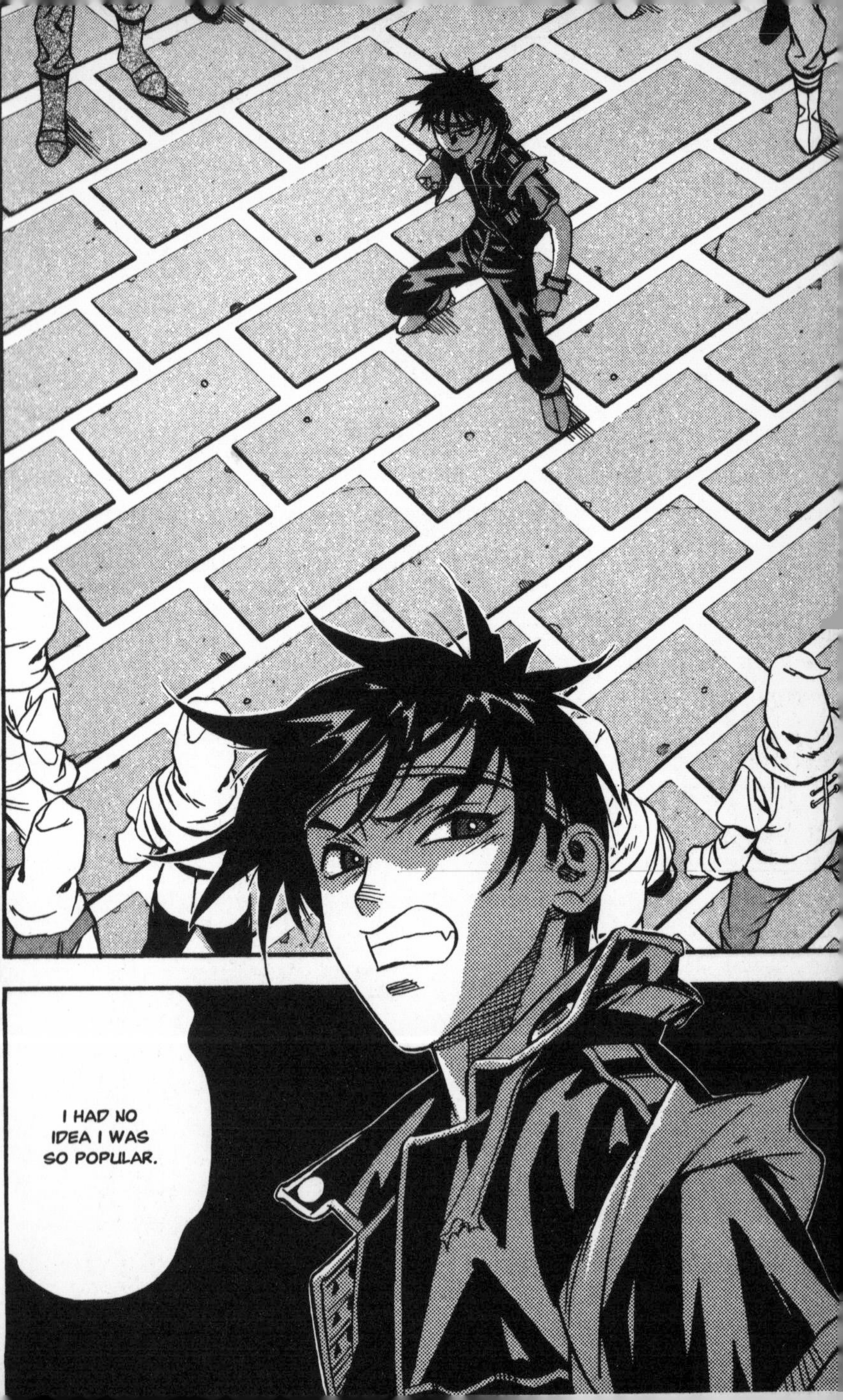
I HAD NO
IDEA I WAS
SO POPULAR.

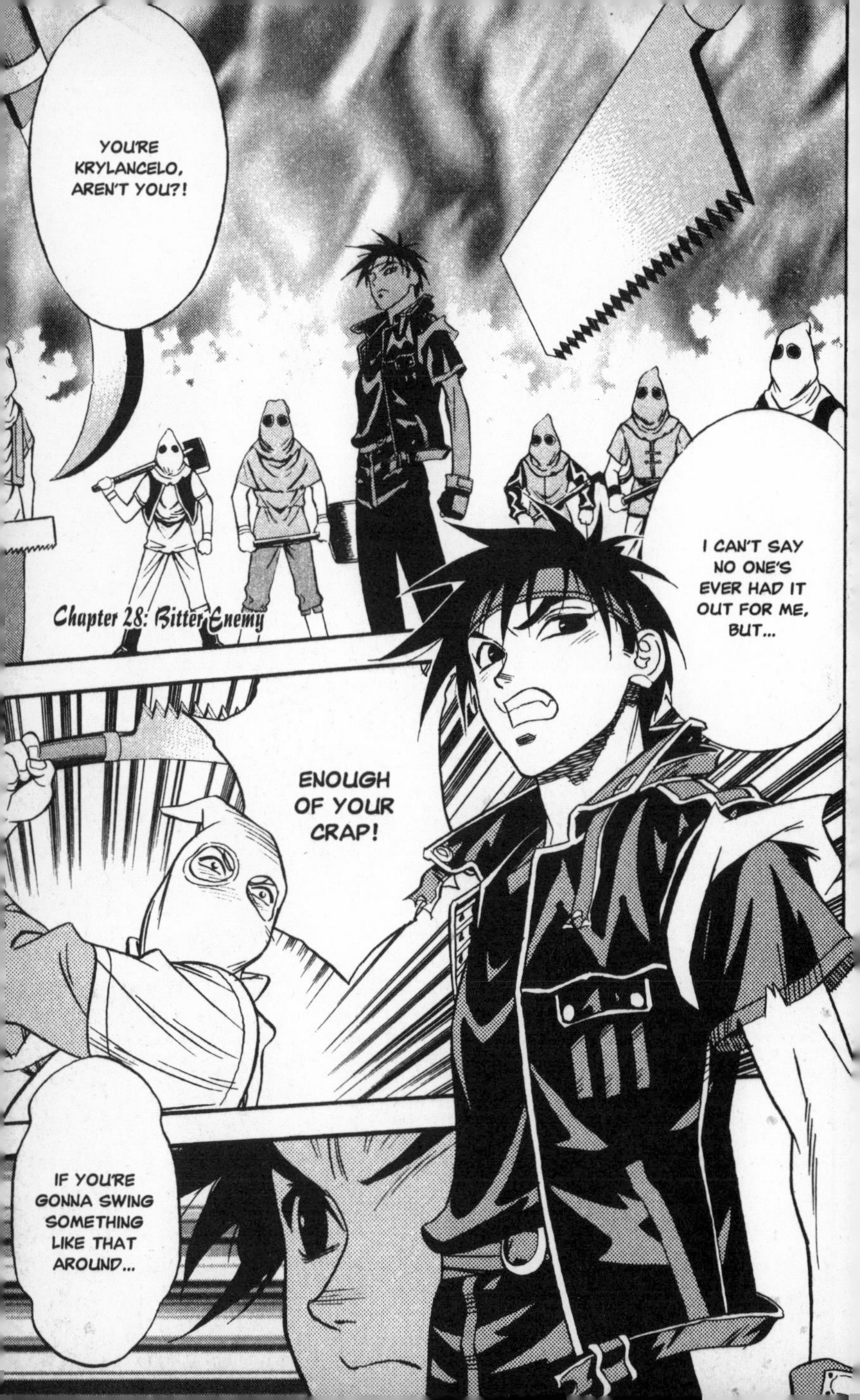
YOU'RE KRYLANCELO, AREN'T YOU?!
I CAN'T SAY NO ONE'S EVER HAD IT OUT FOR ME, BUT...
Chapter 28: Bitter Enemy
ENOUGH OF YOUR CRAP!
IF YOU'RE GONNA SWING SOMETHING LIKE THAT AROUND...

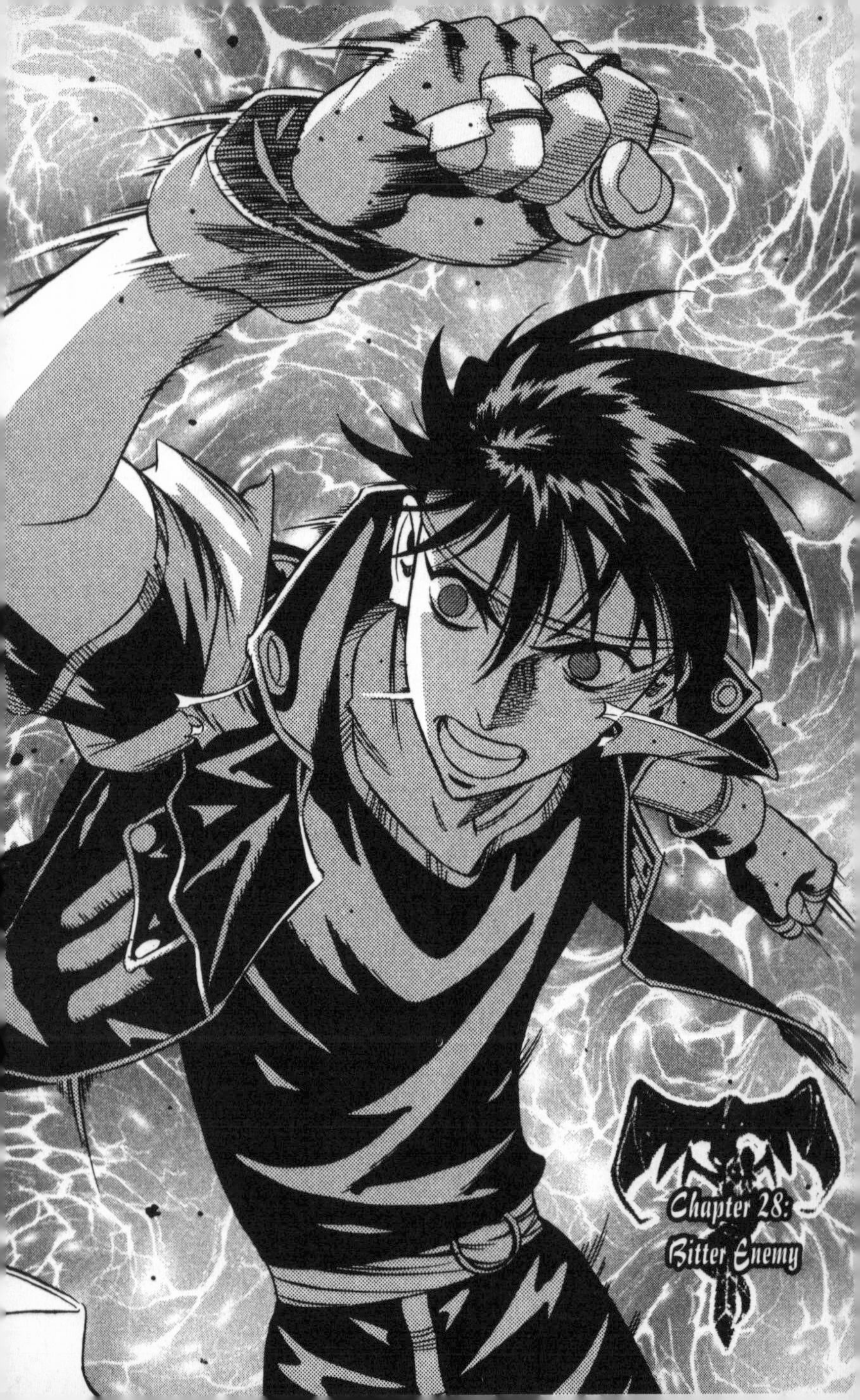
Chapter 28:
Bitter Enemy

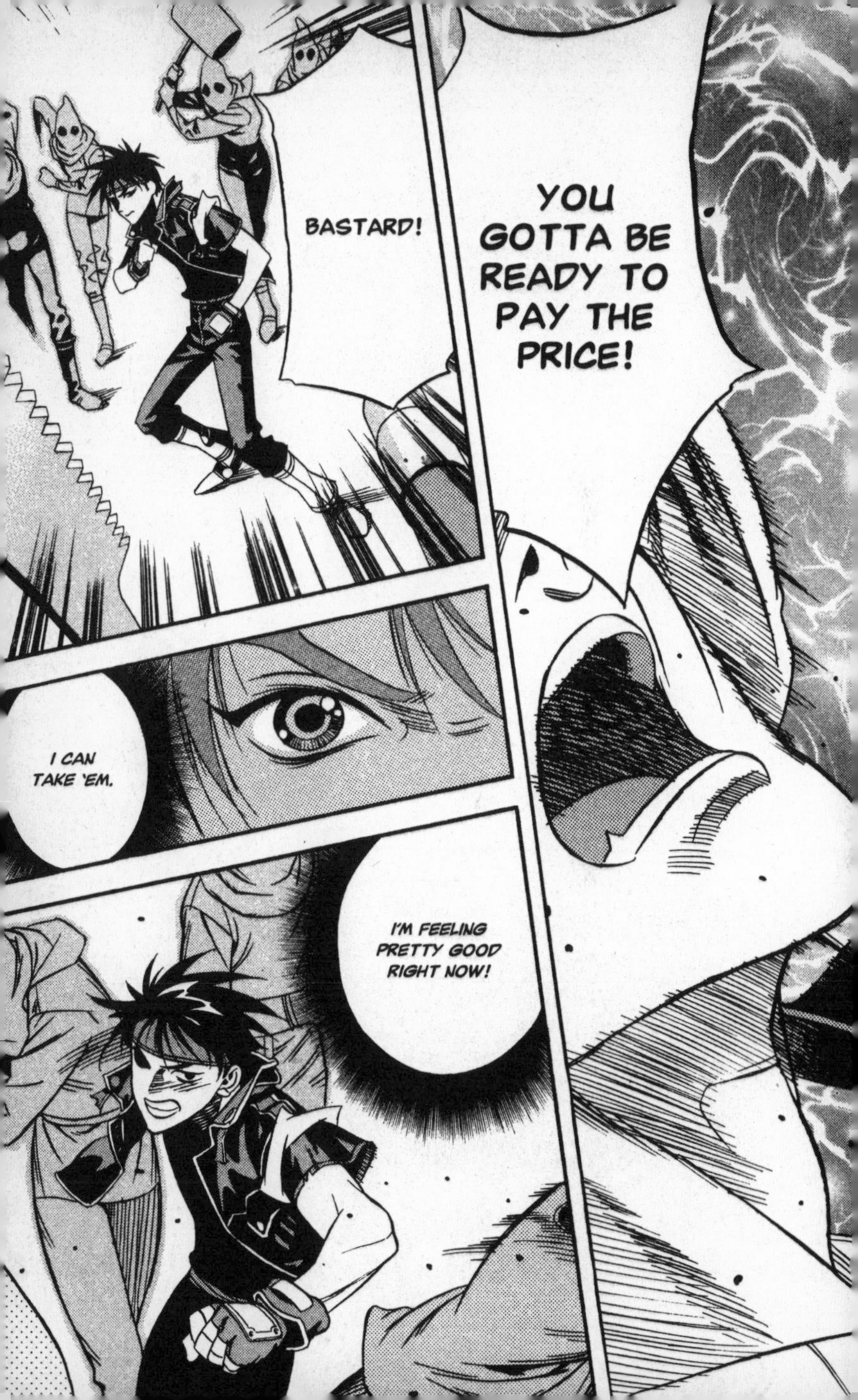
YOU GOTTA BE READY TO PAY THE PRICE!
BASTARD!
I CAN TAKE 'EM.
I'M FEELING PRETTY GOOD RIGHT NOW!

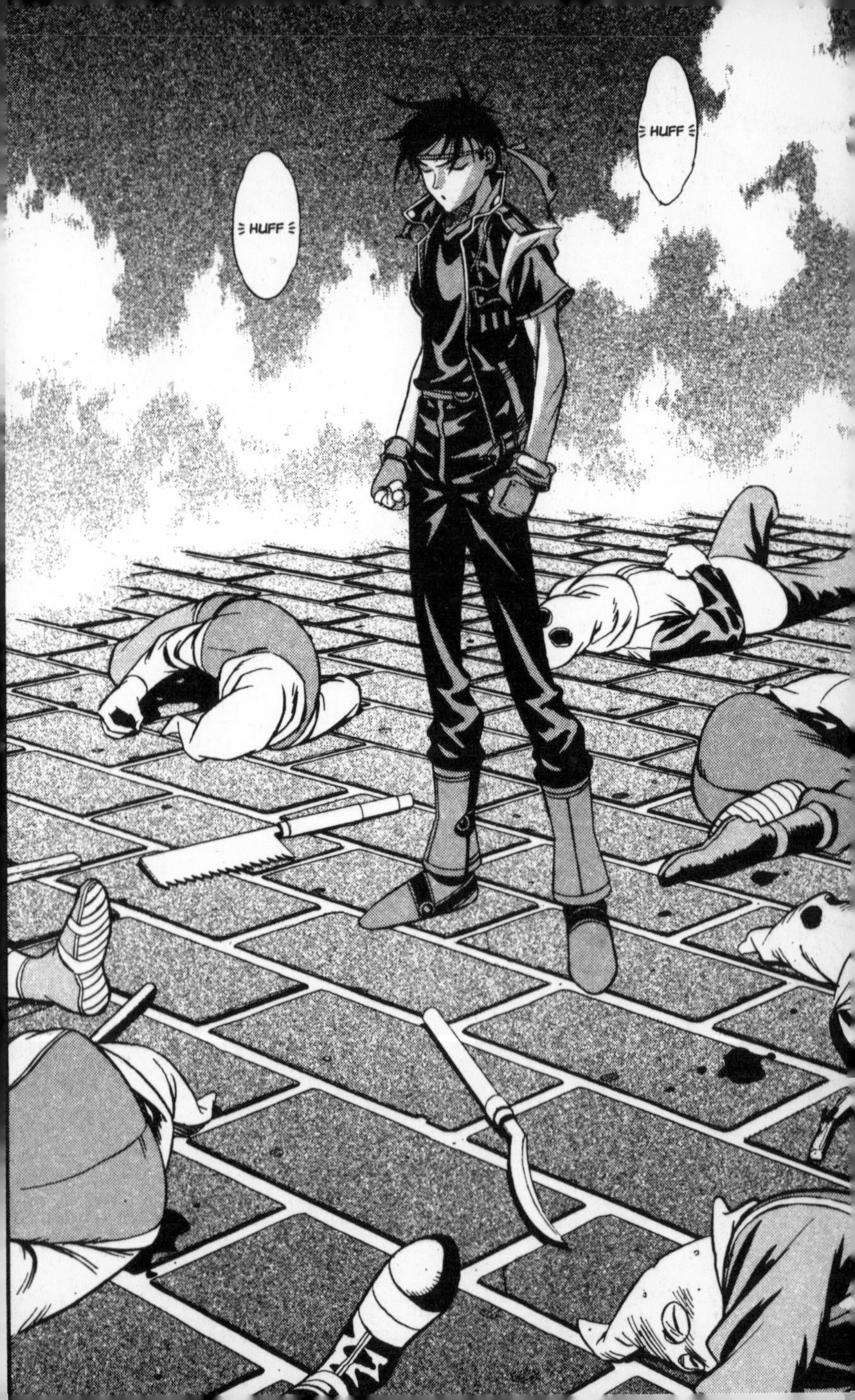
HUFF
HUFF

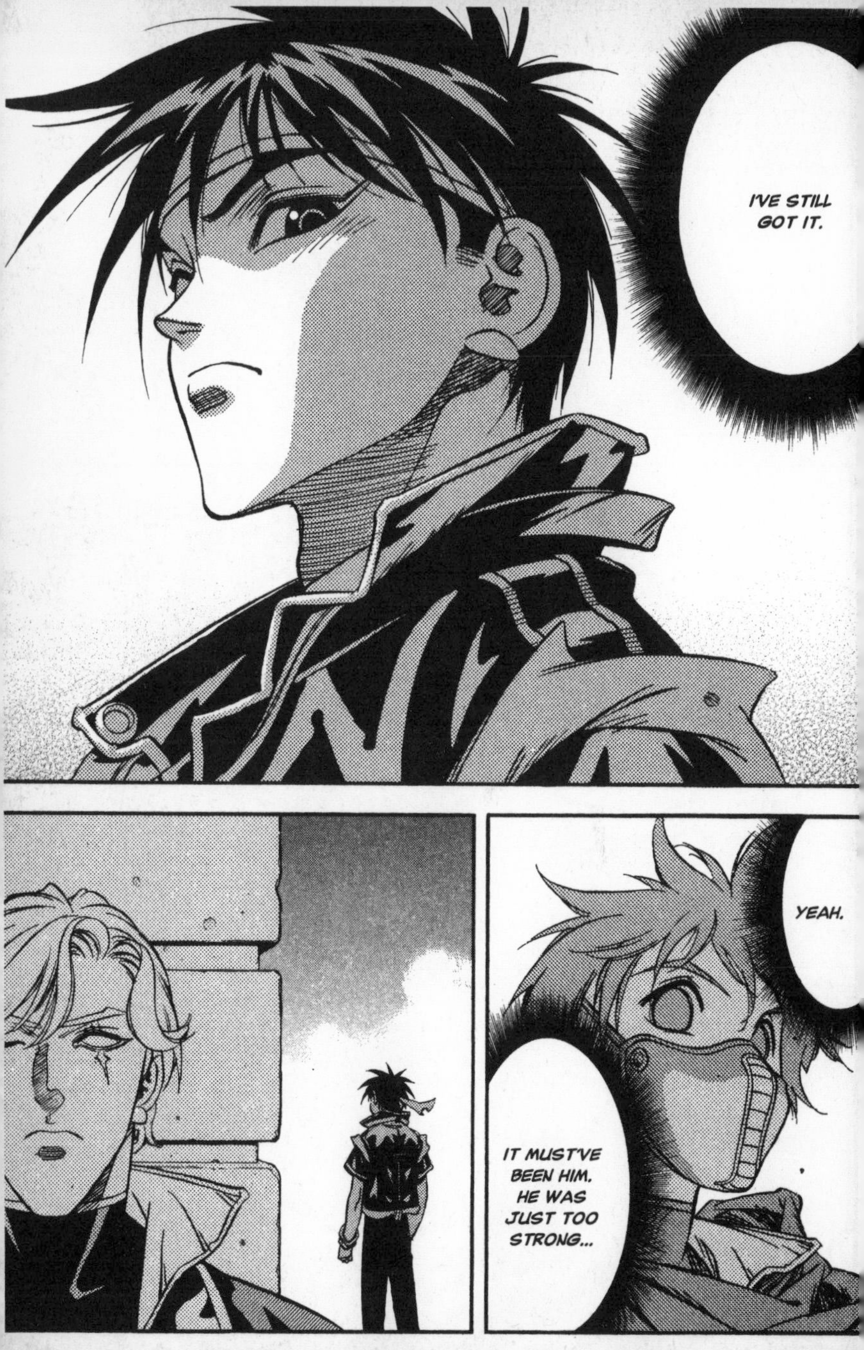
I'VE STILL GOT IT.
YEAH.
IT MUST'VE BEEN HIM. HE WAS JUST TOO STRONG...

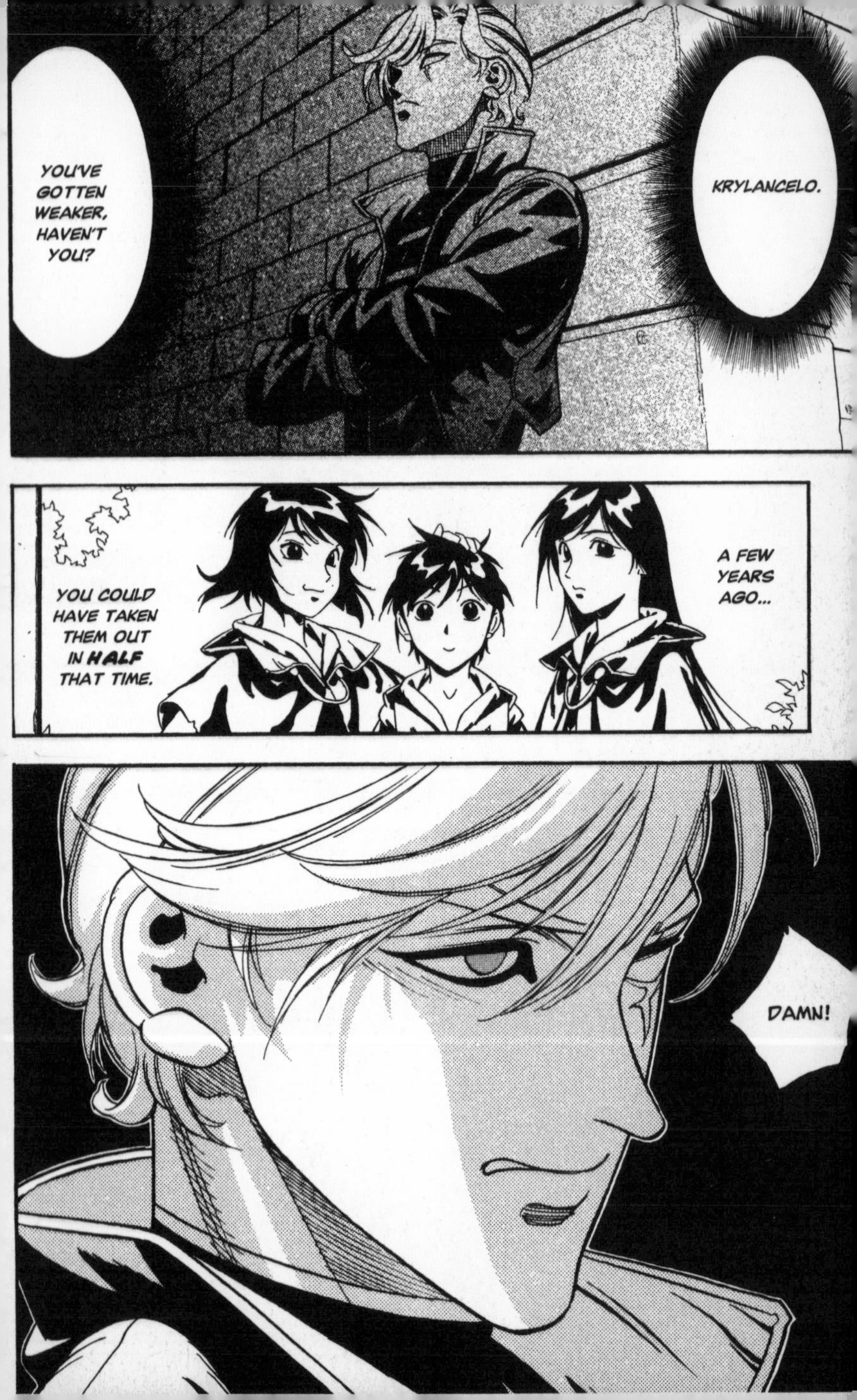
KRYLANCELO.
YOU'VE GOTTEN WEAKER, HAVEN'T YOU?
A FEW YEARS AGO...
YOU COULD HAVE TAKEN THEM OUT IN HALF THAT TIME.
DAMN!

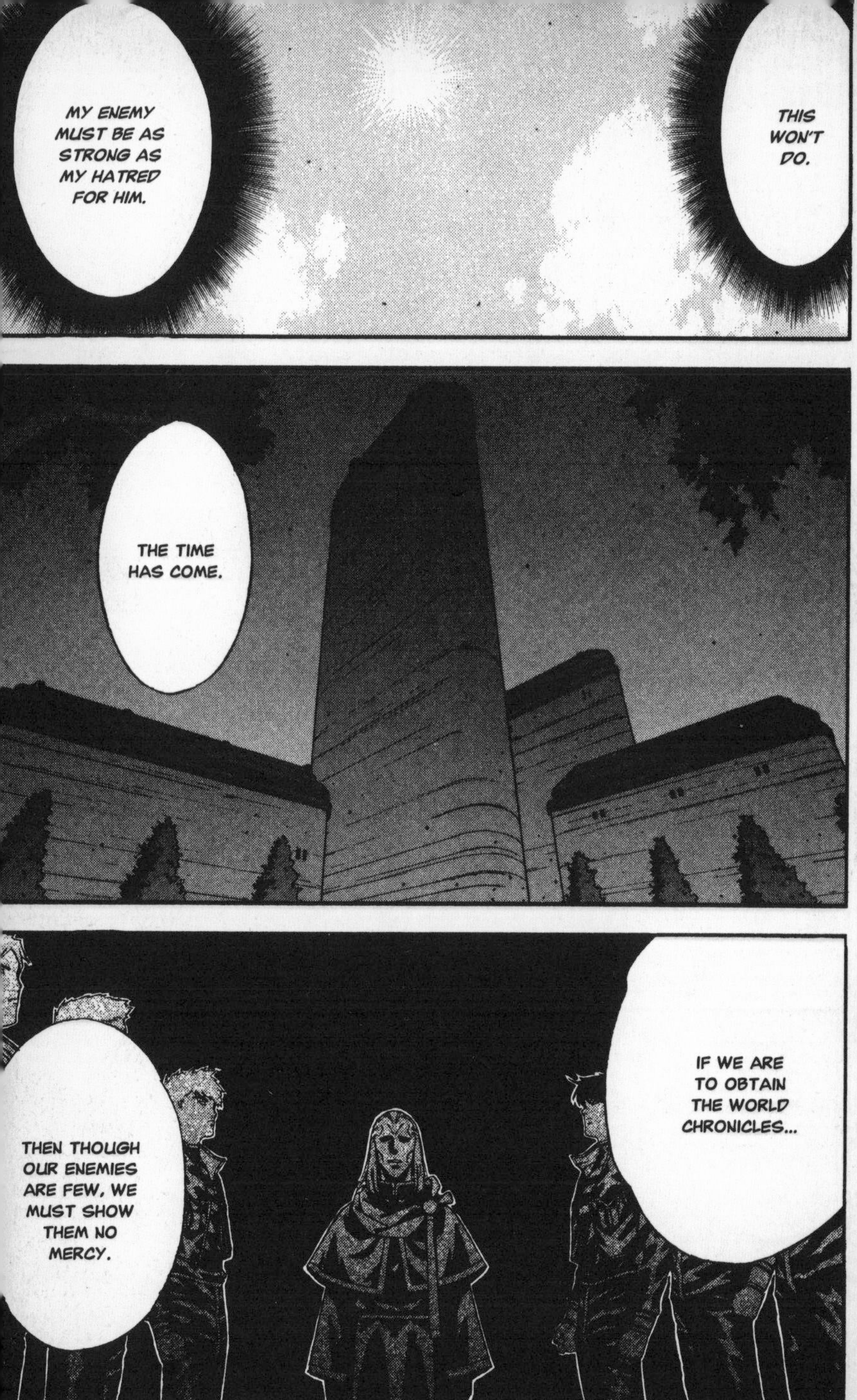

THIS WON'T DO.
MY ENEMY MUST BE AS STRONG AS MY HATRED FOR HIM.
THE TIME HAS COME.
IF WE ARE TO OBTAIN THE WORLD CHRONICLES...
THEN THOUGH OUR ENEMIES ARE FEW, WE MUST SHOW THEM NO MERCY.

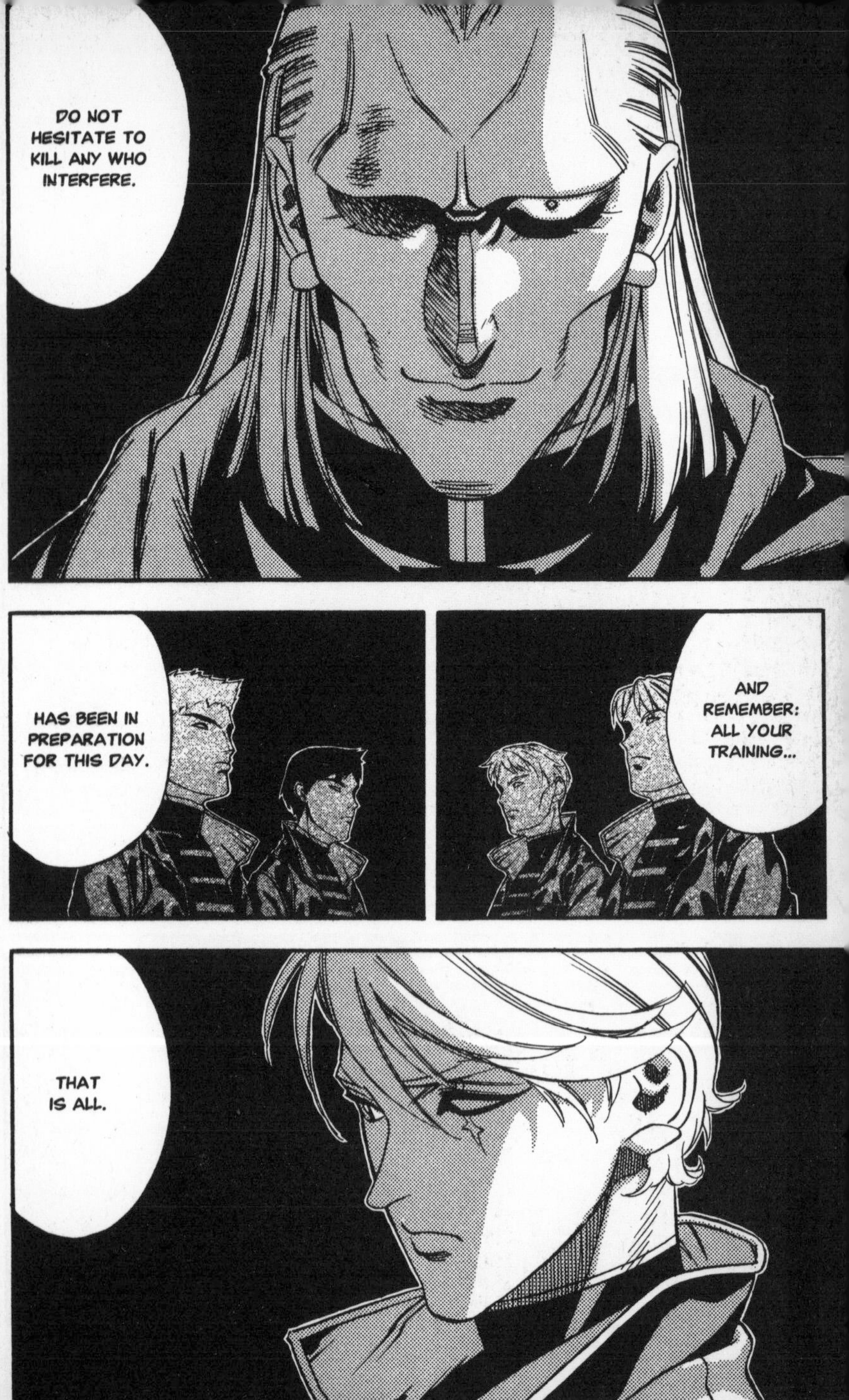
DO NOT HESITATE TO KILL ANY WHO INTERFERE.
AND REMEMBER: ALL YOUR TRAINING...
HAS BEEN IN PREPARATION FOR THIS DAY.
THAT IS ALL.

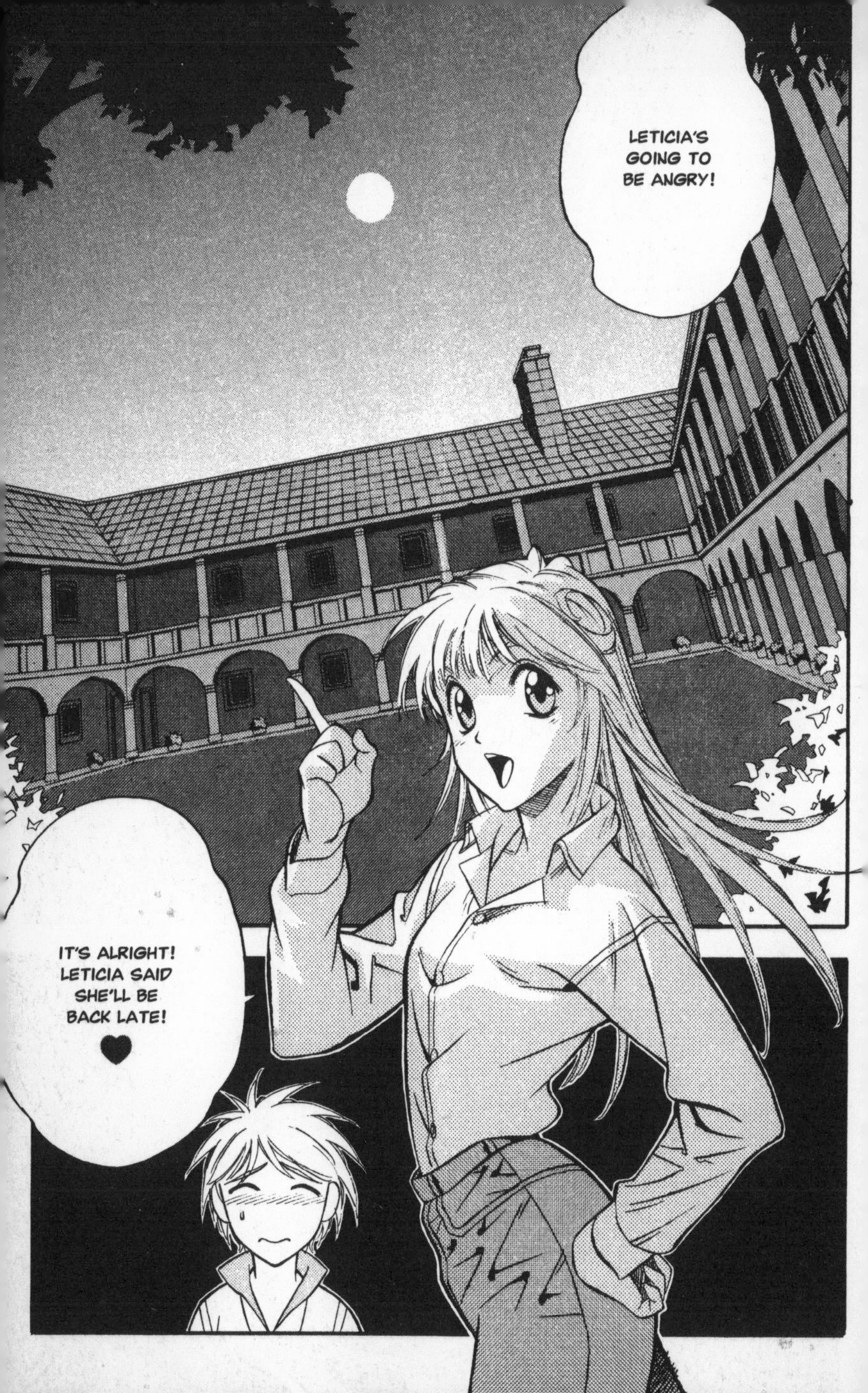
LETICIA'S GOING TO BE ANGRY!
IT'S ALRIGHT! LETICIA SAID SHE'LL BE BACK LATE! ♥

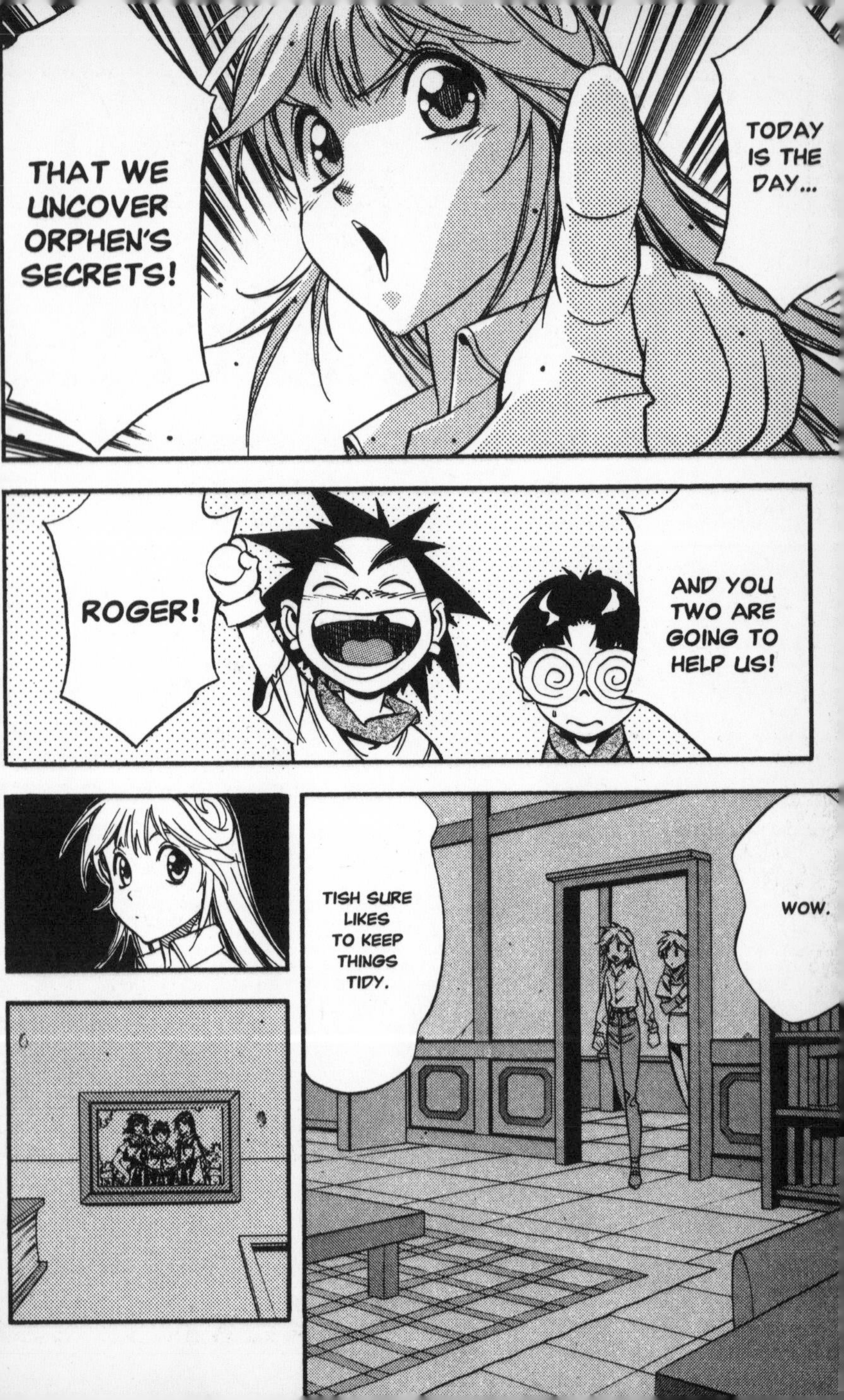
TODAY IS THE DAY...
THAT WE UNCOVER ORPHEN'S SECRETS!
AND YOU TWO ARE GOING TO HELP US!
ROGER!
WOW.
TISH SURE LIKES TO KEEP THINGS TIDY.

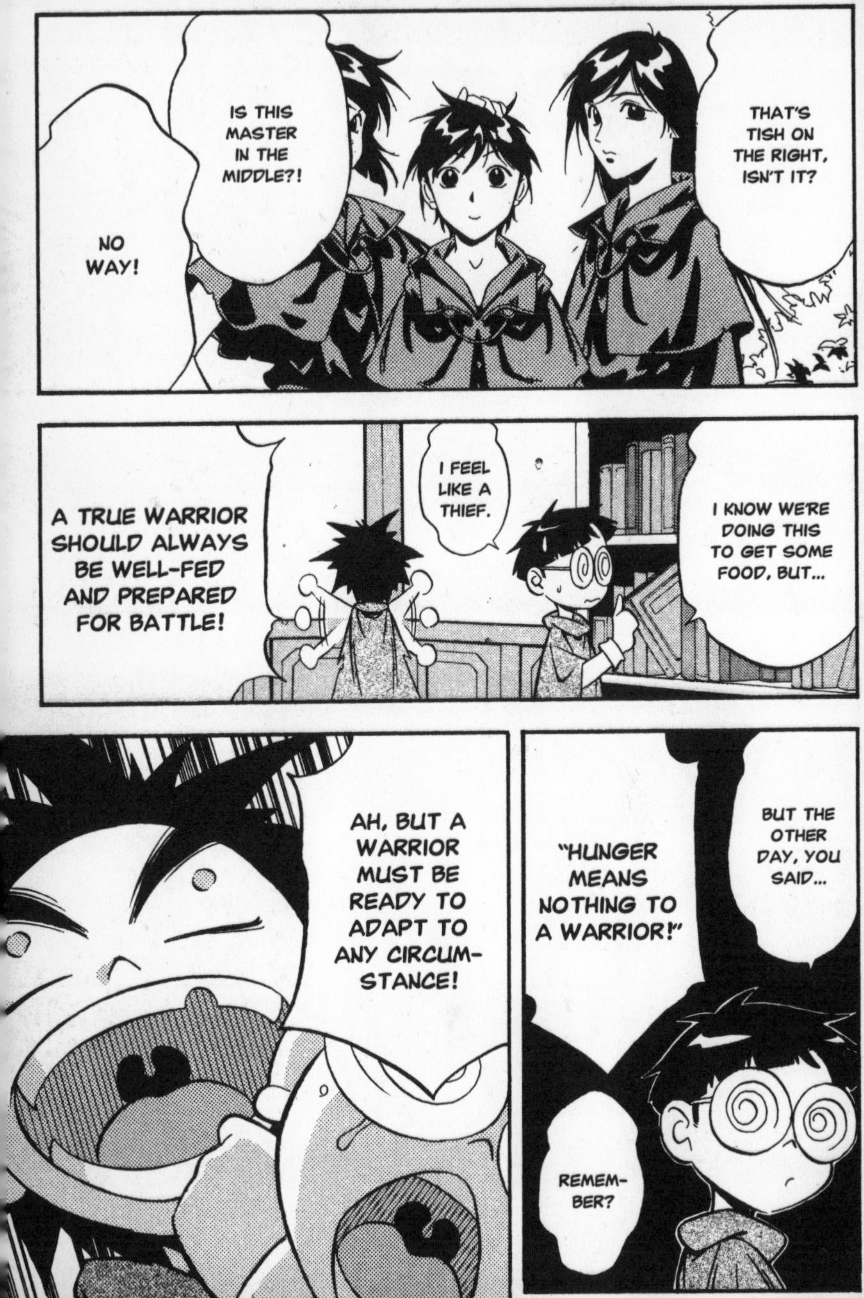
THAT'S TISH ON THE RIGHT, ISN'T IT?
IS THIS MASTER IN THE MIDDLE?!
NO WAY!
I KNOW WE'RE DOING THIS TO GET SOME FOOD, BUT...
I FEEL LIKE A THIEF.
A TRUE WARRIOR SHOULD ALWAYS BE WELL-FED AND PREPARED FOR BATTLE!
BUT THE OTHER DAY, YOU SAID...
"HUNGER MEANS NOTHING TO A WARRIOR!"
REMEMBER?
AH, BUT A WARRIOR MUST BE READY TO ADAPT TO ANY CIRCUM-STANCE!

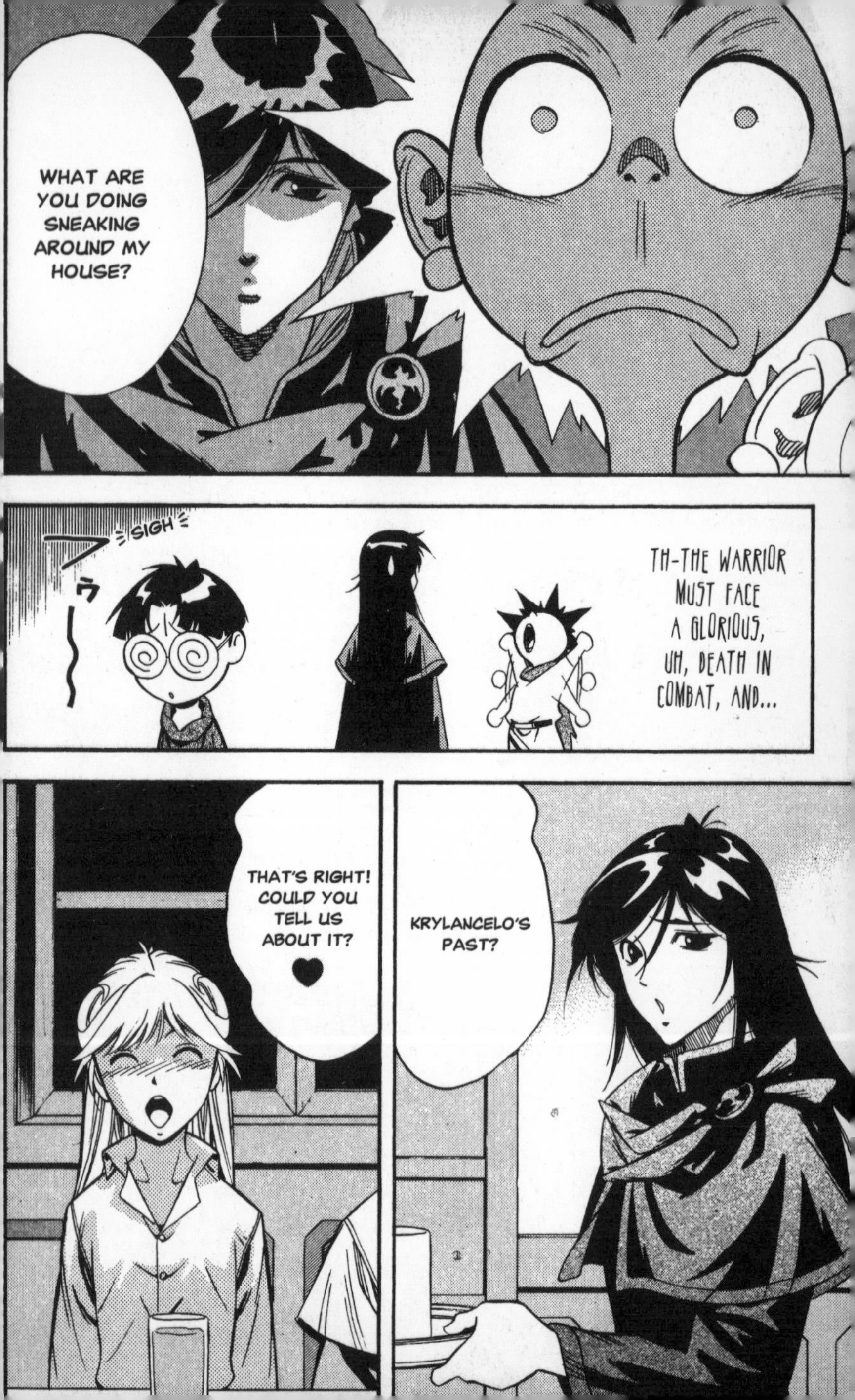
WHAT ARE YOU DOING SNEAKING AROUND MY HOUSE?
TH-THE WARRIOR MUST FACE A GLORIOUS, UH, DEATH IN COMBAT, AND...
SIGH
KRYLANCELO'S PAST?
THAT'S RIGHT! COULD YOU TELL US ABOUT IT? ♥

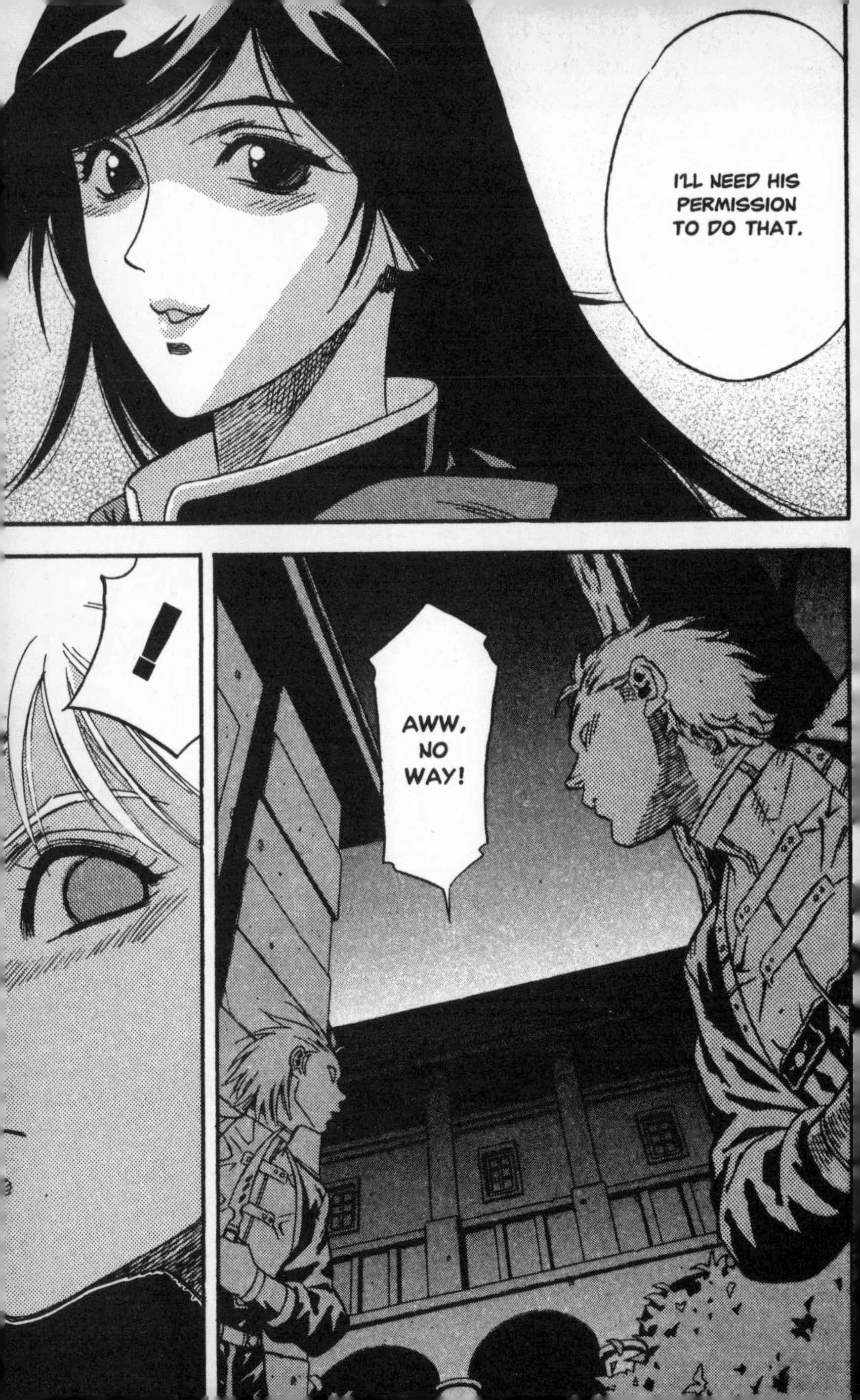
I'LL NEED HIS PERMISSION TO DO THAT.
AWW, NO WAY!
!

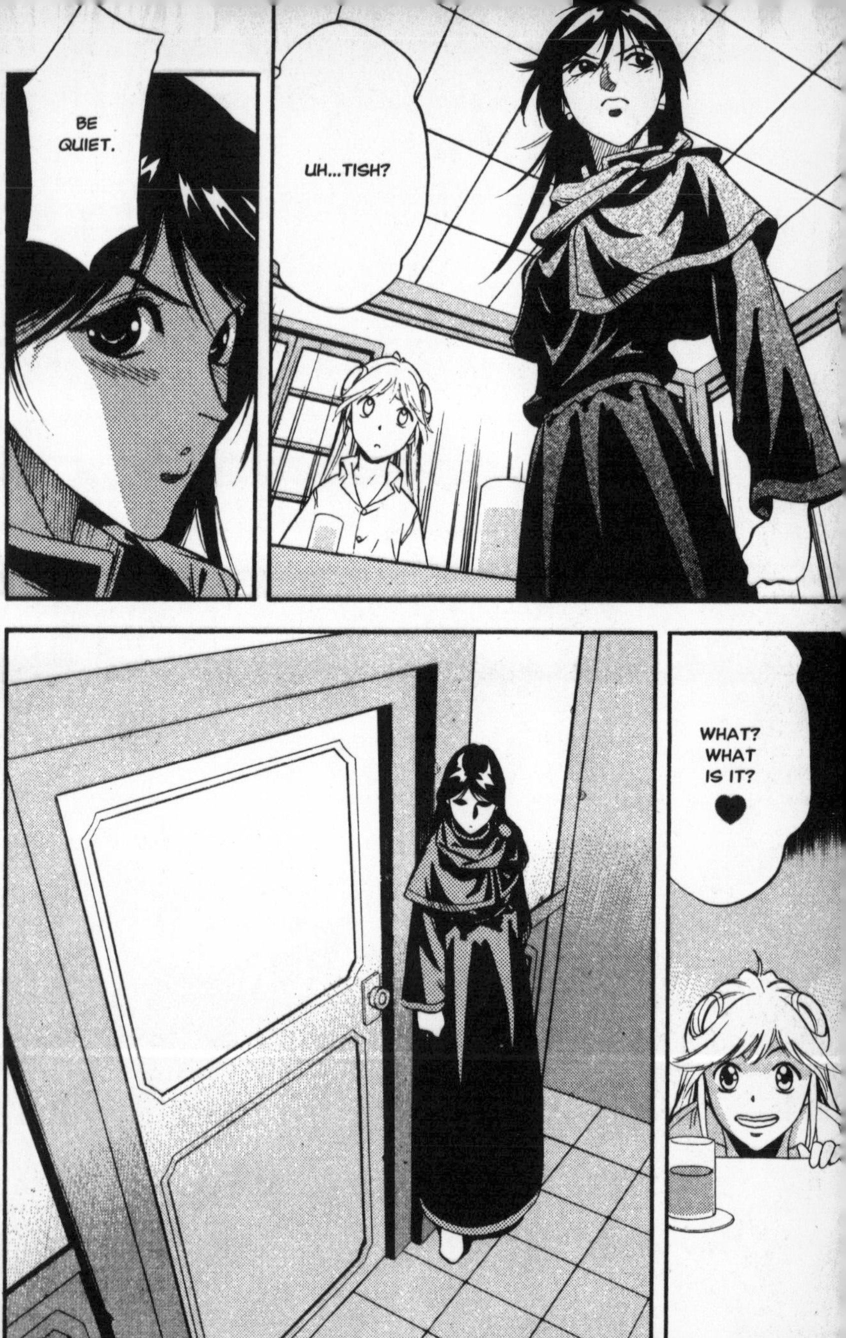
UH...TISH?
BE QUIET.
WHAT? WHAT IS IT? ♥

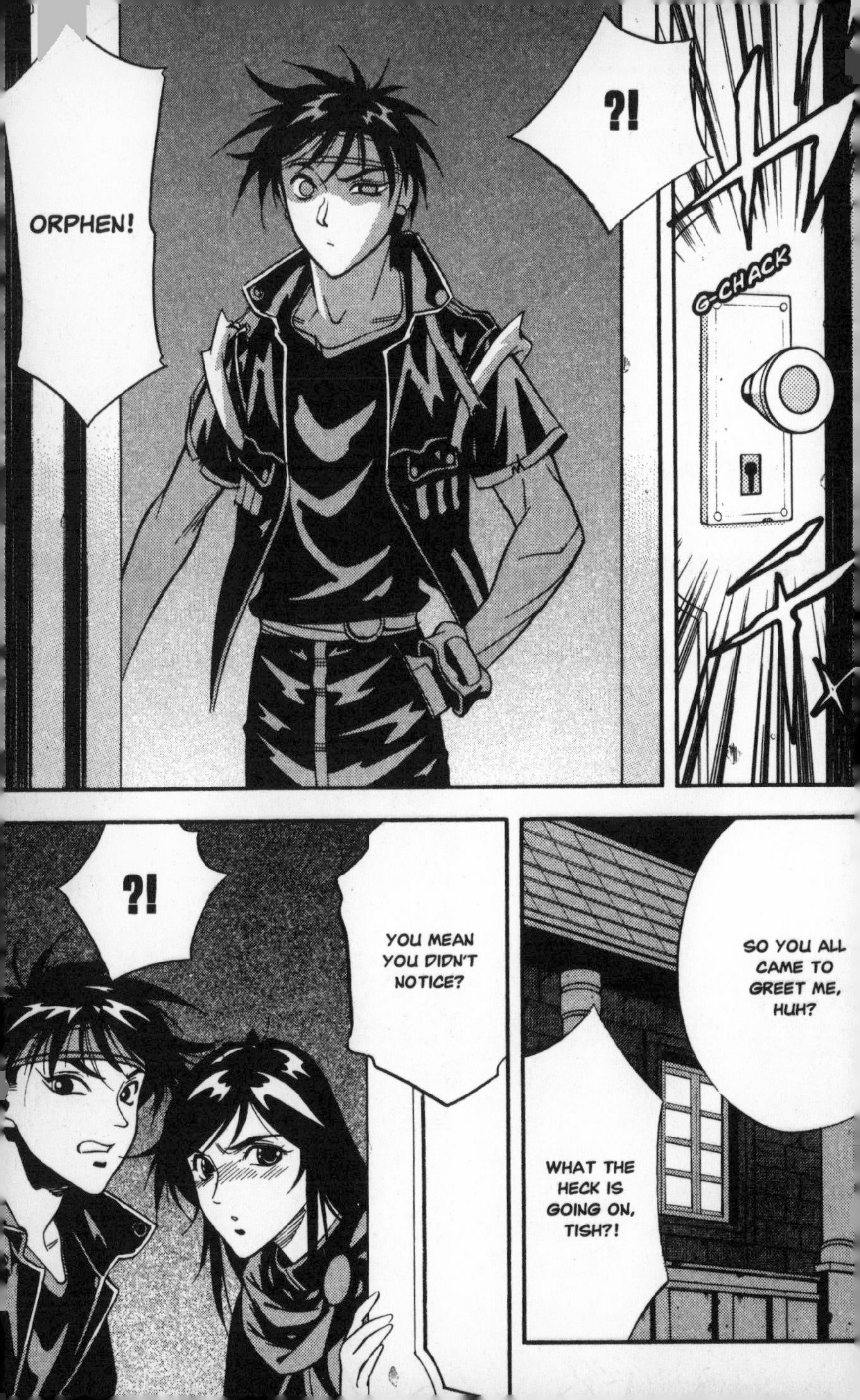
G-CHACK
?!
ORPHEN!
SO YOU ALL CAME TO GREET ME, HUH?
WHAT THE HECK IS GOING ON, TISH?!
YOU MEAN YOU DIDN'T NOTICE?
?!

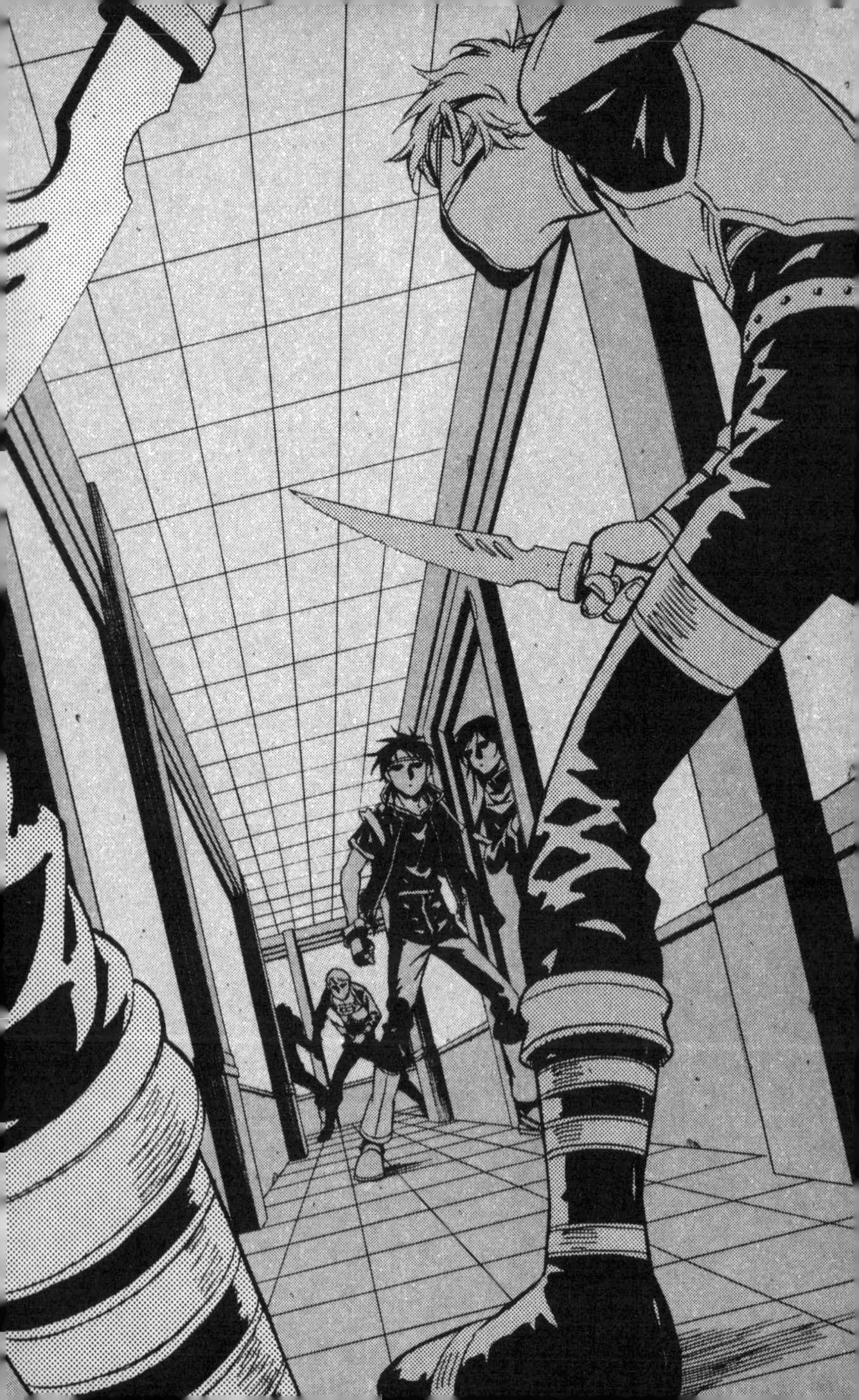

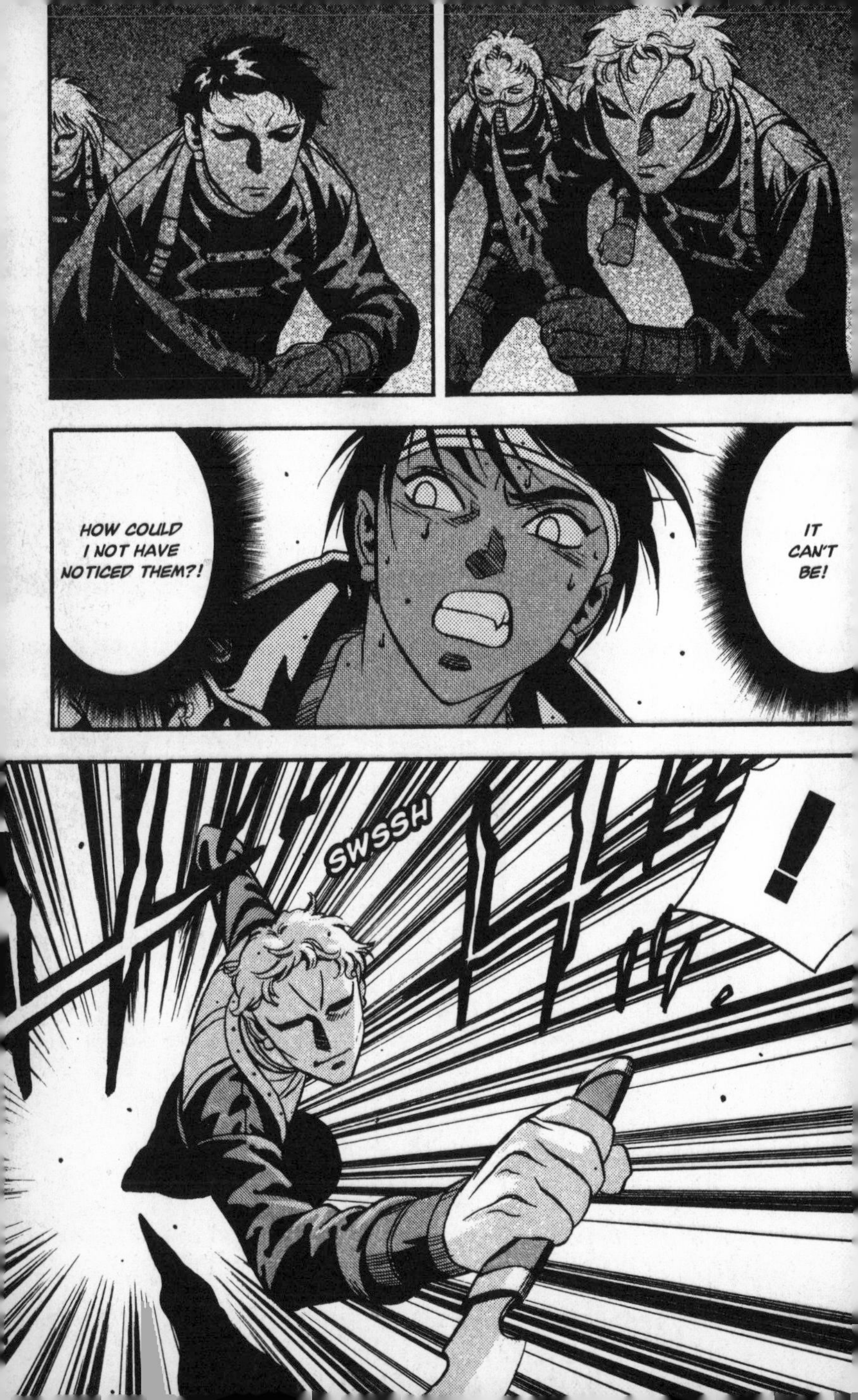
IT CAN'T BE!
HOW COULD I NOT HAVE NOTICED THEM?!
!
SWSSH

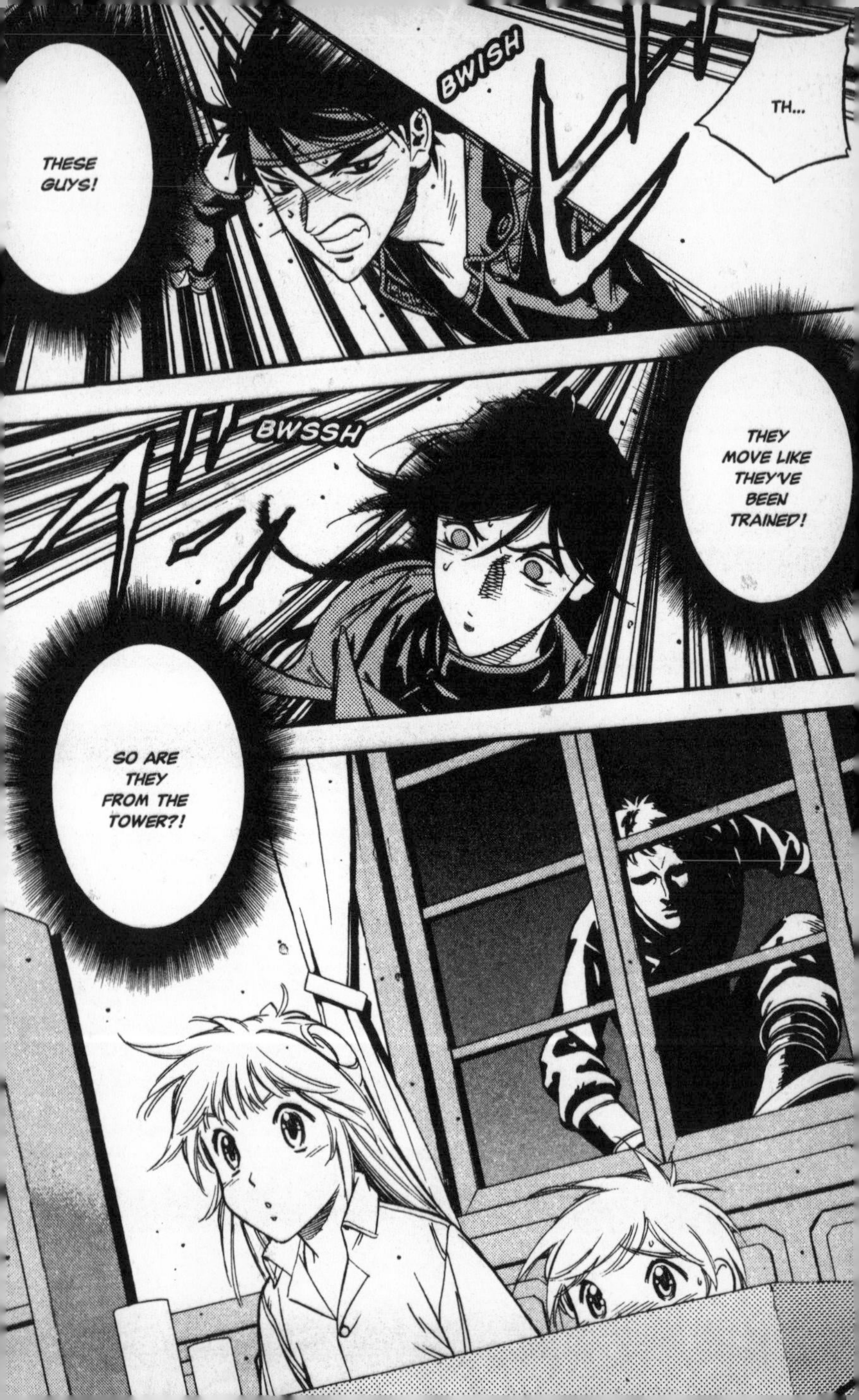
TH...
BWISH
THESE GUYS!
BWSSH
THEY MOVE LIKE THEY'VE BEEN TRAINED!
SO ARE THEY FROM THE TOWER?!

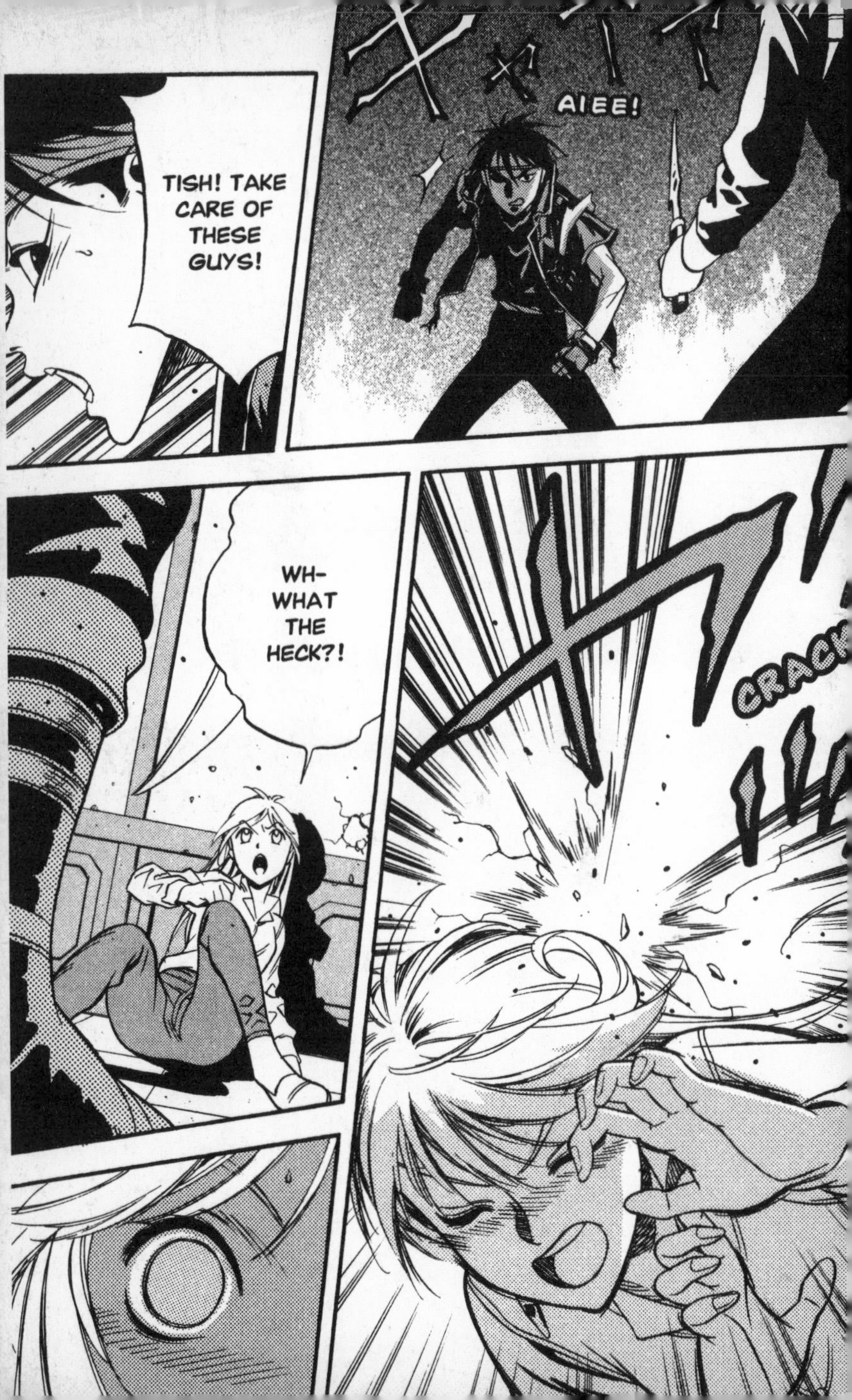
AIEE!
TISH! TAKE CARE OF THESE GUYS!
WH- WHAT THE HECK?!

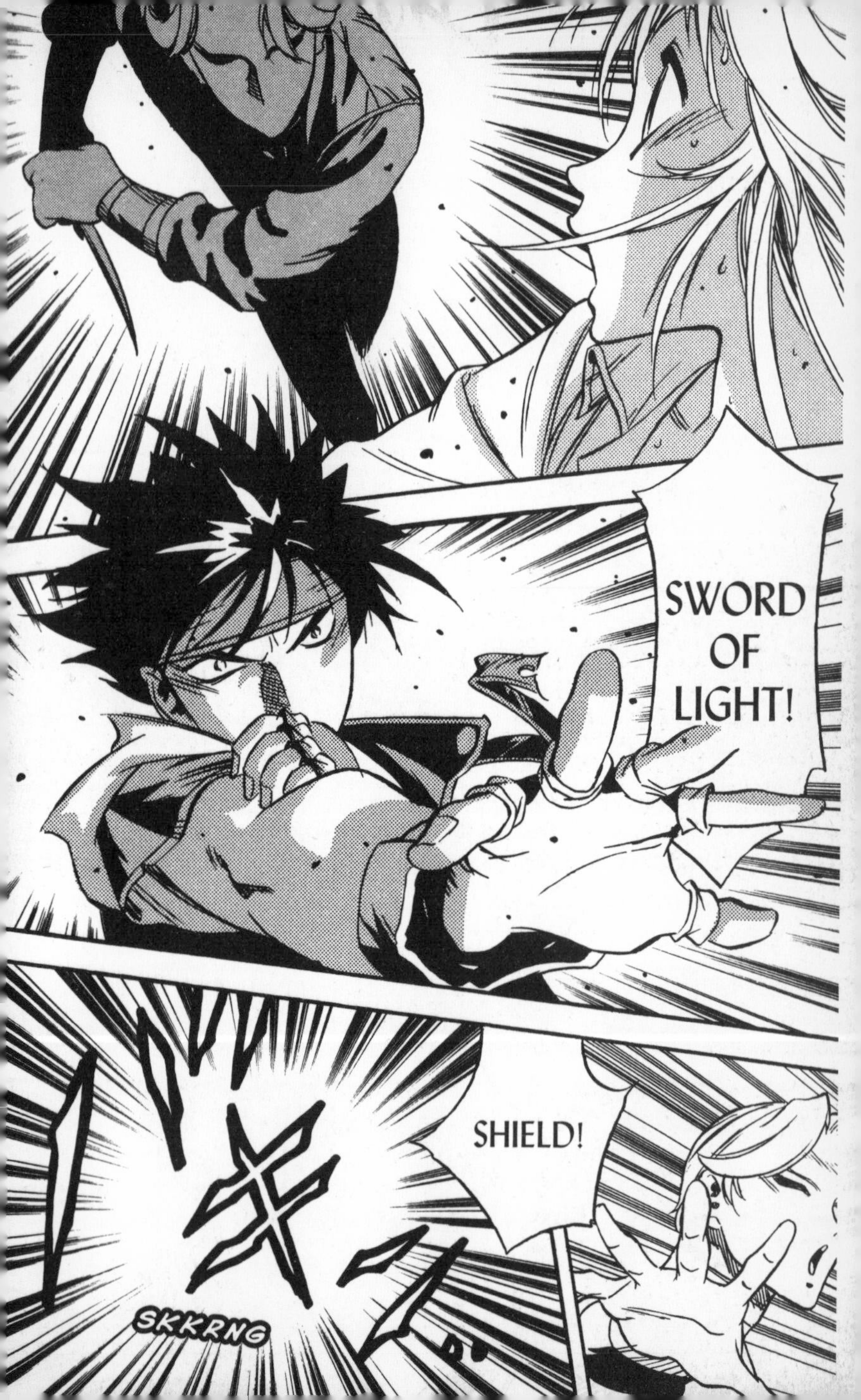
SWORD OF LIGHT!
SHIELD!
SKKRNG

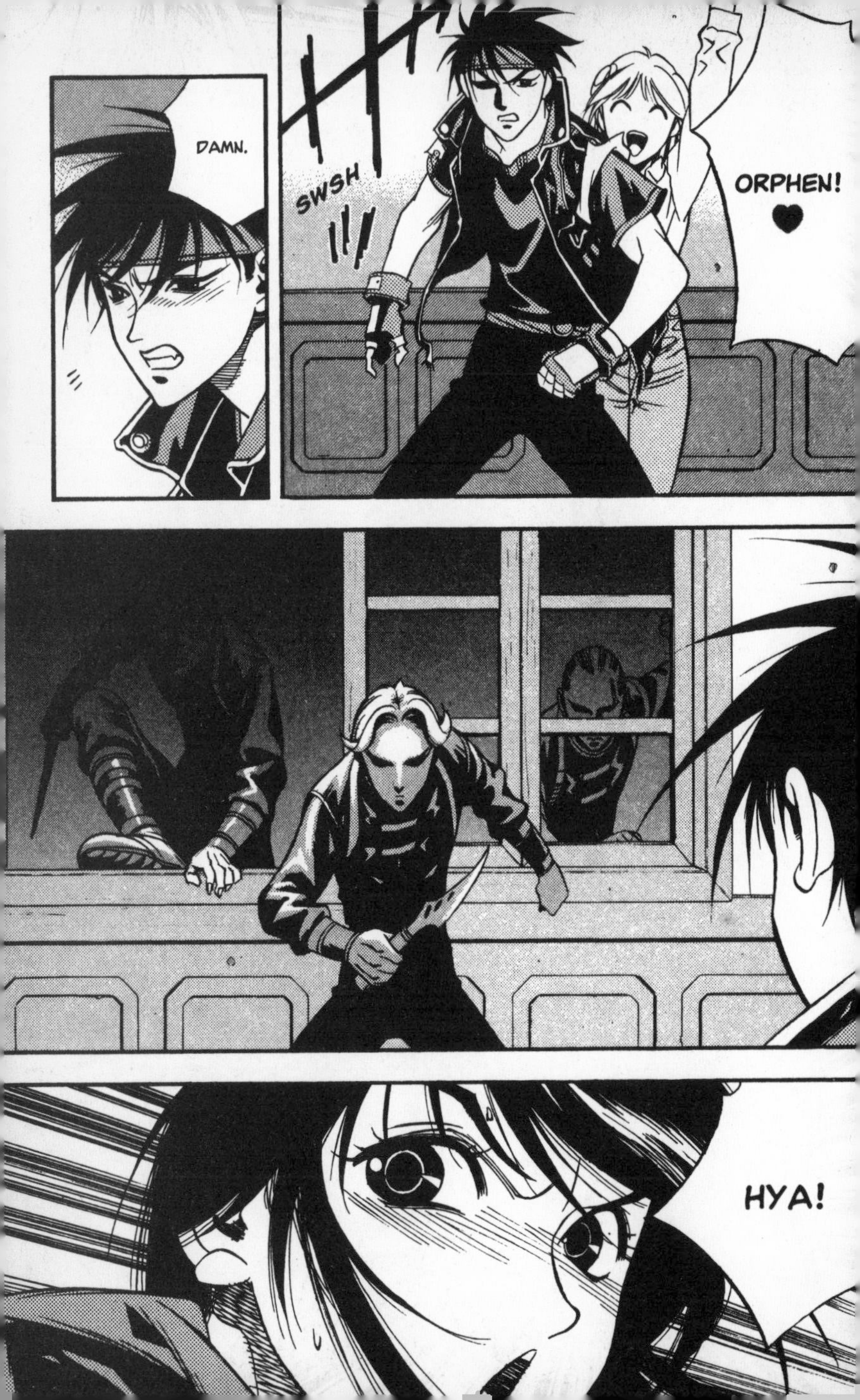
ORPHEN!
SWSH
DAMN.
HYA!

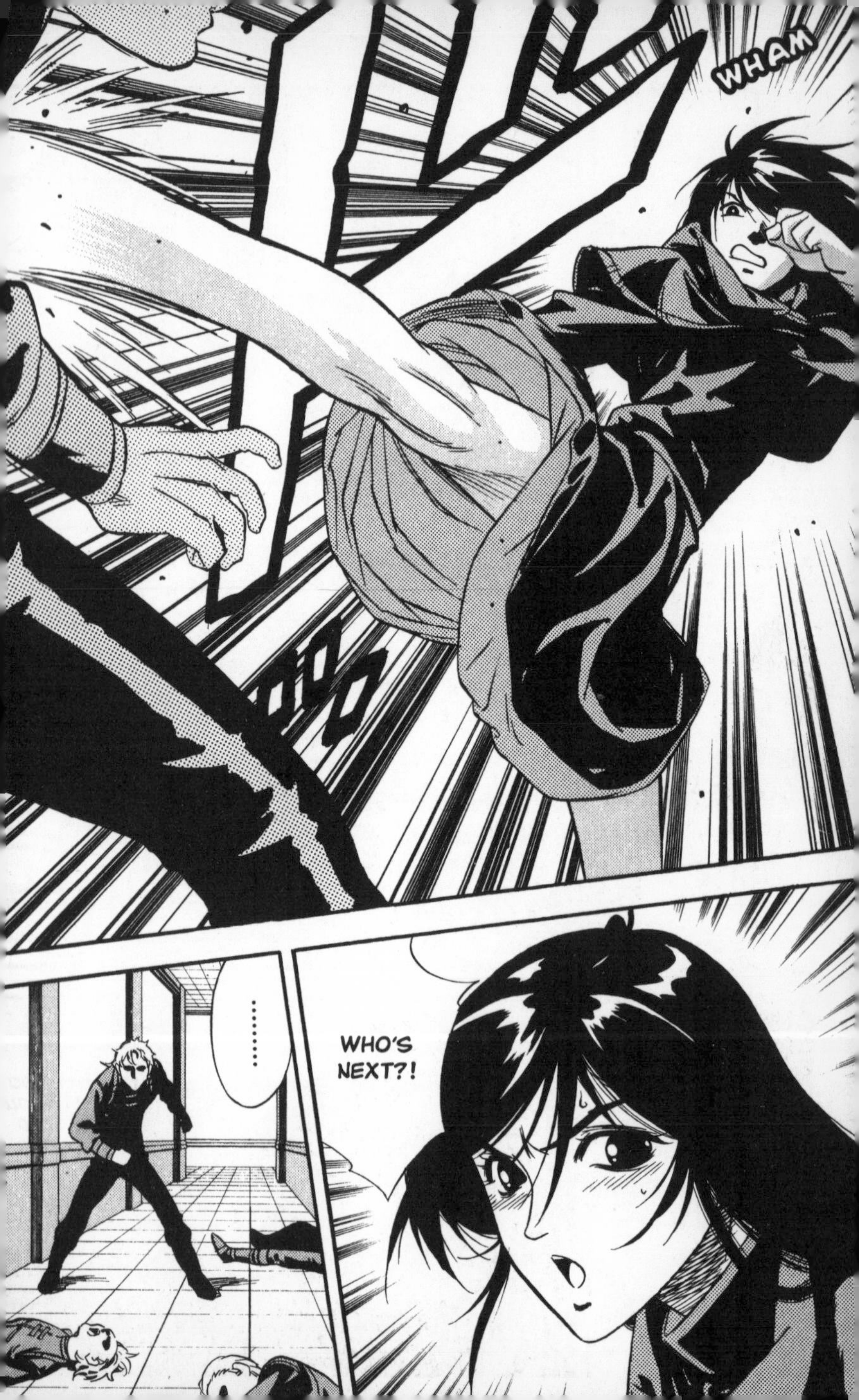
WHAM
WHO'S NEXT?!
....

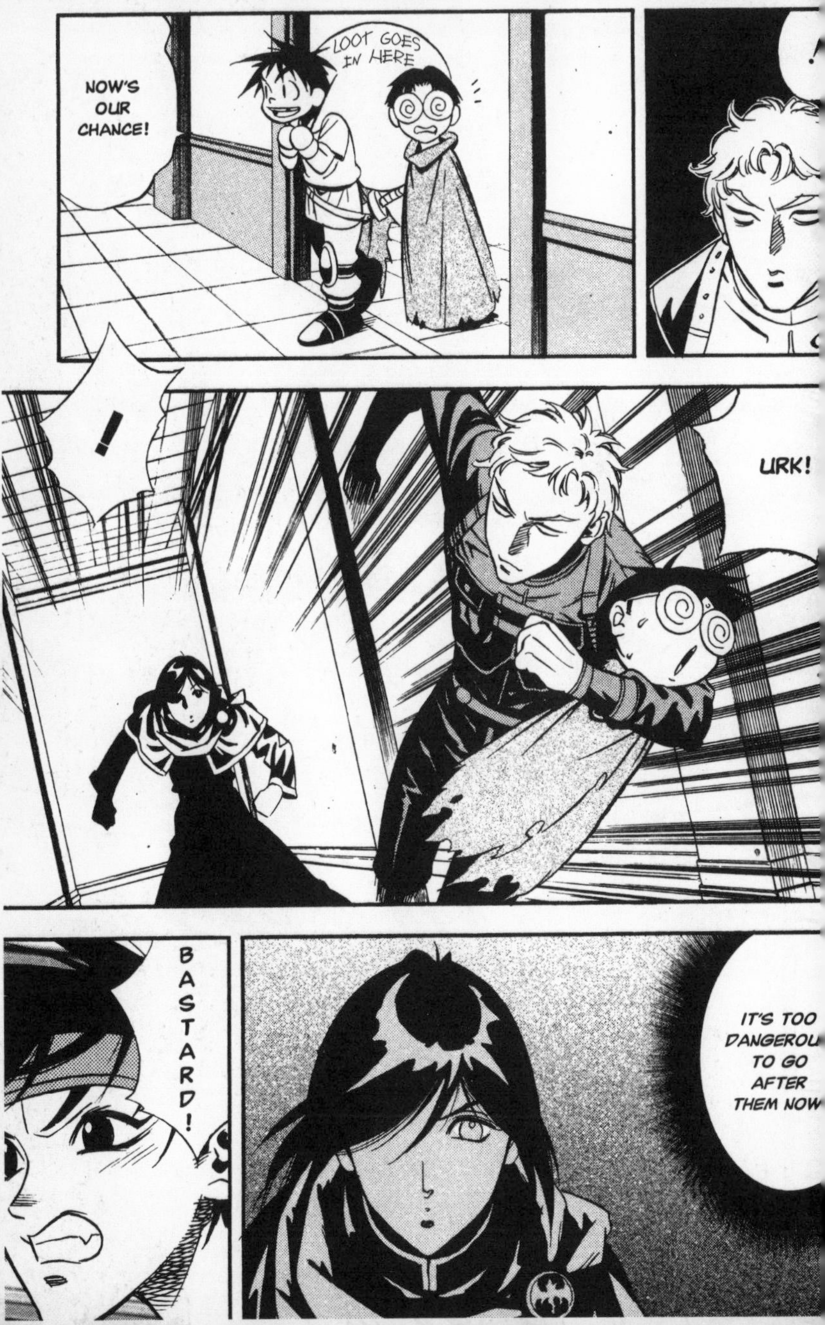
!
LOOT GOES IN HERE
NOW'S OUR CHANCE!
URK!
!
IT'S TOO DANGEROU
TO GO AFTER THEM NOW
BASTARD!

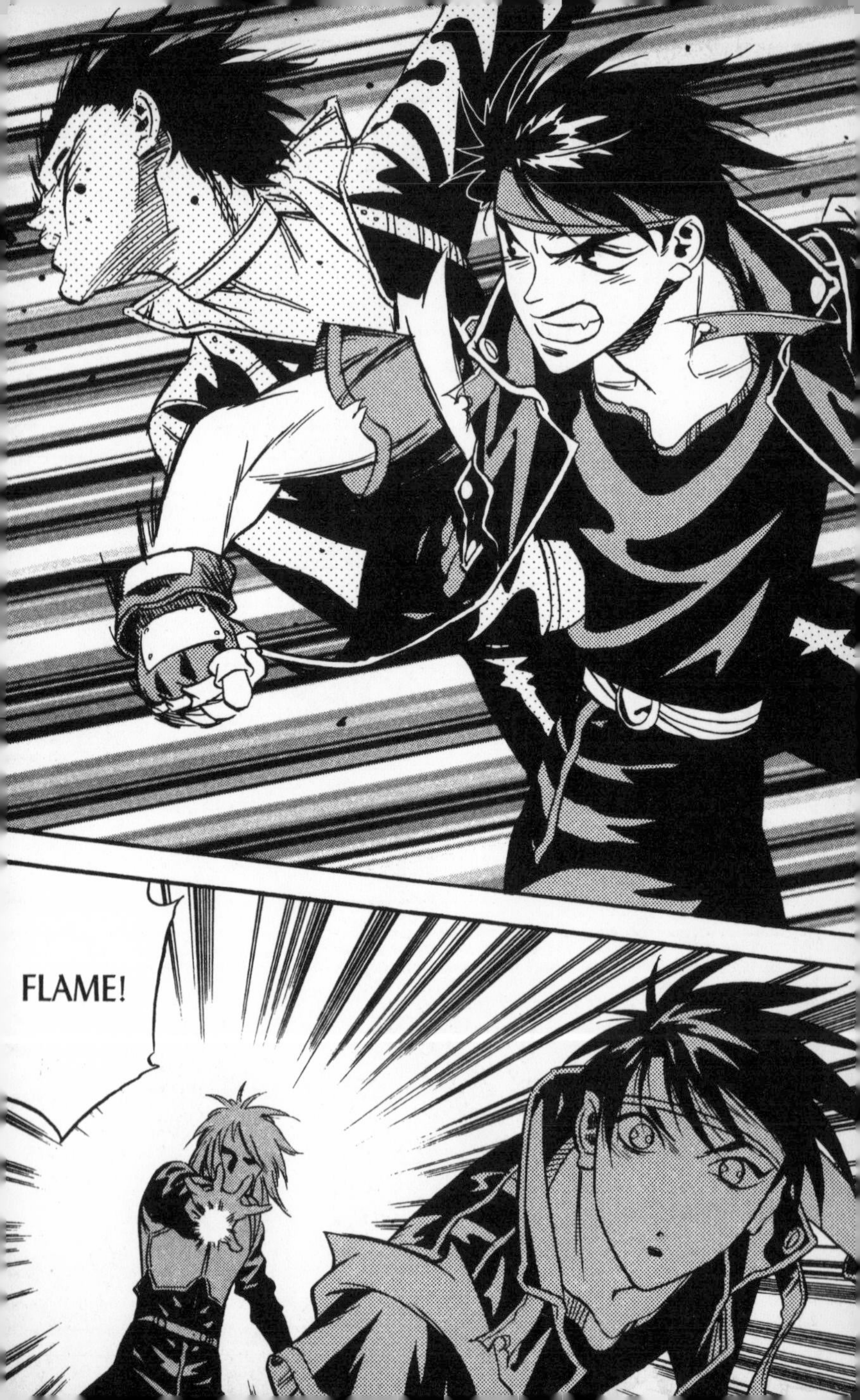
FLAME!

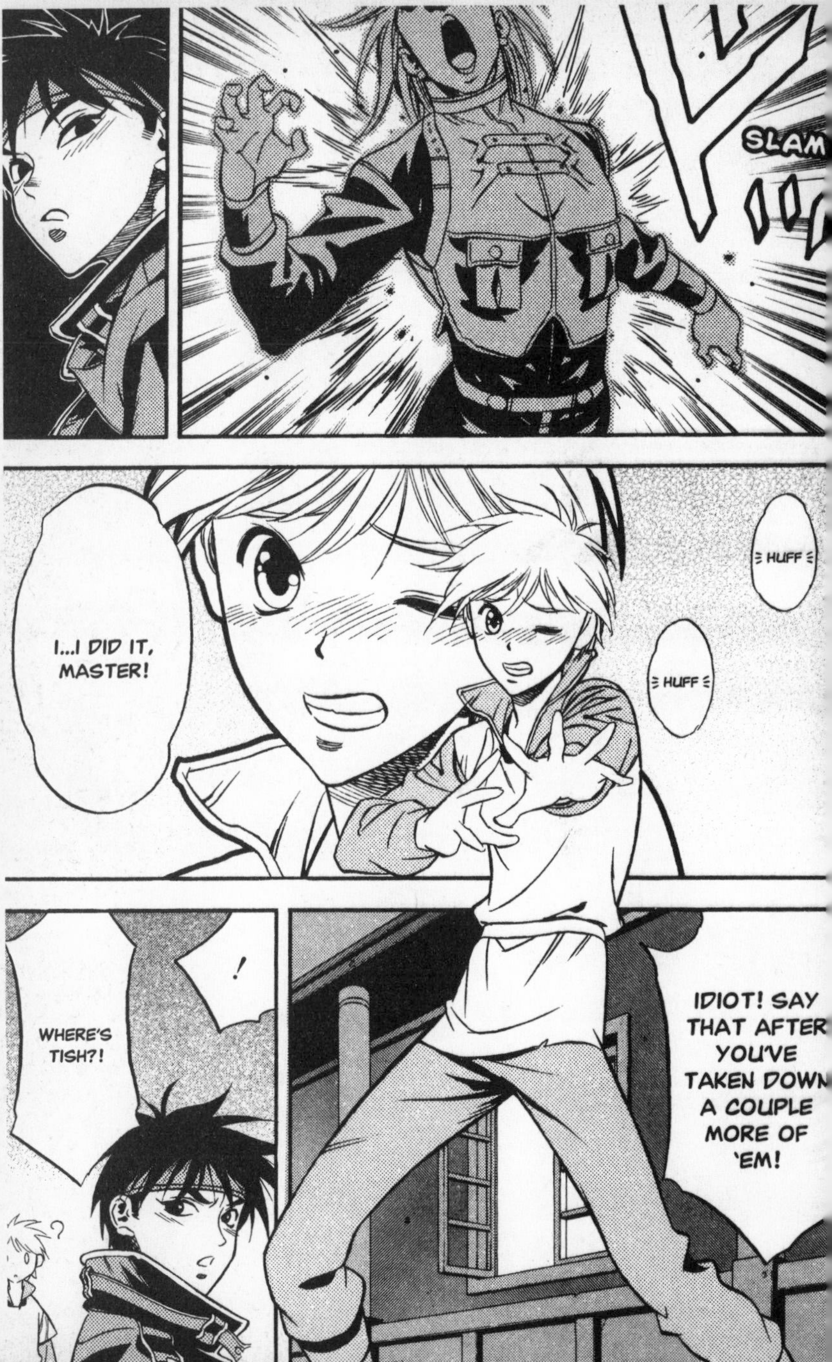
SLAM
HUFF
HUFF
I...I DID IT, MASTER!
IDIOT! SAY THAT AFTER YOU'VE TAKEN DOWN A COUPLE MORE OF 'EM!
!
WHERE'S TISH?!
?

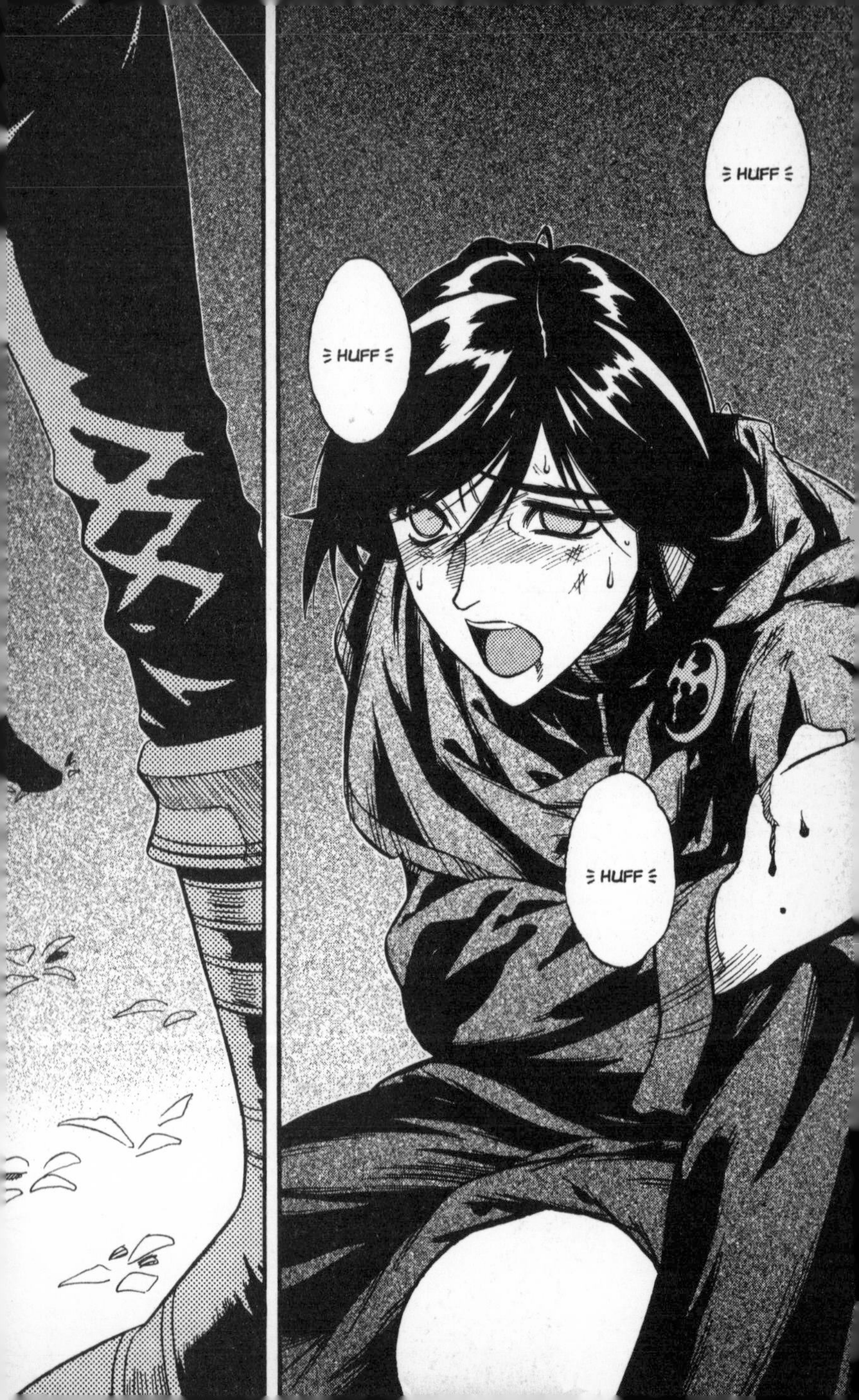
HUFF
HUFF
HUFF

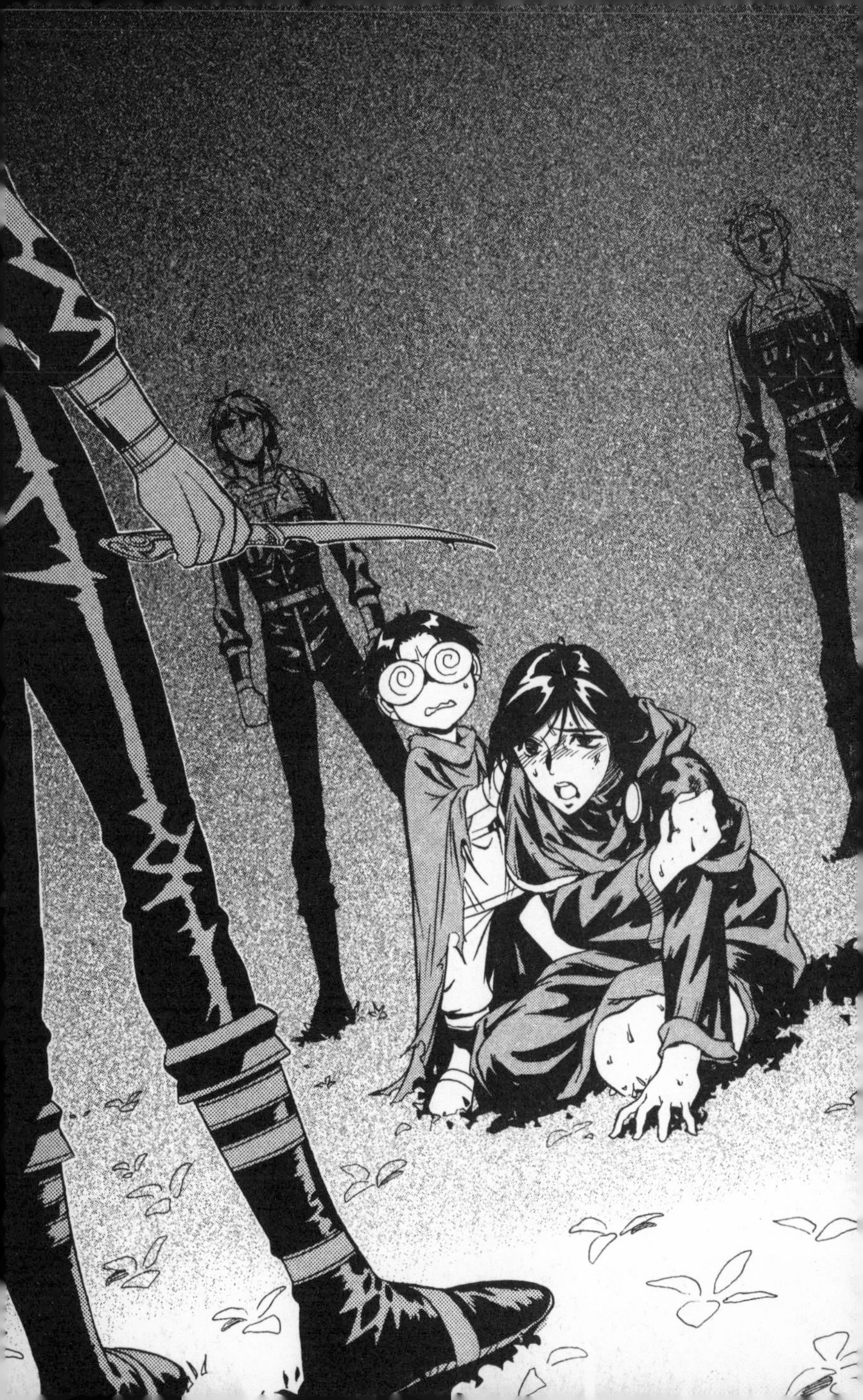

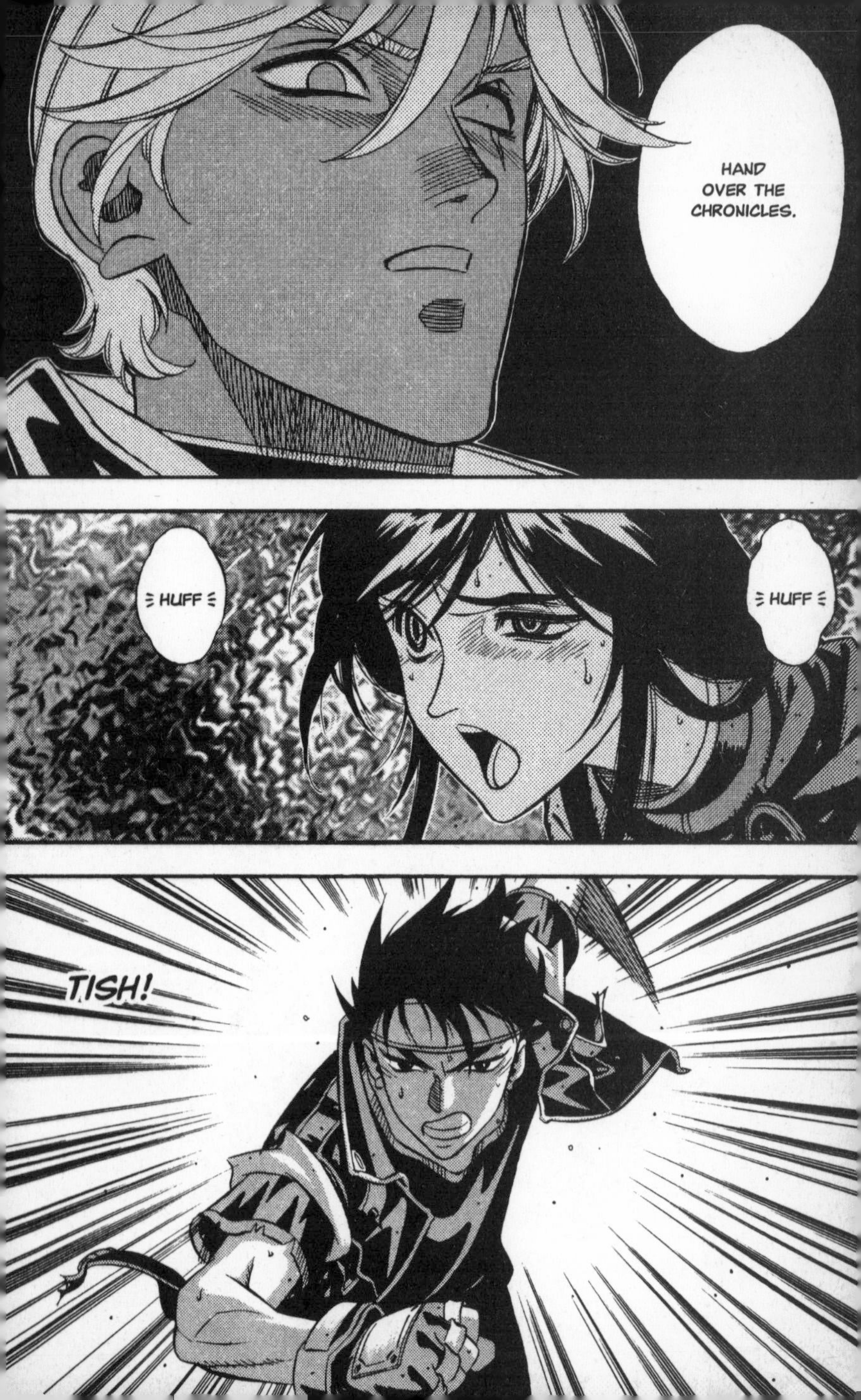
HAND OVER THE CHRONICLES.
HUFF
HUFF
TISH!

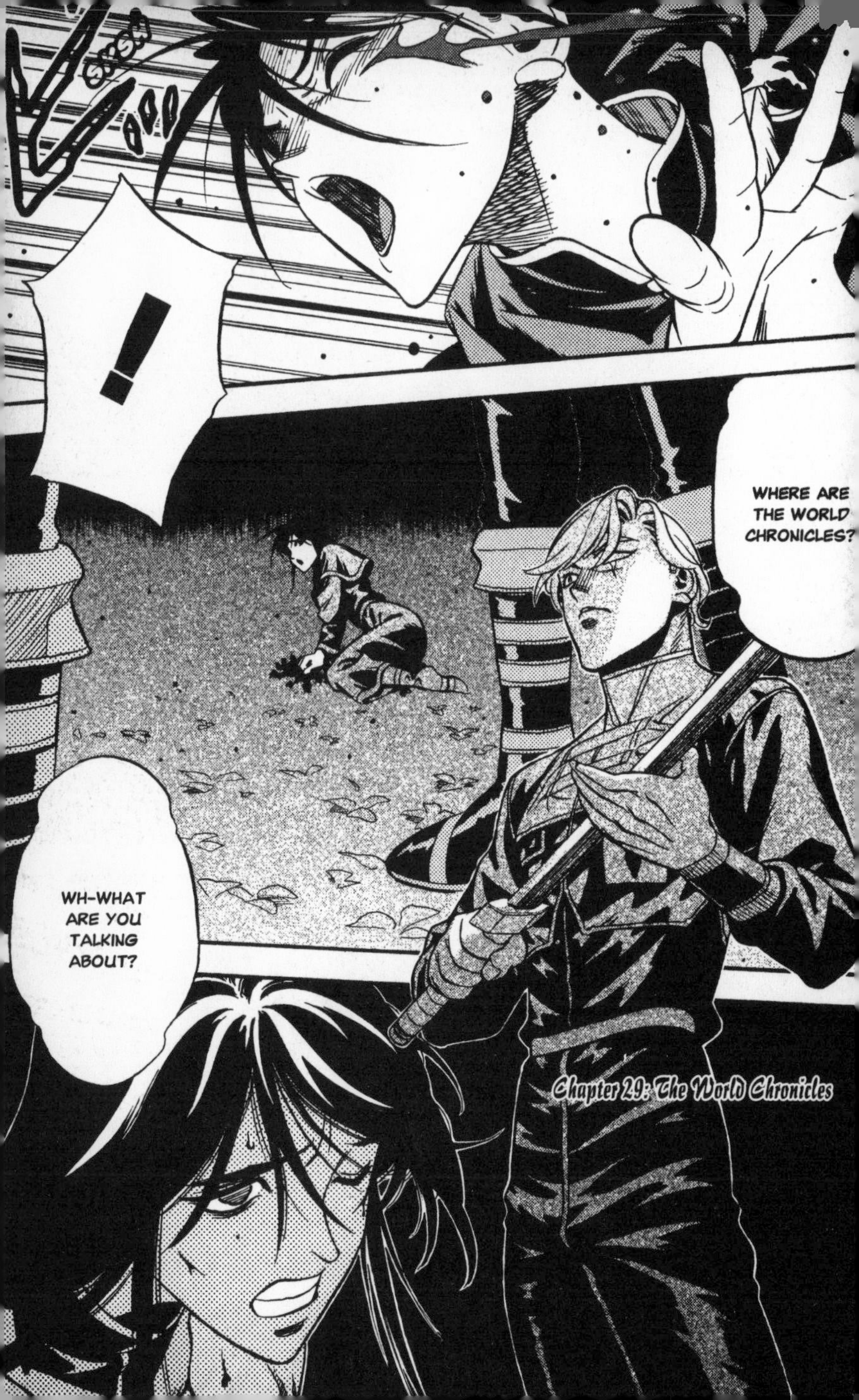
!
WHERE ARE THE WORLD CHRONICLES?
WH-WHAT ARE YOU TALKING ABOUT?
Chapter 29: The World Chronicles

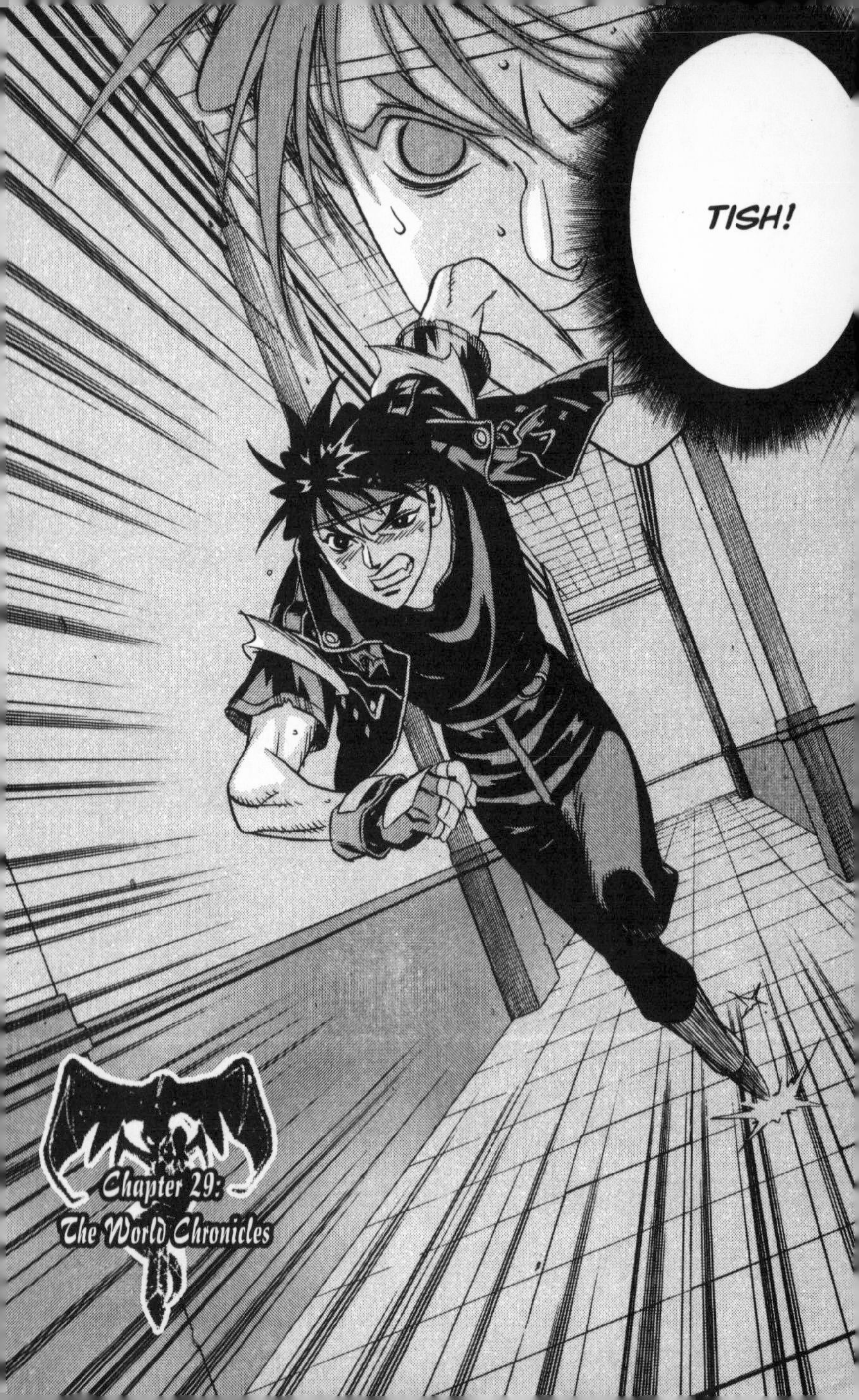
TISH!
Chapter 29:
The World Chronicles

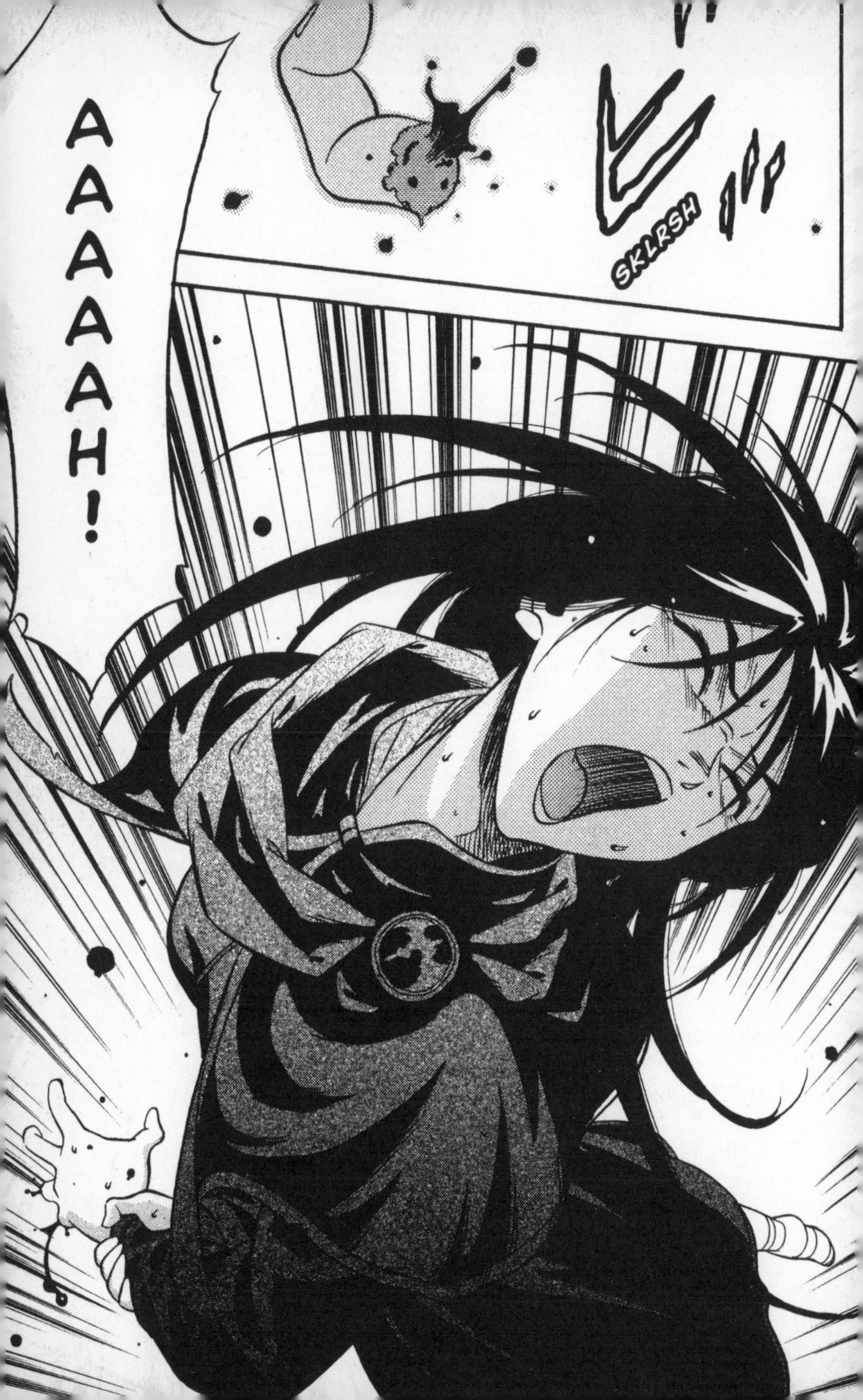
AAAAAAH!
SKLRSH

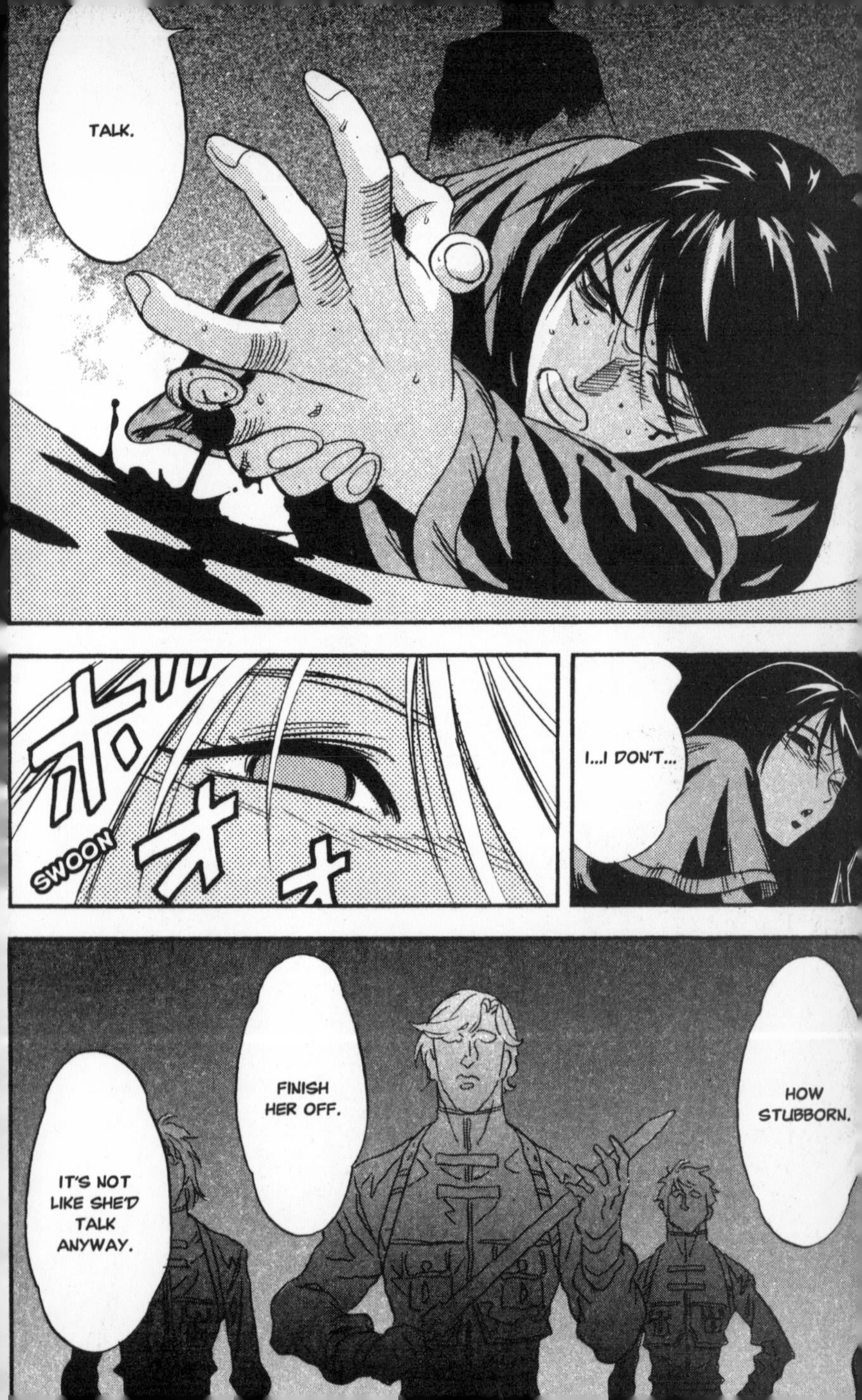
TALK.
I...I DON'T...
SWOON
HOW STUBBORN.
FINISH HER OFF.
IT'S NOT LIKE SHE'D TALK ANYWAY.

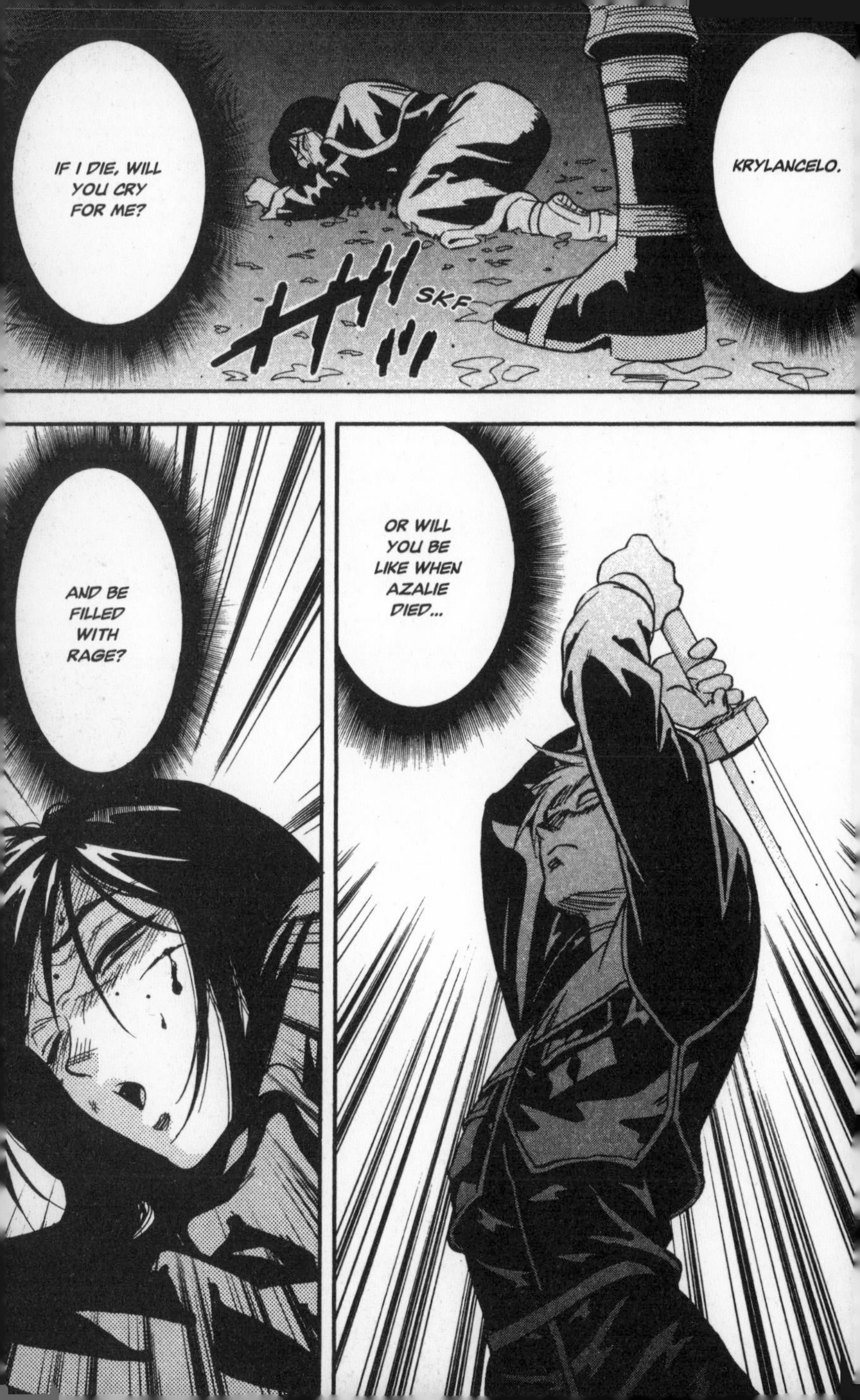
KRYLANCELO.
IF I DIE, WILL YOU CRY FOR ME?
SKF
OR WILL YOU BE LIKE WHEN AZALIE DIED...
AND BE FILLED WITH RAGE?

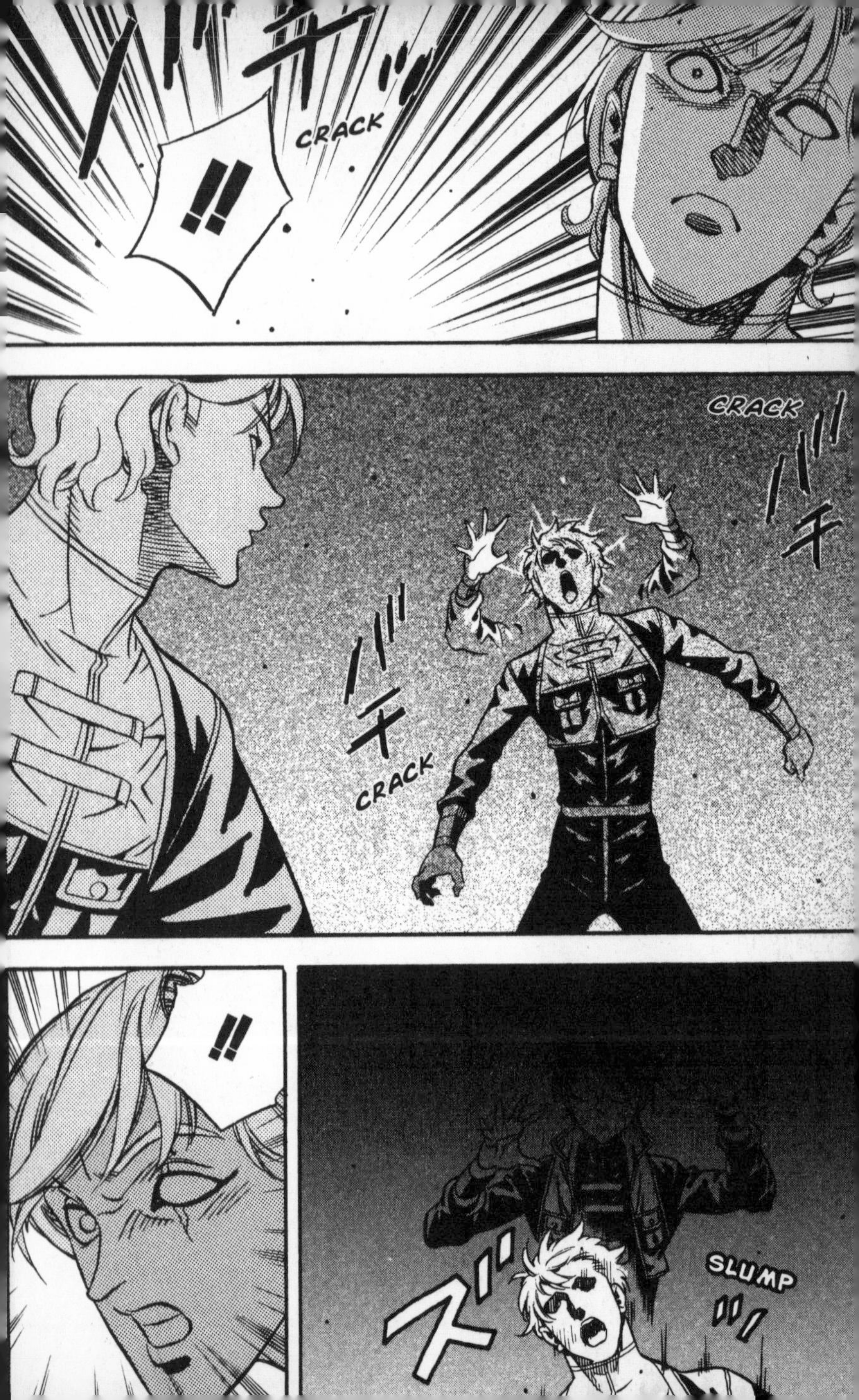

CRACK
!!
CRACK
CRACK
!!
SLUMP

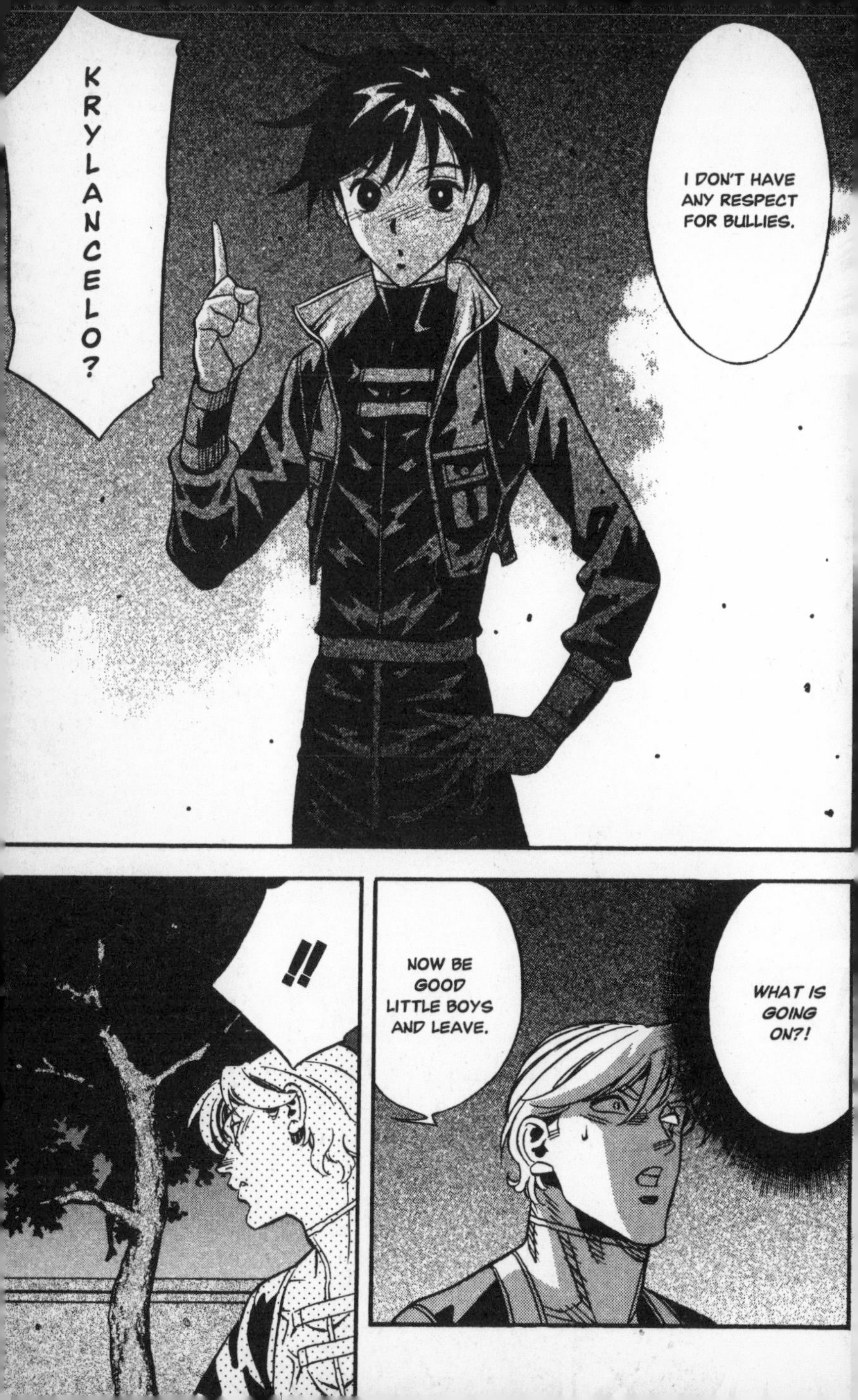
I DON'T HAVE ANY RESPECT FOR BULLIES.
KRYLANCELO?
WHAT IS GOING ON?!
NOW BE GOOD LITTLE BOYS AND LEAVE.
!!

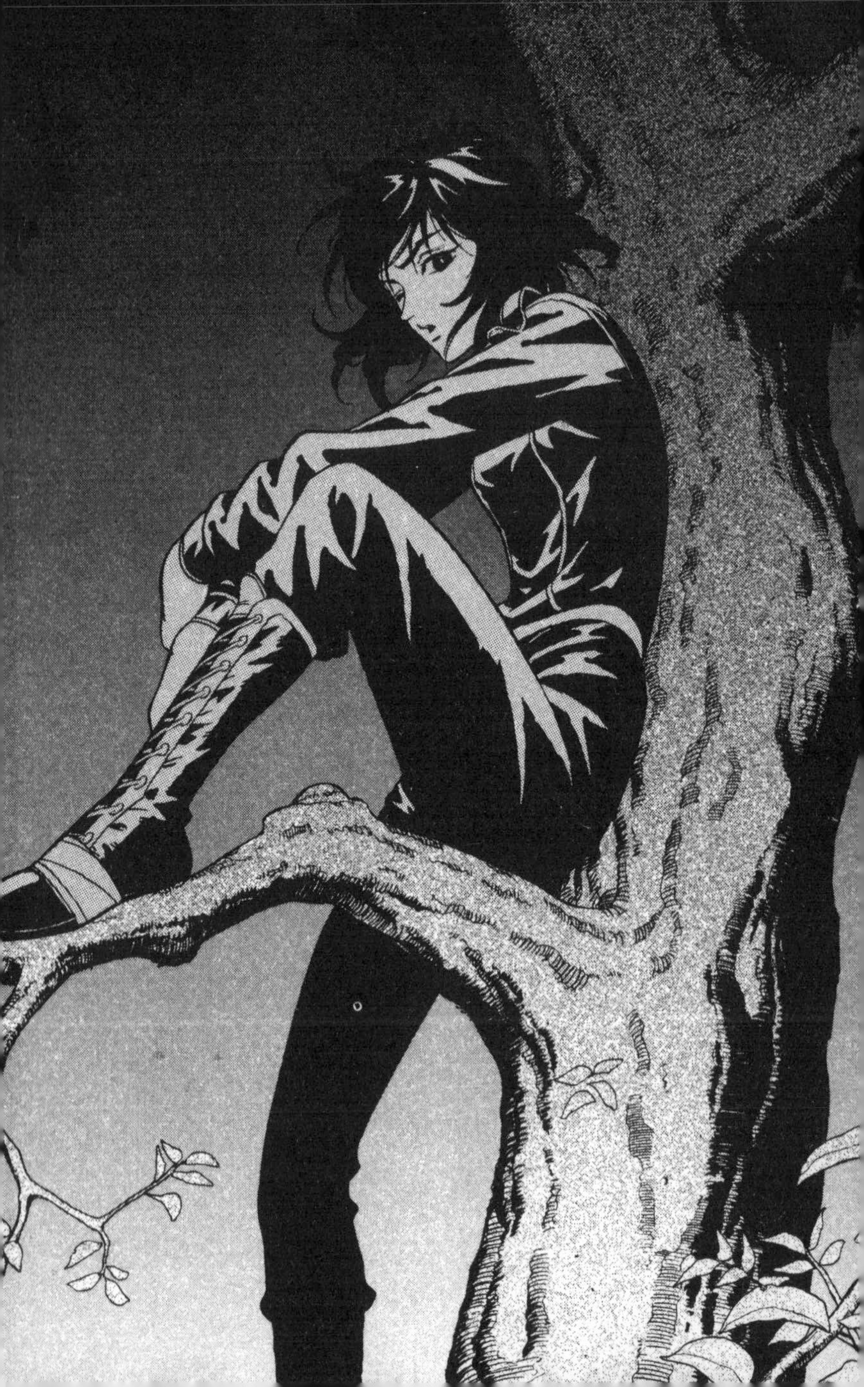

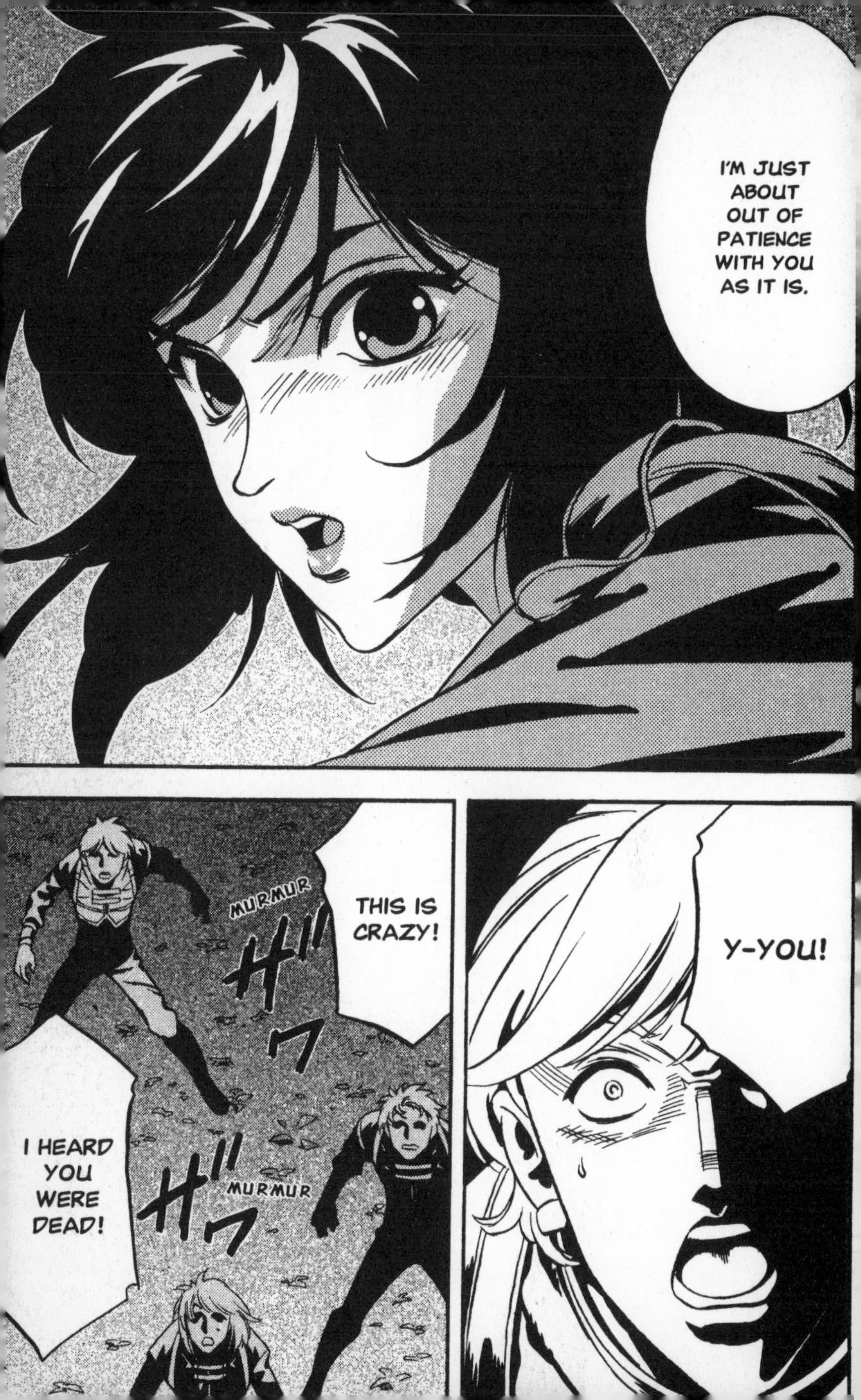
I'M JUST ABOUT OUT OF PATIENCE WITH YOU AS IT IS.
Y-YOU!
THIS IS CRAZY!
MURMUR
ザワ
I HEARD YOU WERE DEAD!
MURMUR
ザワ

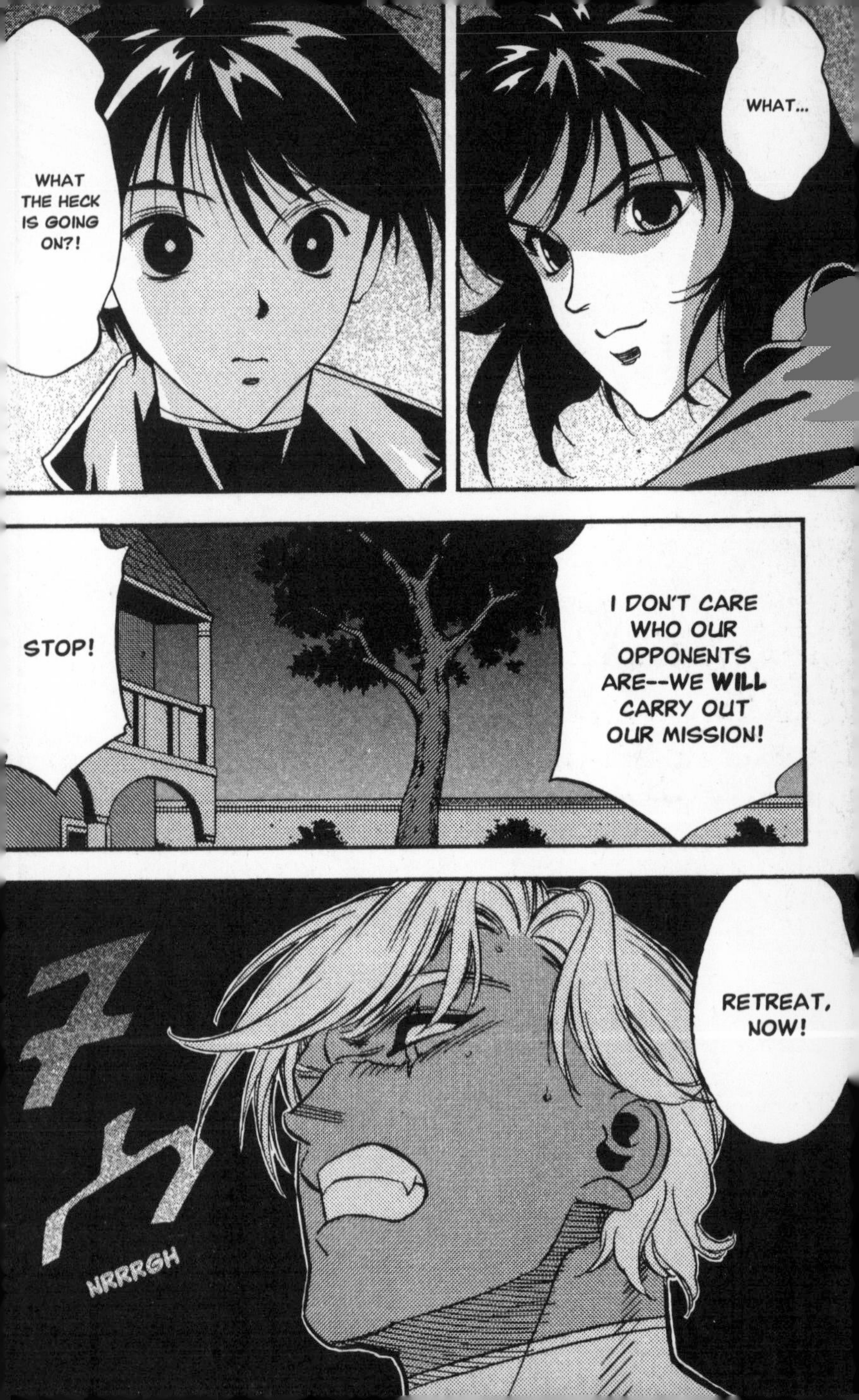
WHAT...
WHAT THE HECK IS GOING ON?!
I DON'T CARE WHO OUR OPPONENTS ARE--WE **WILL** CARRY OUT OUR MISSION!
STOP!
RETREAT, NOW!
NRRRGH

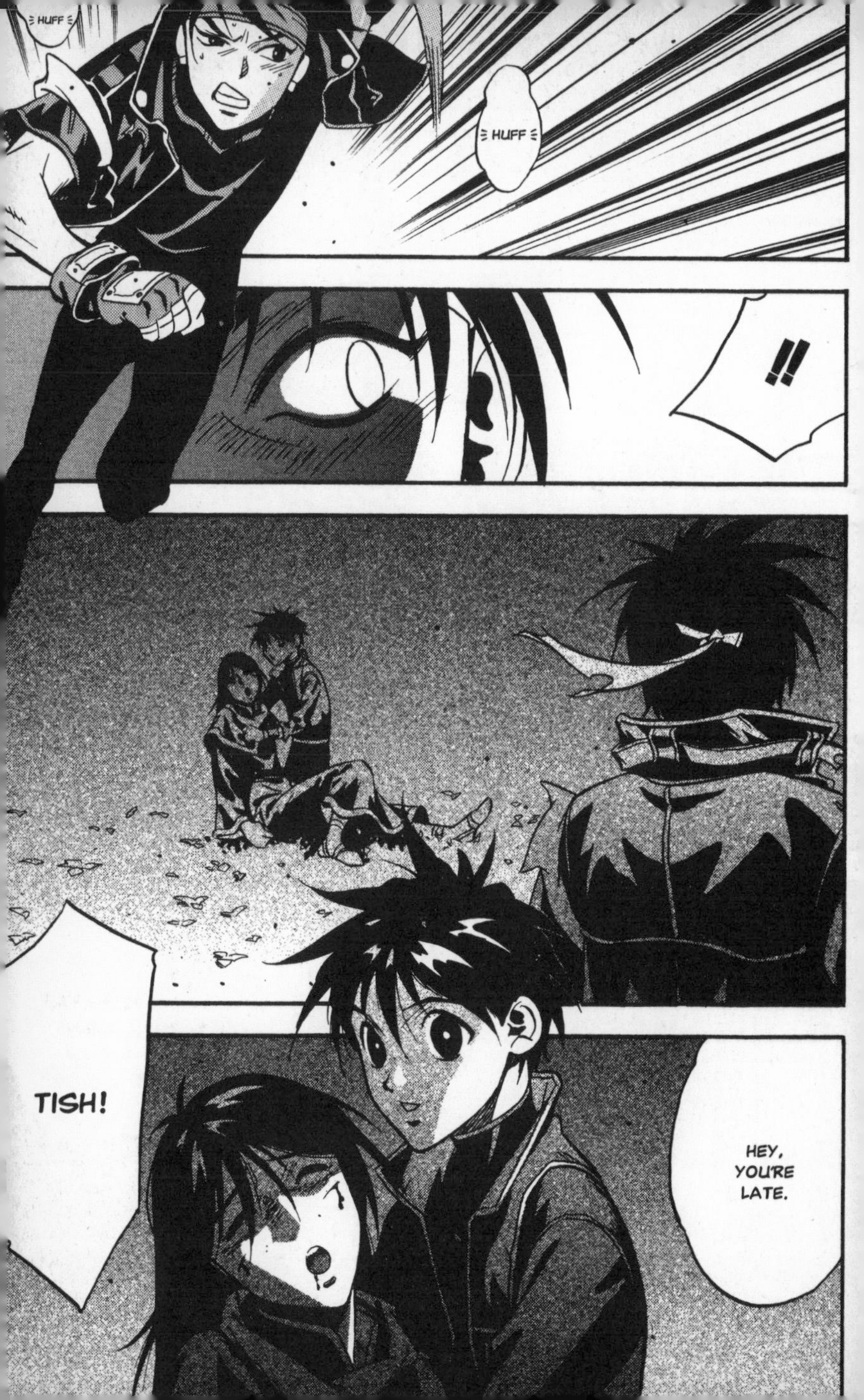
HUFF
HUFF
!!
TISH!
HEY, YOU'RE LATE.

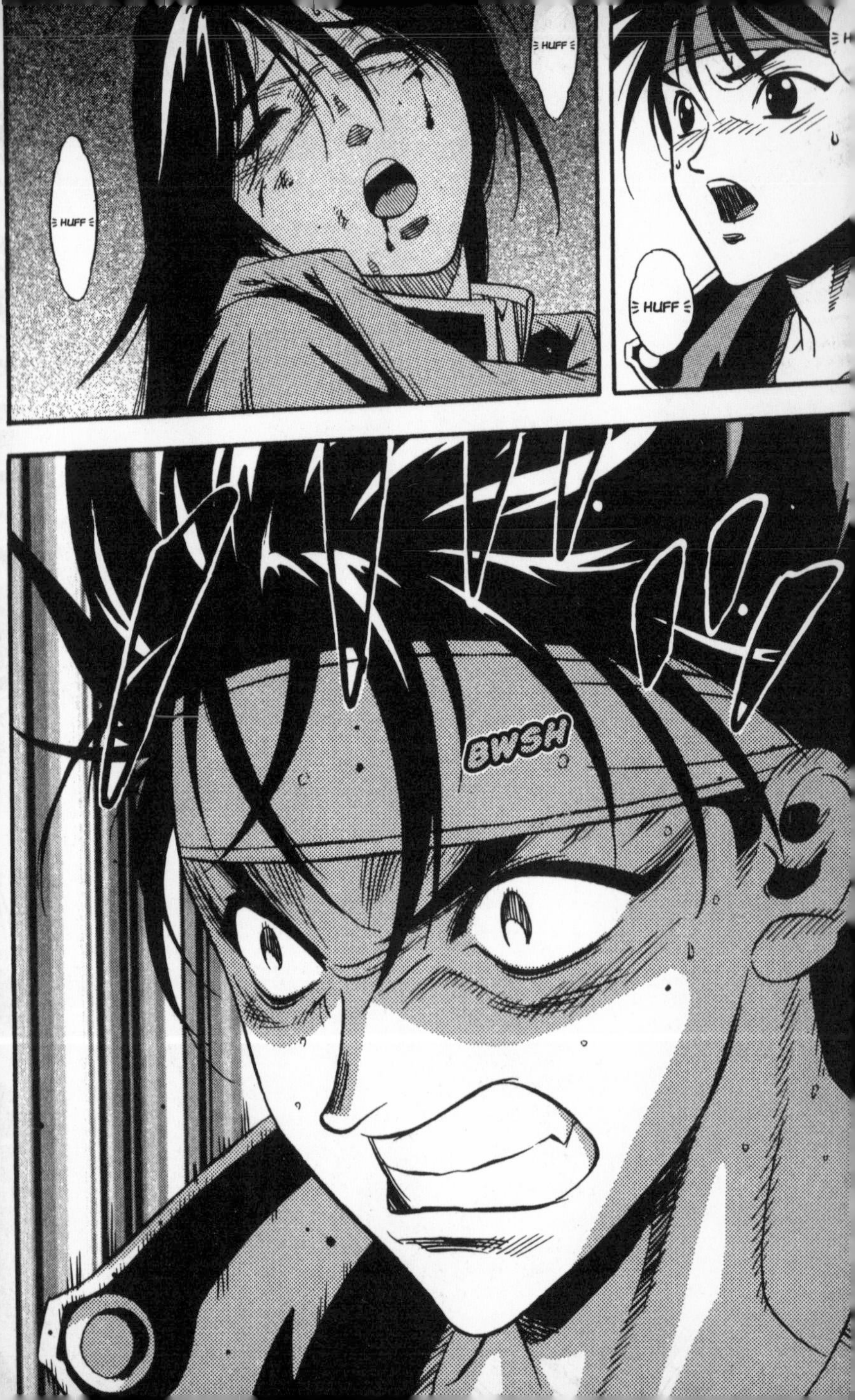
HUFF
HUFF
HUFF
BWSH

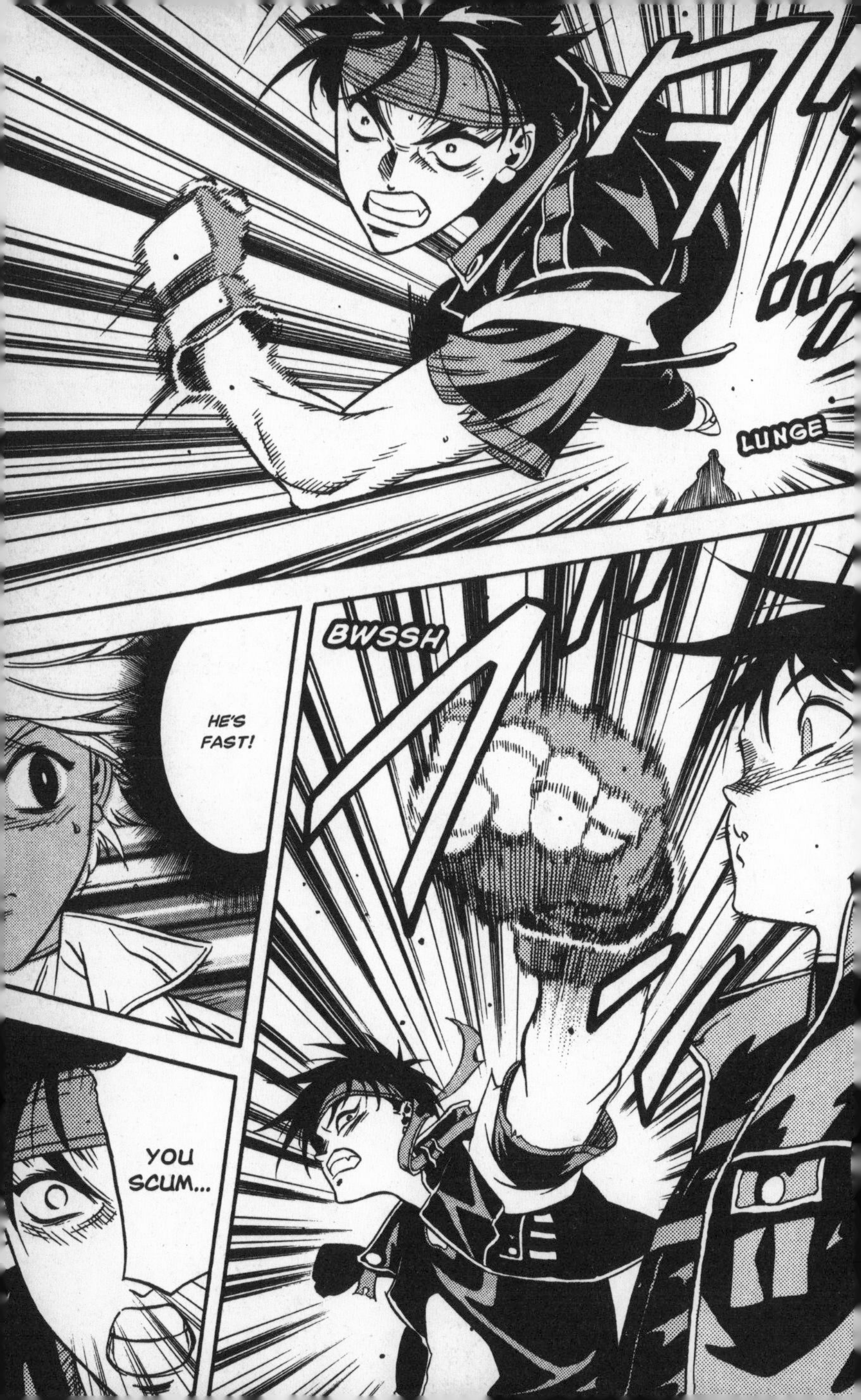
LUNGE
BWSSH
HE'S FAST!
YOU SCUM...

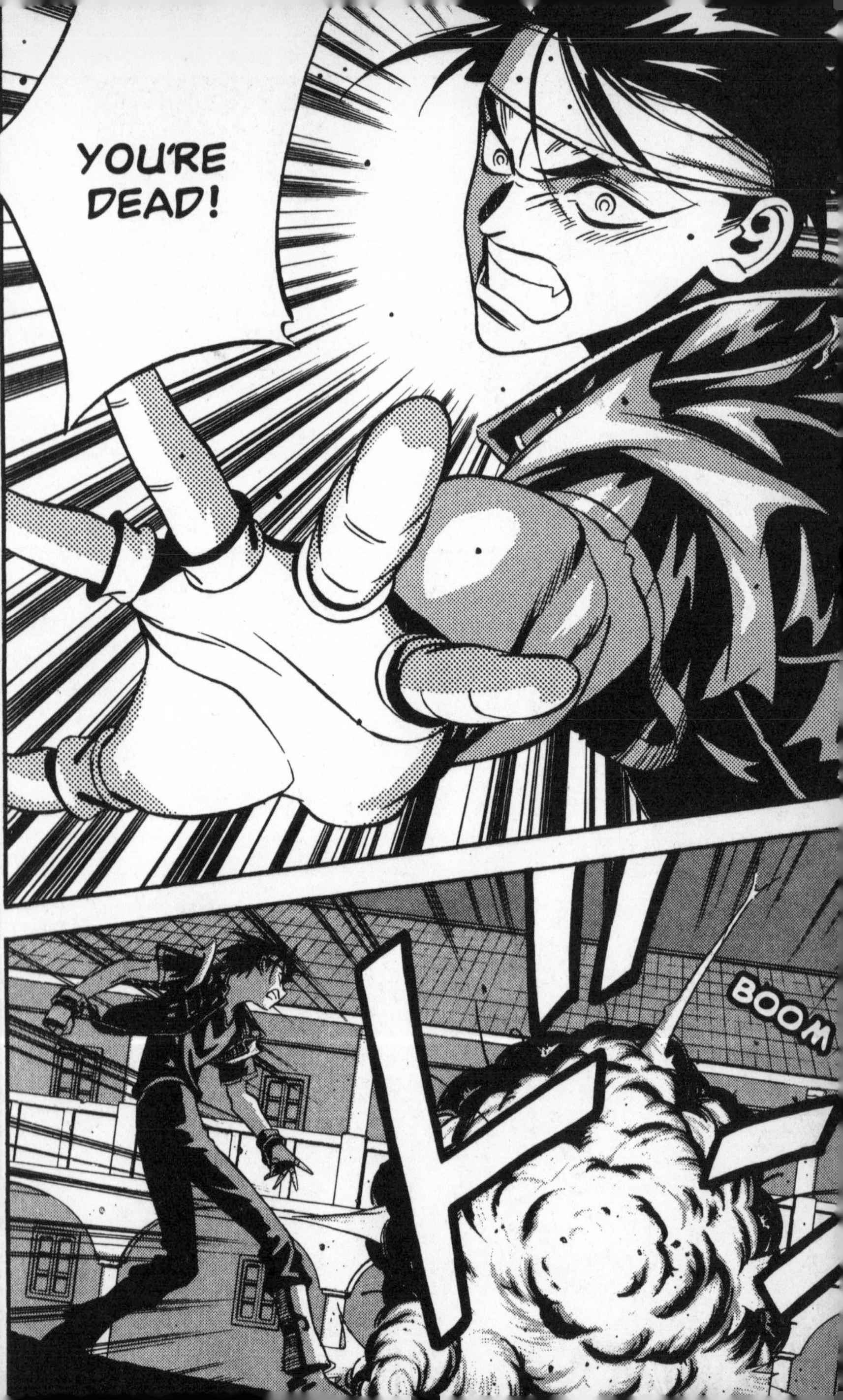
YOU'RE DEAD!
BOOM

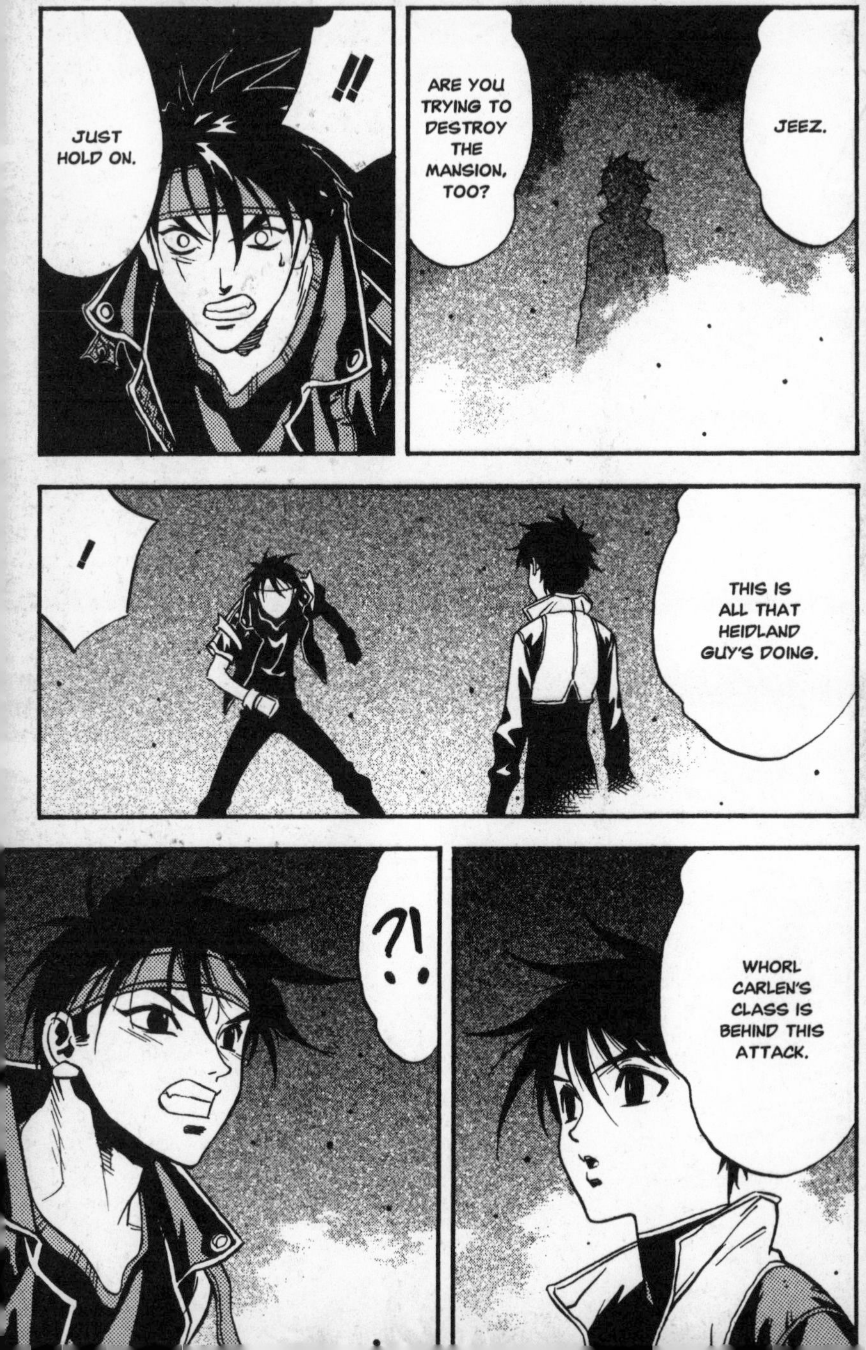
JEEZ.
ARE YOU TRYING TO DESTROY THE MANSION, TOO?
!!
JUST HOLD ON.
THIS IS ALL THAT HEIDLAND GUY'S DOING.
!
WHORL CARLEN'S CLASS IS BEHIND THIS ATTACK.
?!

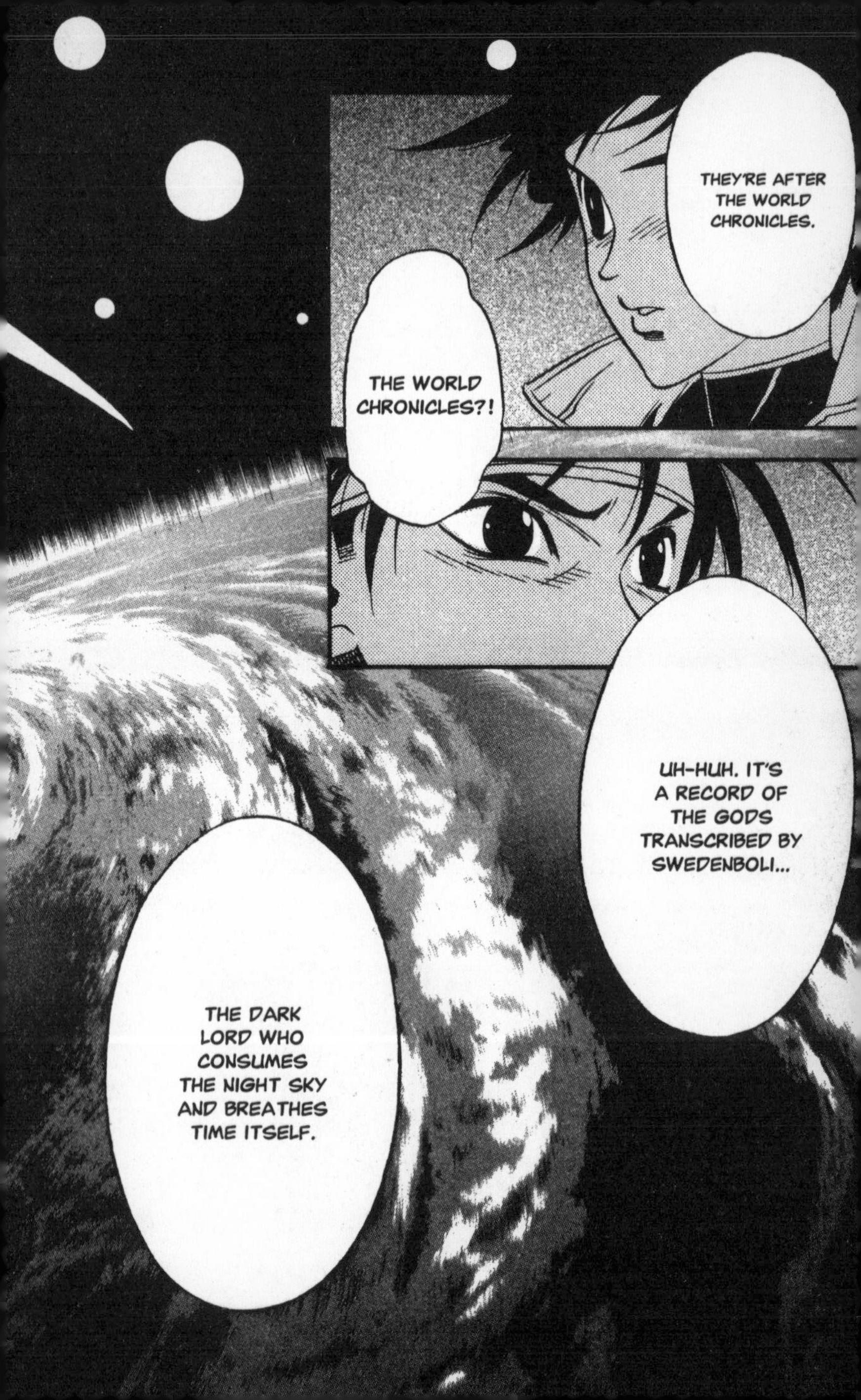
THEY'RE AFTER THE WORLD CHRONICLES.
THE WORLD CHRONICLES?!
UH-HUH. IT'S A RECORD OF THE GODS TRANSCRIBED BY SWEDENBOLI...
THE DARK LORD WHO CONSUMES THE NIGHT SKY AND BREATHES TIME ITSELF.

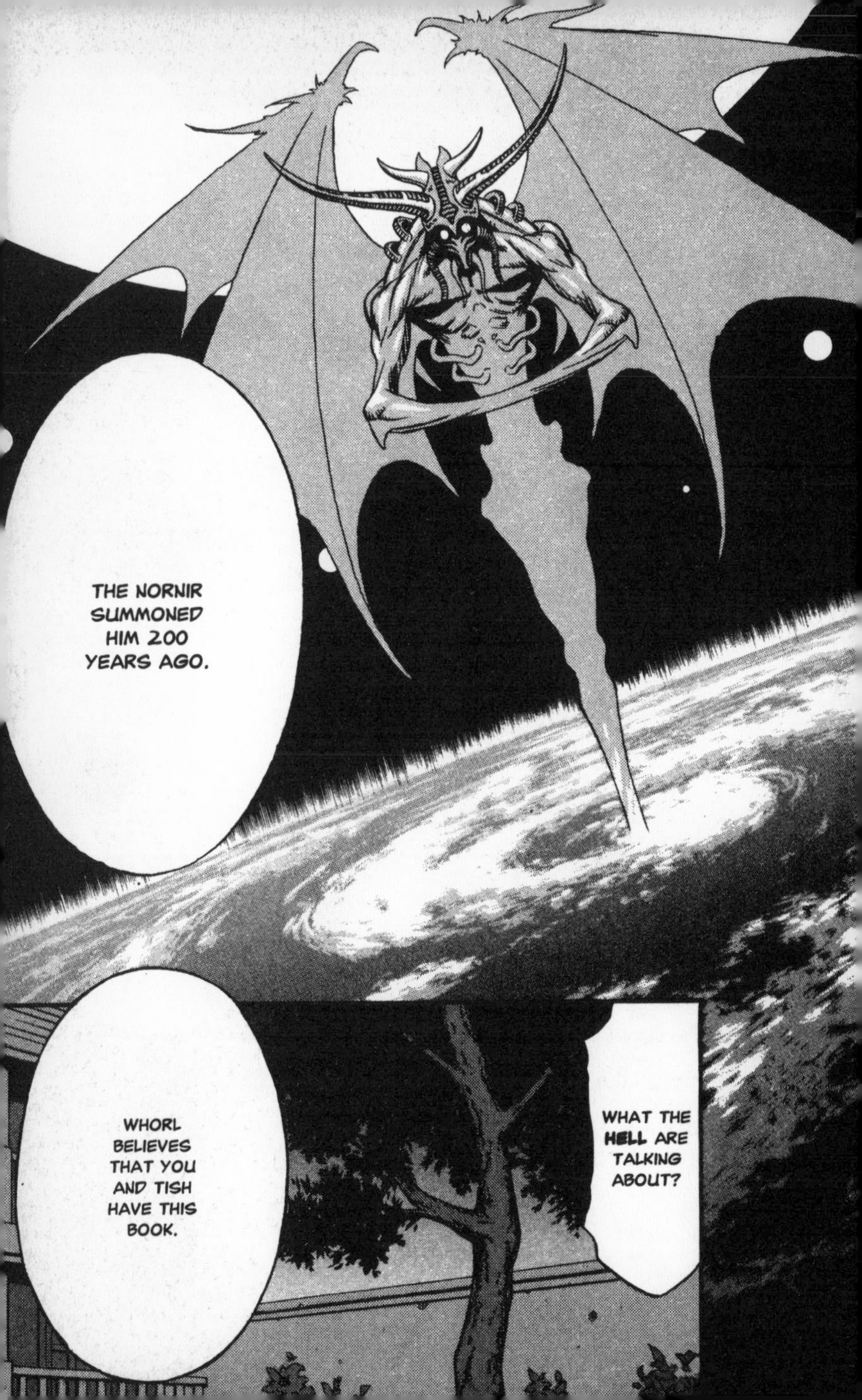
THE NORNIR SUMMONED HIM 200 YEARS AGO.
WHAT THE HELL ARE TALKING ABOUT?
WHORL BELIEVES THAT YOU AND TISH HAVE THIS BOOK.

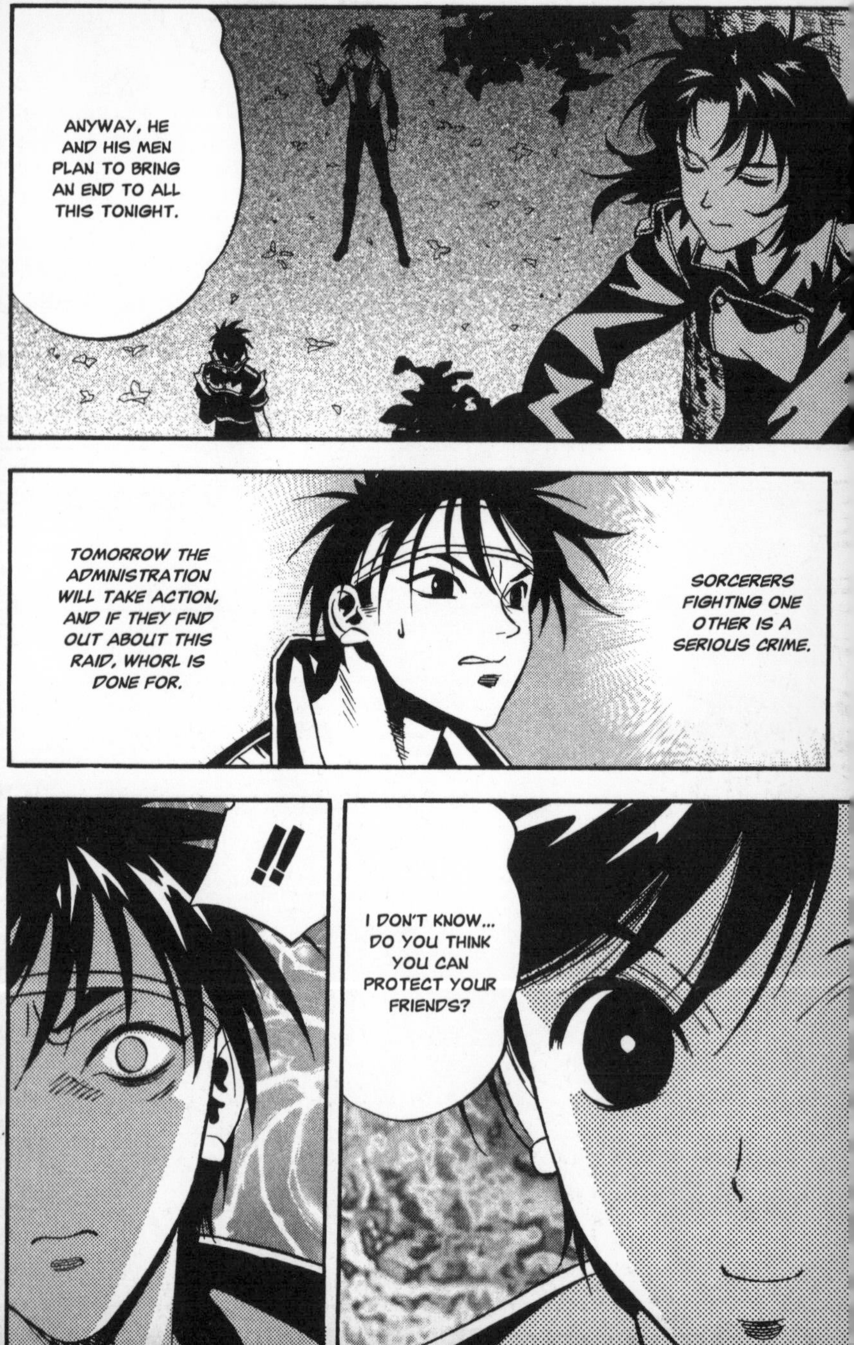
ANYWAY, HE AND HIS MEN PLAN TO BRING AN END TO ALL THIS TONIGHT.
SORCERERS FIGHTING ONE OTHER IS A SERIOUS CRIME.
TOMORROW THE ADMINISTRATION WILL TAKE ACTION, AND IF THEY FIND OUT ABOUT THIS RAID, WHORL IS DONE FOR.
I DON'T KNOW... DO YOU THINK YOU CAN PROTECT YOUR FRIENDS?
!!

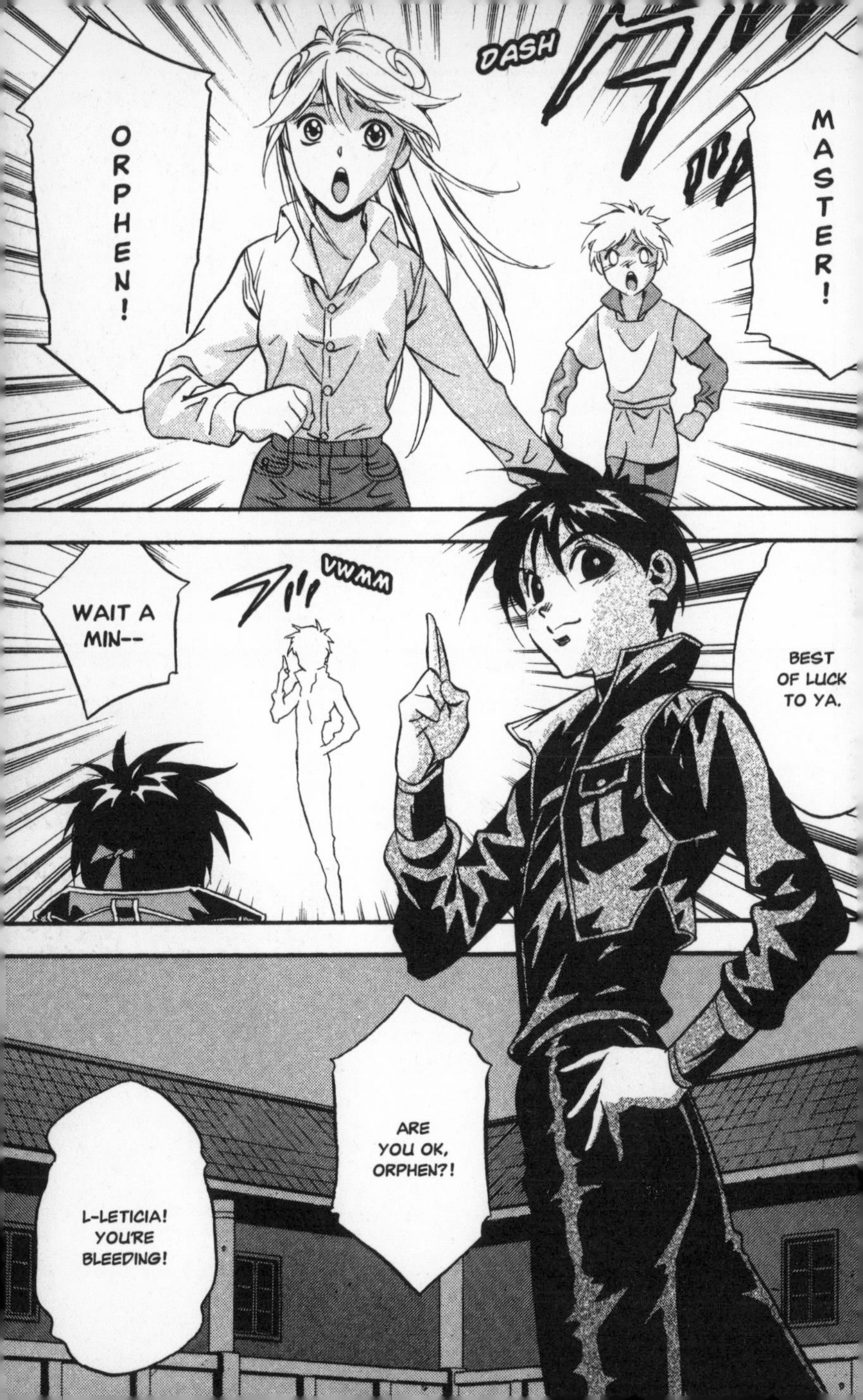
DASH
MASTER!
ORPHEN!
BEST OF LUCK TO YA.
VWMM
WAIT A MIN--
ARE YOU OK, ORPHEN?!
L-LETICIA! YOU'RE BLEEDING!

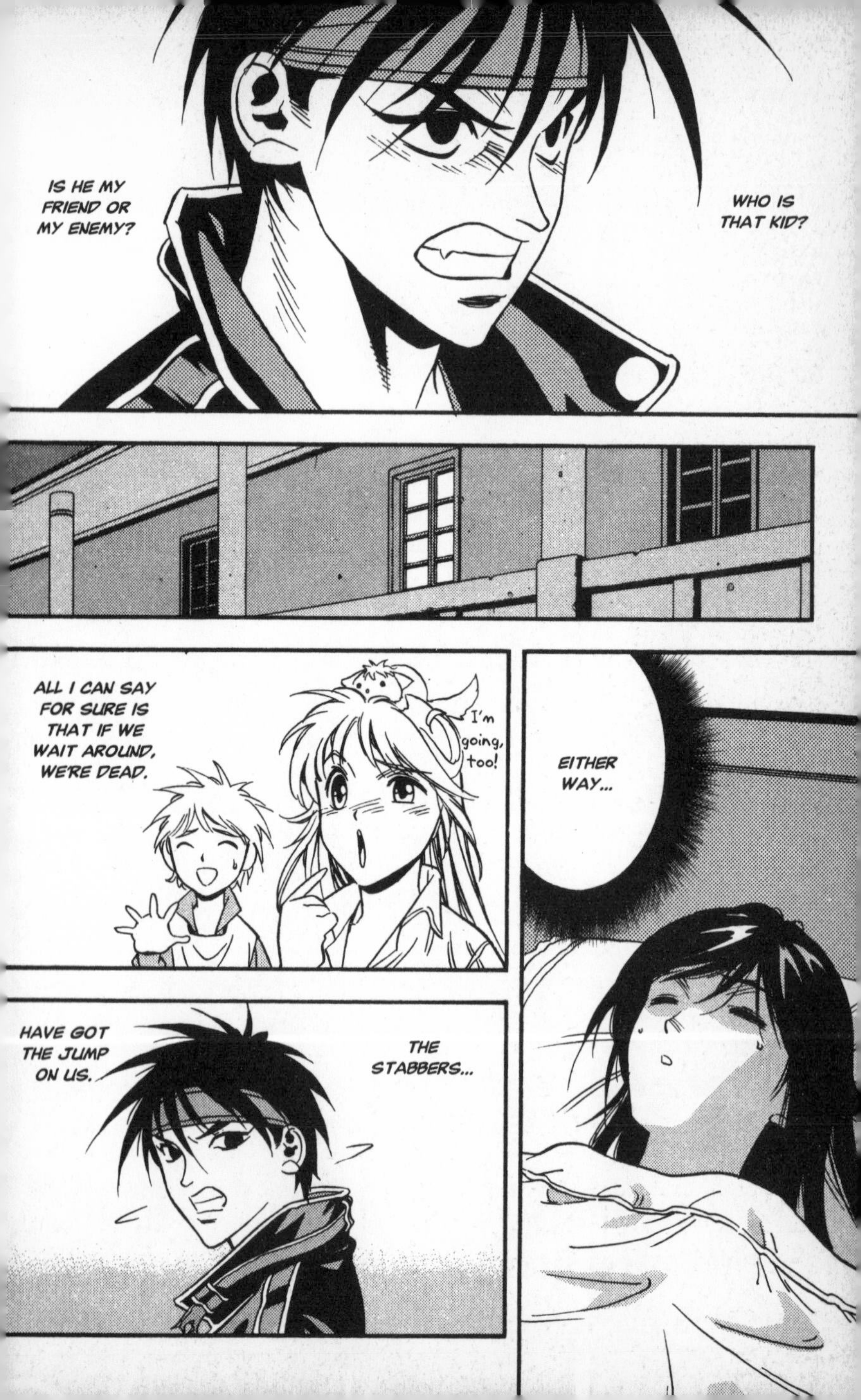
WHO IS THAT KID?
IS HE MY FRIEND OR MY ENEMY?
EITHER WAY...
ALL I CAN SAY FOR SURE IS THAT IF WE WAIT AROUND, WE'RE DEAD.
I'm going, too!
THE STABBERS...
HAVE GOT THE JUMP ON US.

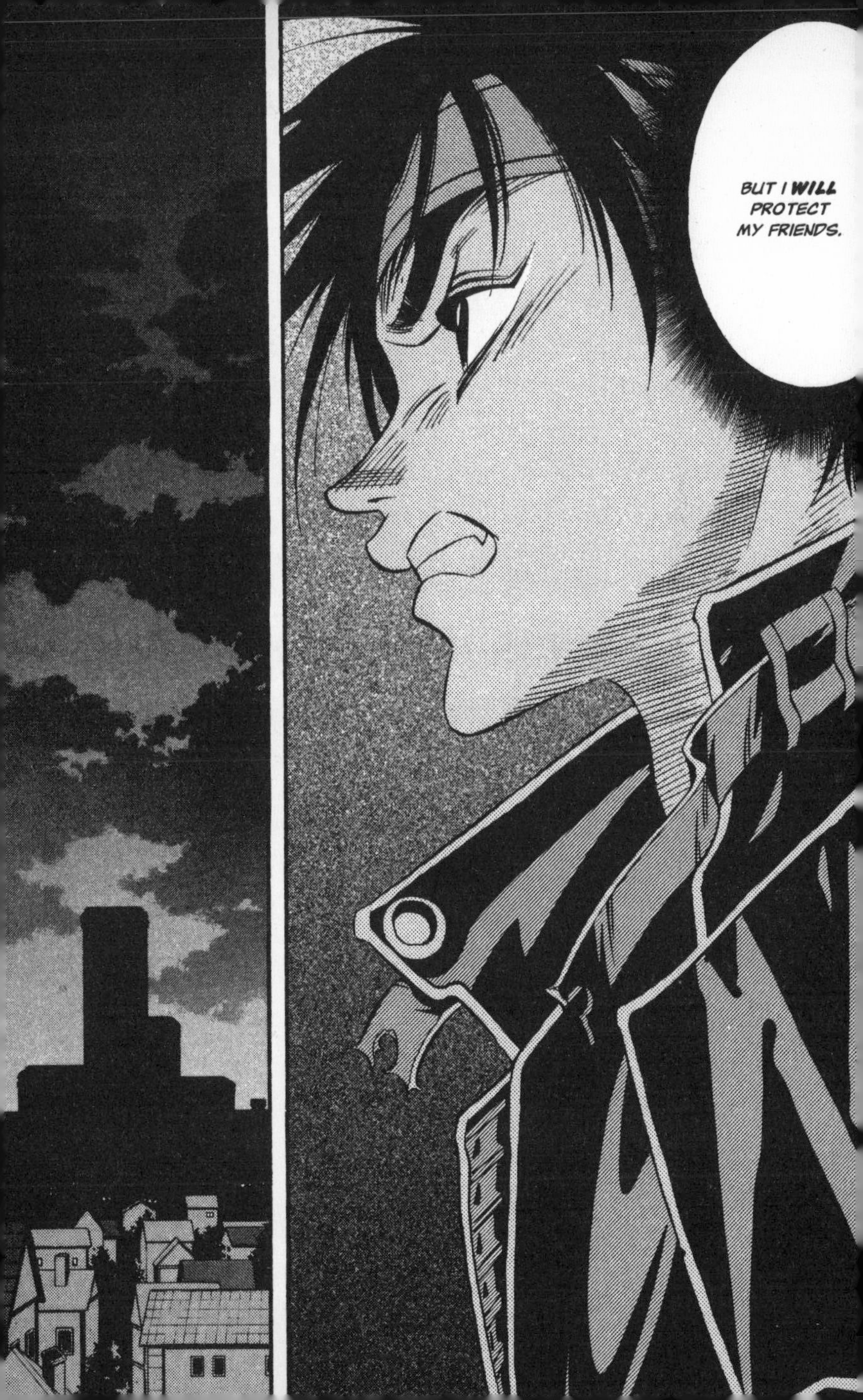
BUT I WILL PROTECT MY FRIENDS.

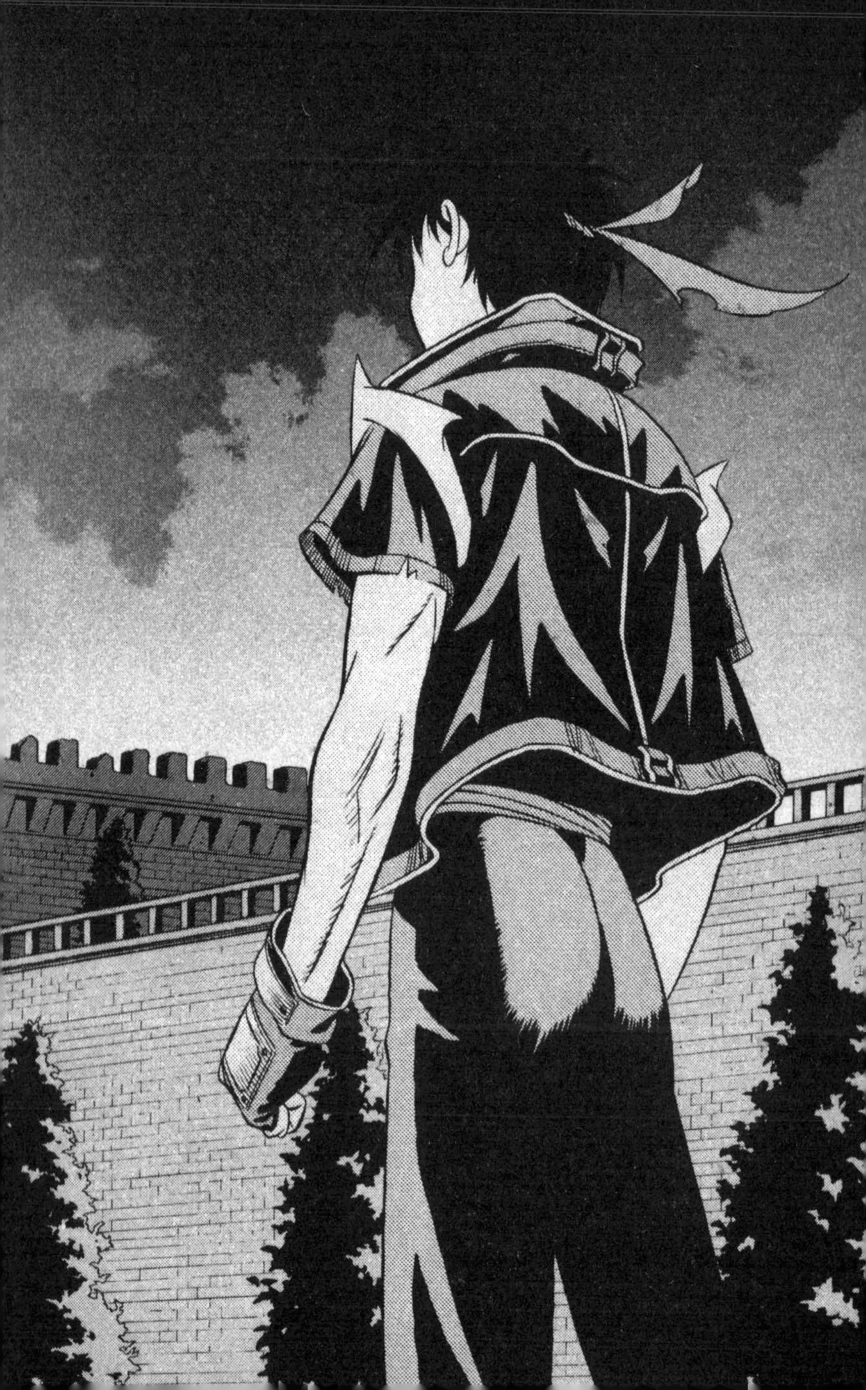

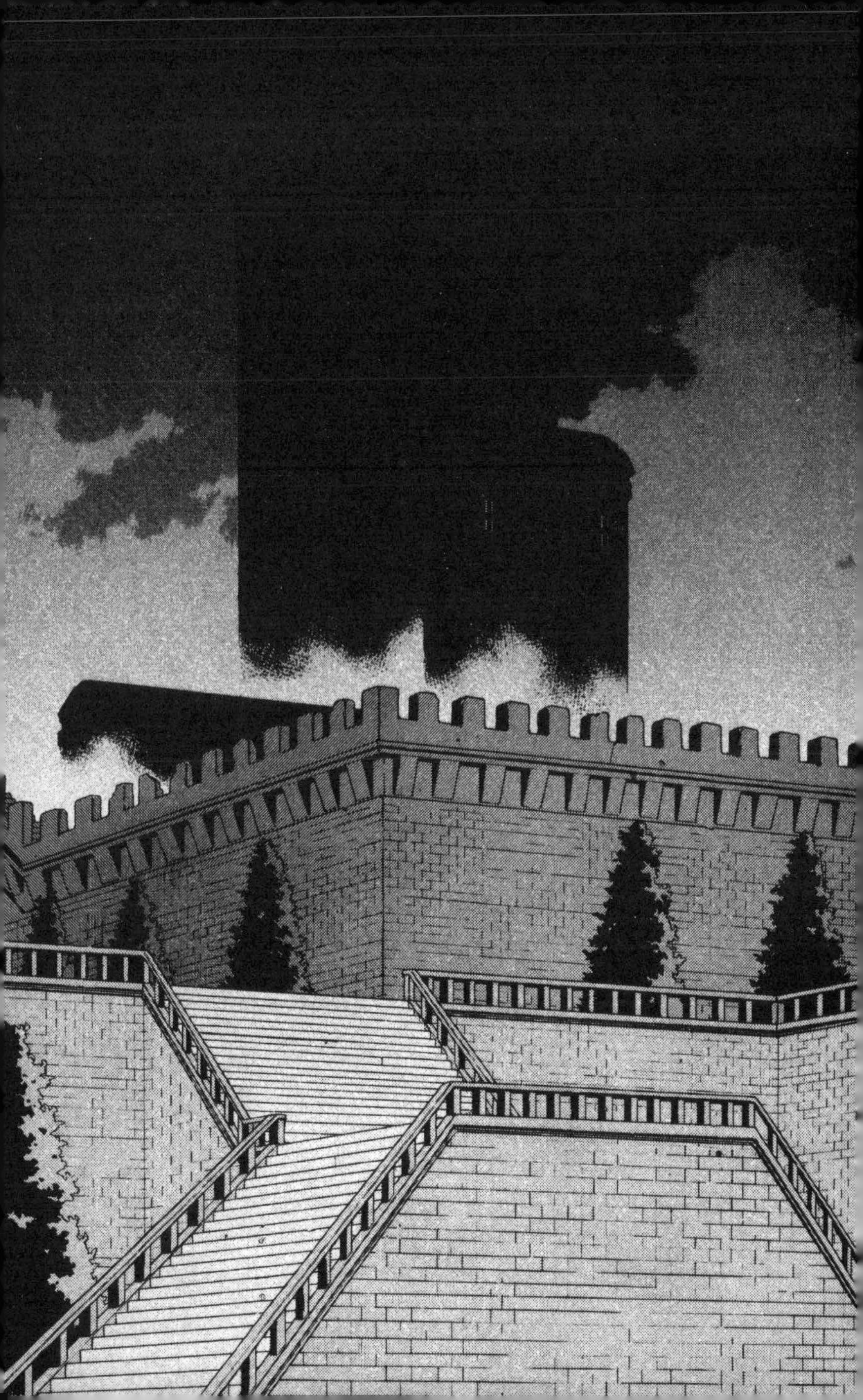

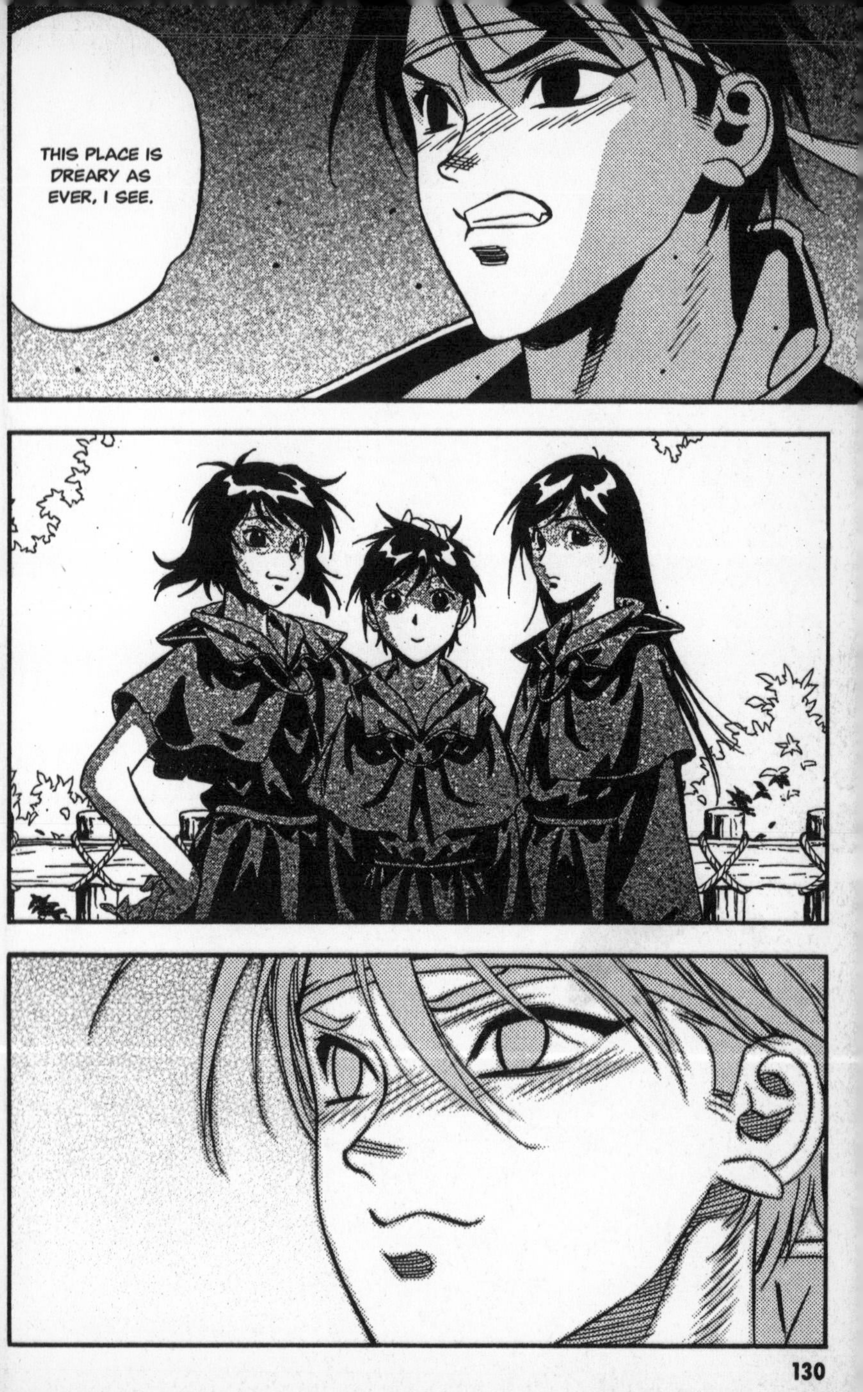
THIS PLACE IS DREARY AS EVER, I SEE.

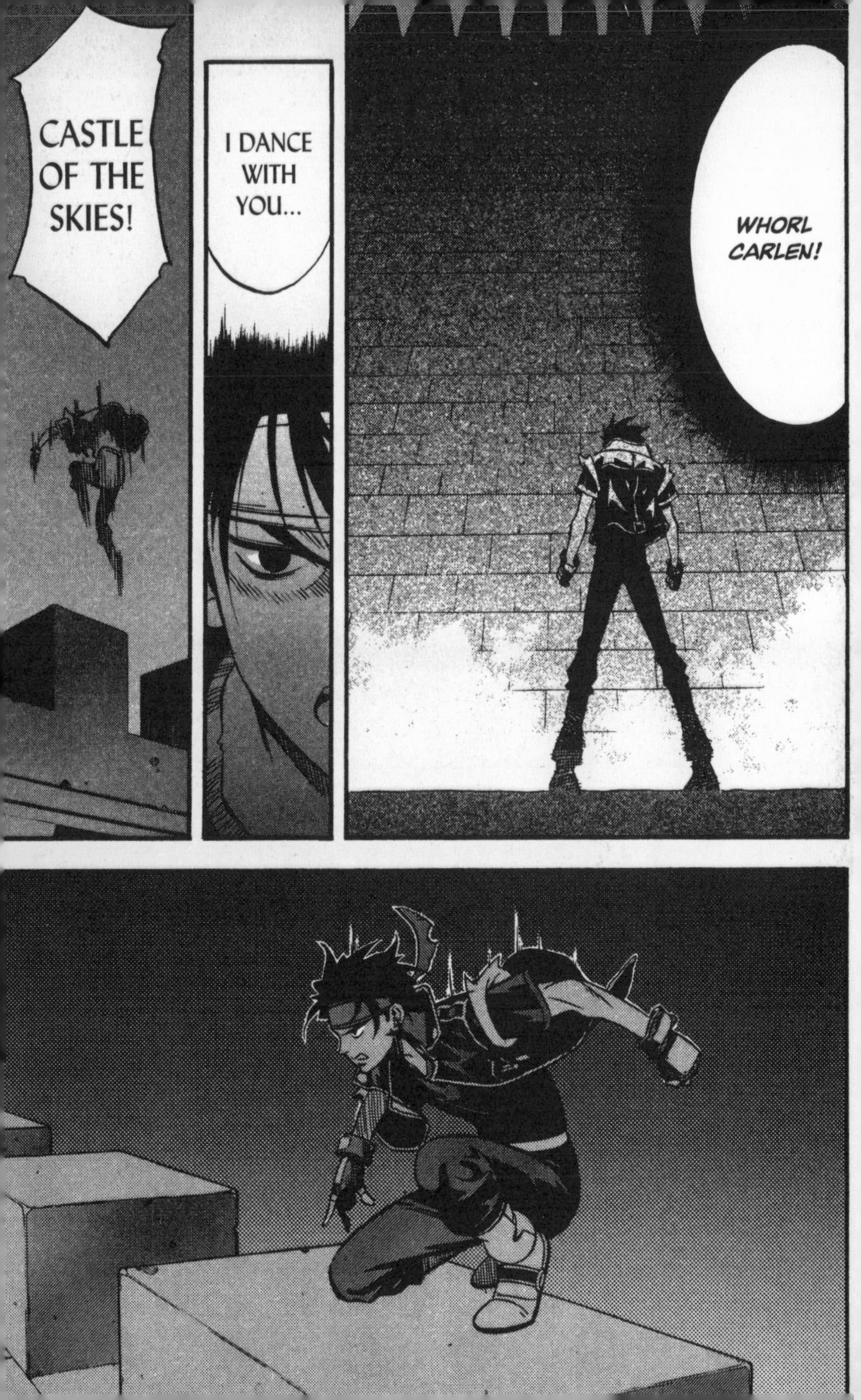
CASTLE OF THE SKIES!
I DANCE WITH YOU...
WHORL CARLEN!

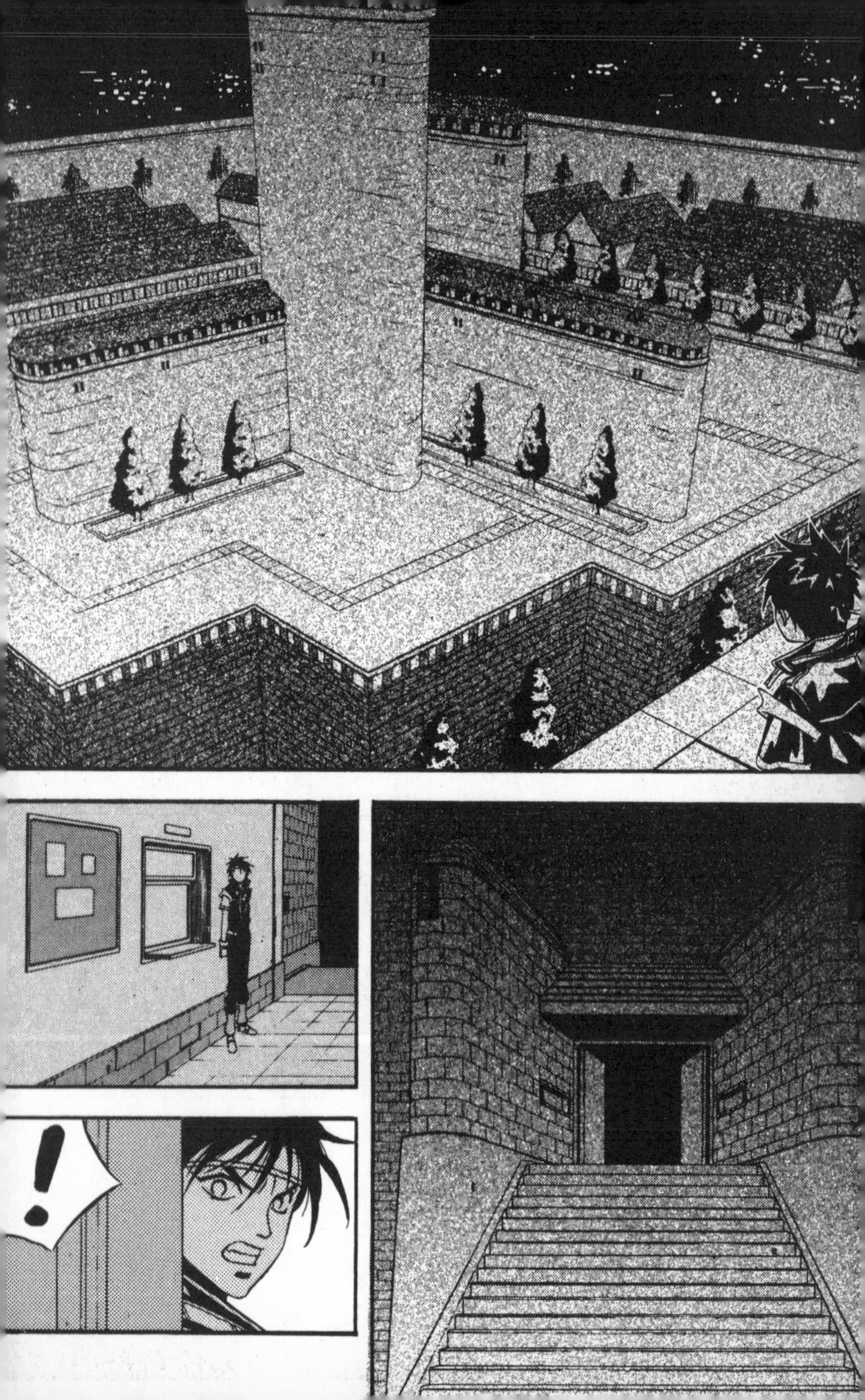
!

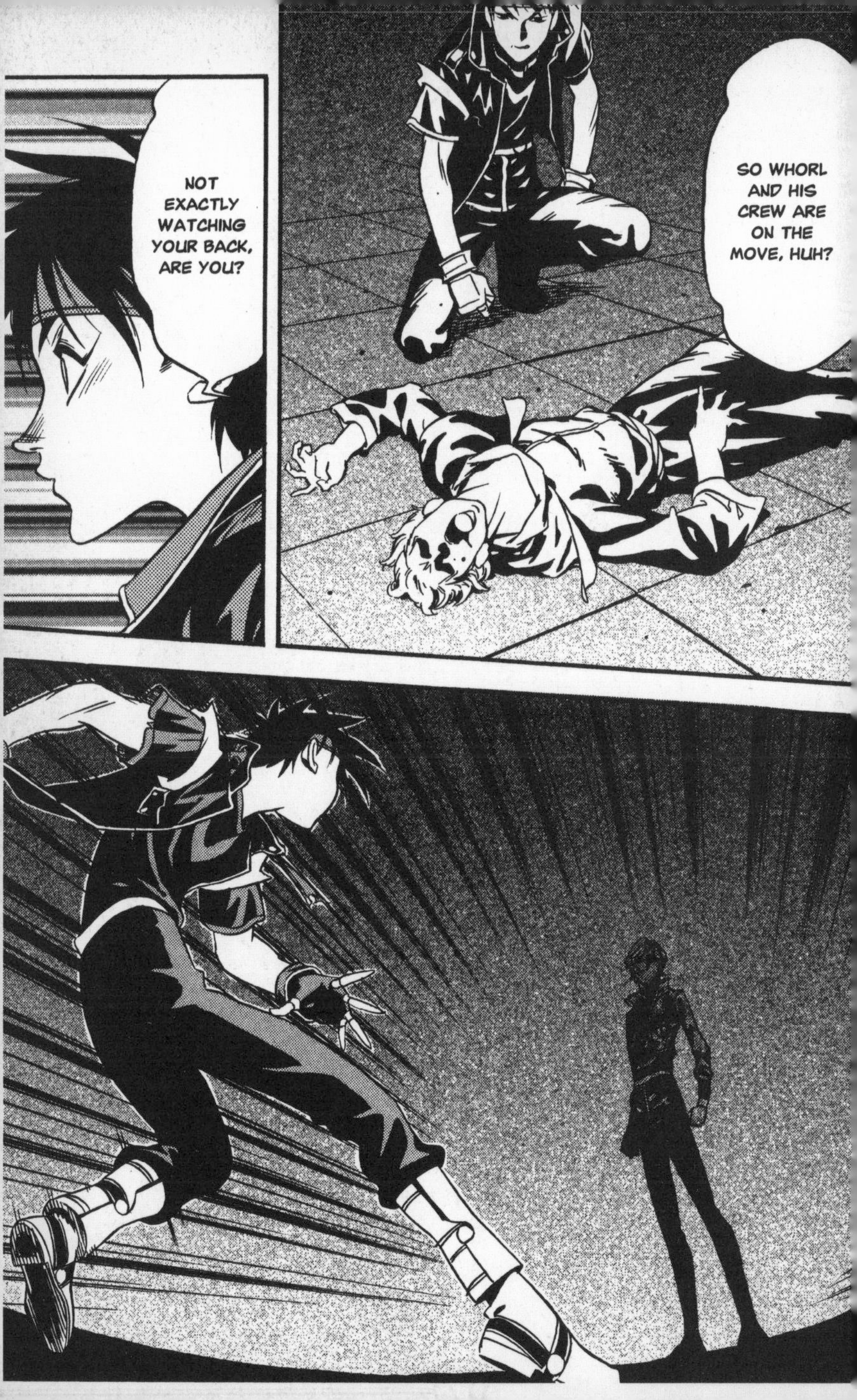
SO WHORL AND HIS CREW ARE ON THE MOVE, HUH?
NOT EXACTLY WATCHING YOUR BACK, ARE YOU?

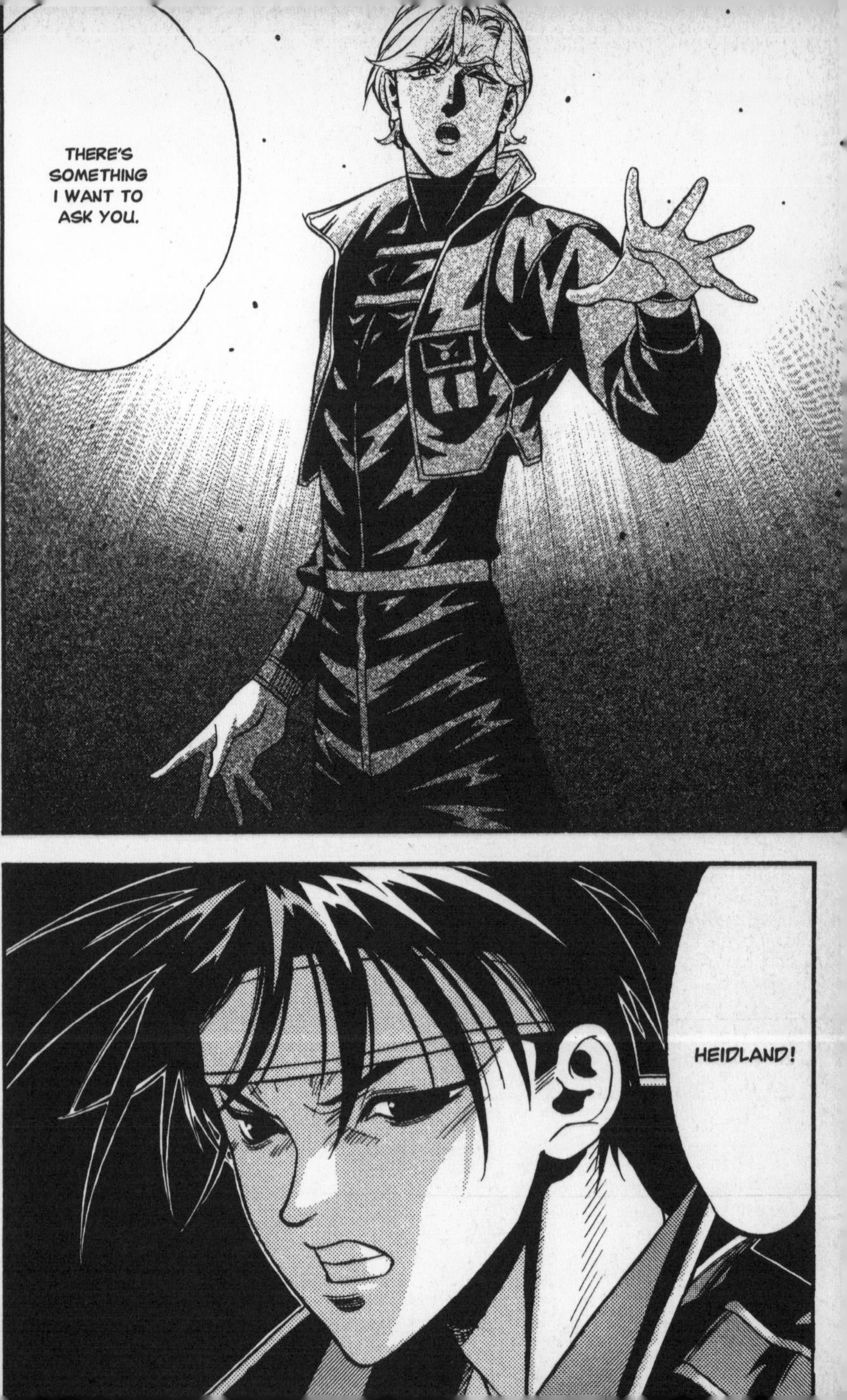
THERE'S SOMETHING I WANT TO ASK YOU.
HEIDLAND!

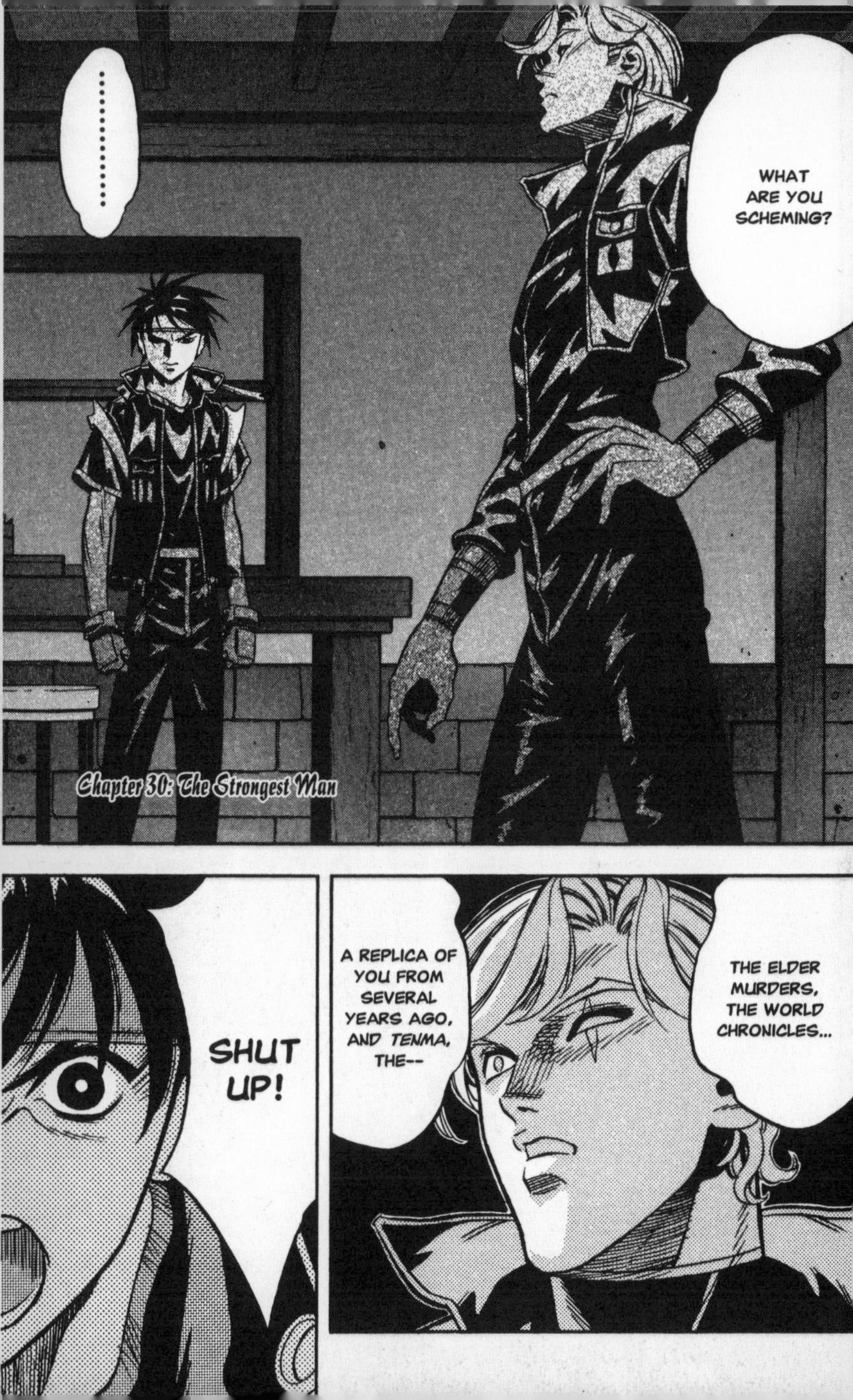
WHAT ARE YOU SCHEMING?
......
Chapter 30: The Strongest Man
THE ELDER MURDERS, THE WORLD CHRONICLES...
A REPLICA OF YOU FROM SEVERAL YEARS AGO, AND *TENMA*, THE--
SHUT UP!

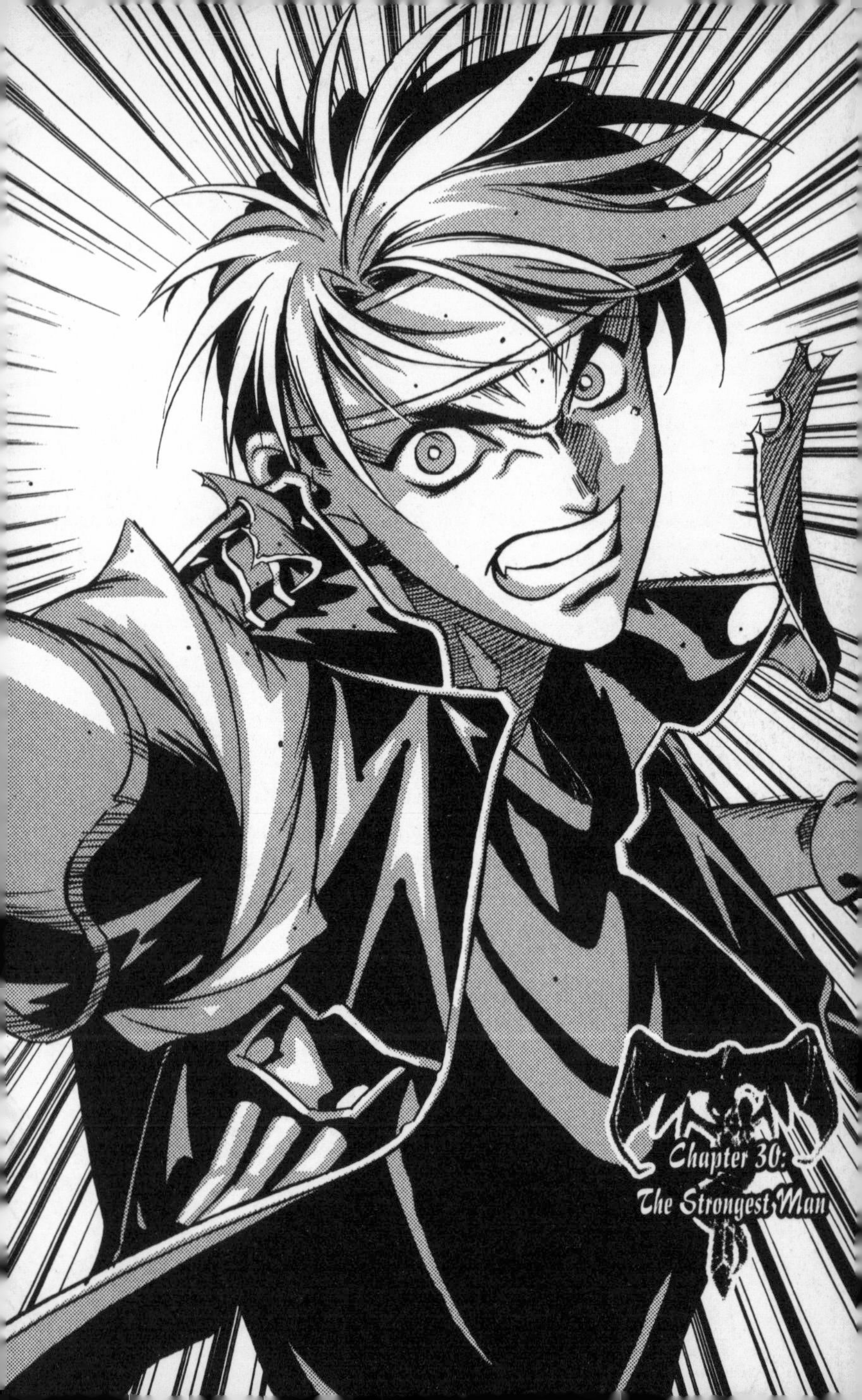
Chapter 30:
The Strongest Man

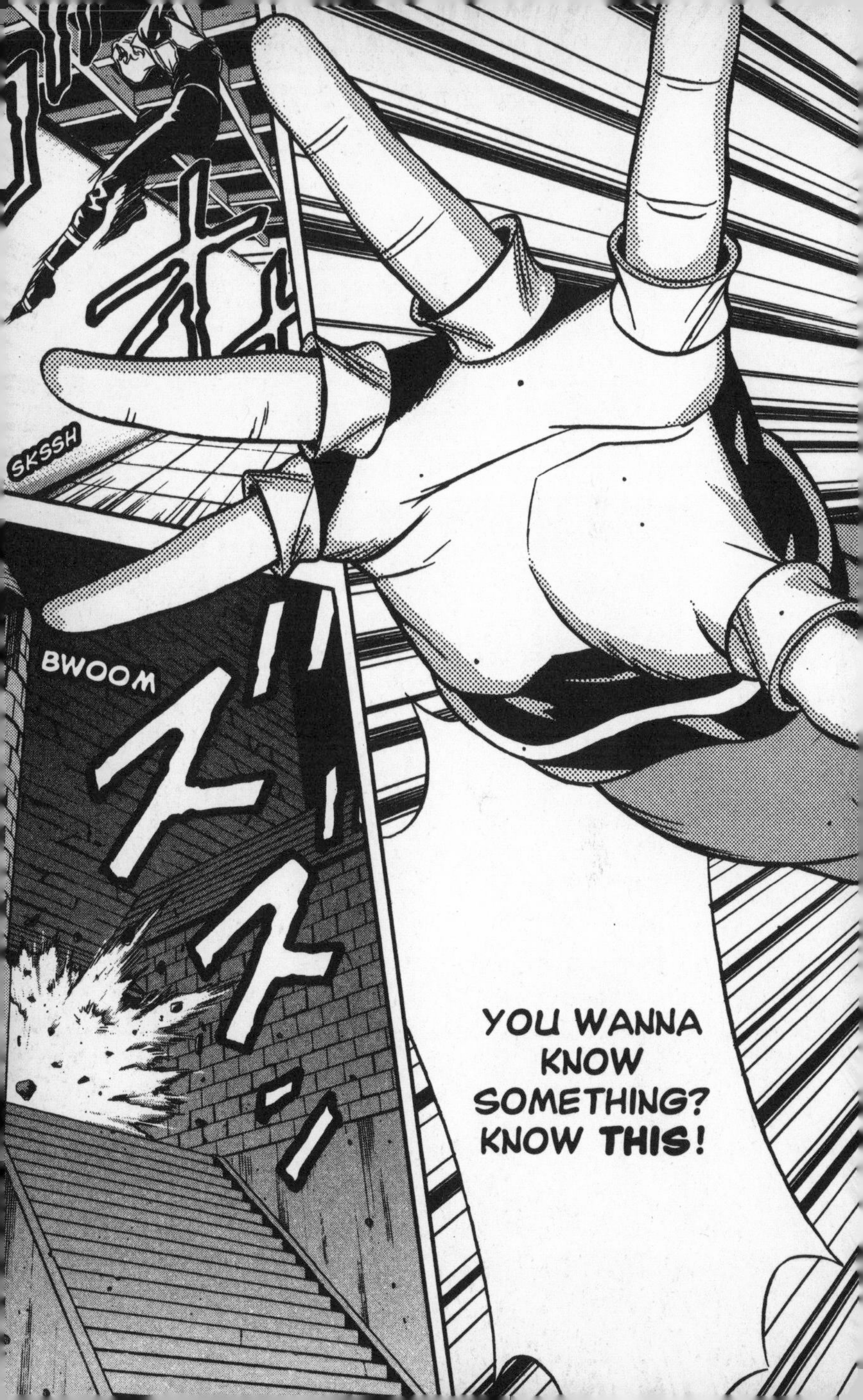
SKSSH
BWOOM
YOU WANNA KNOW SOMETHING? KNOW THIS!

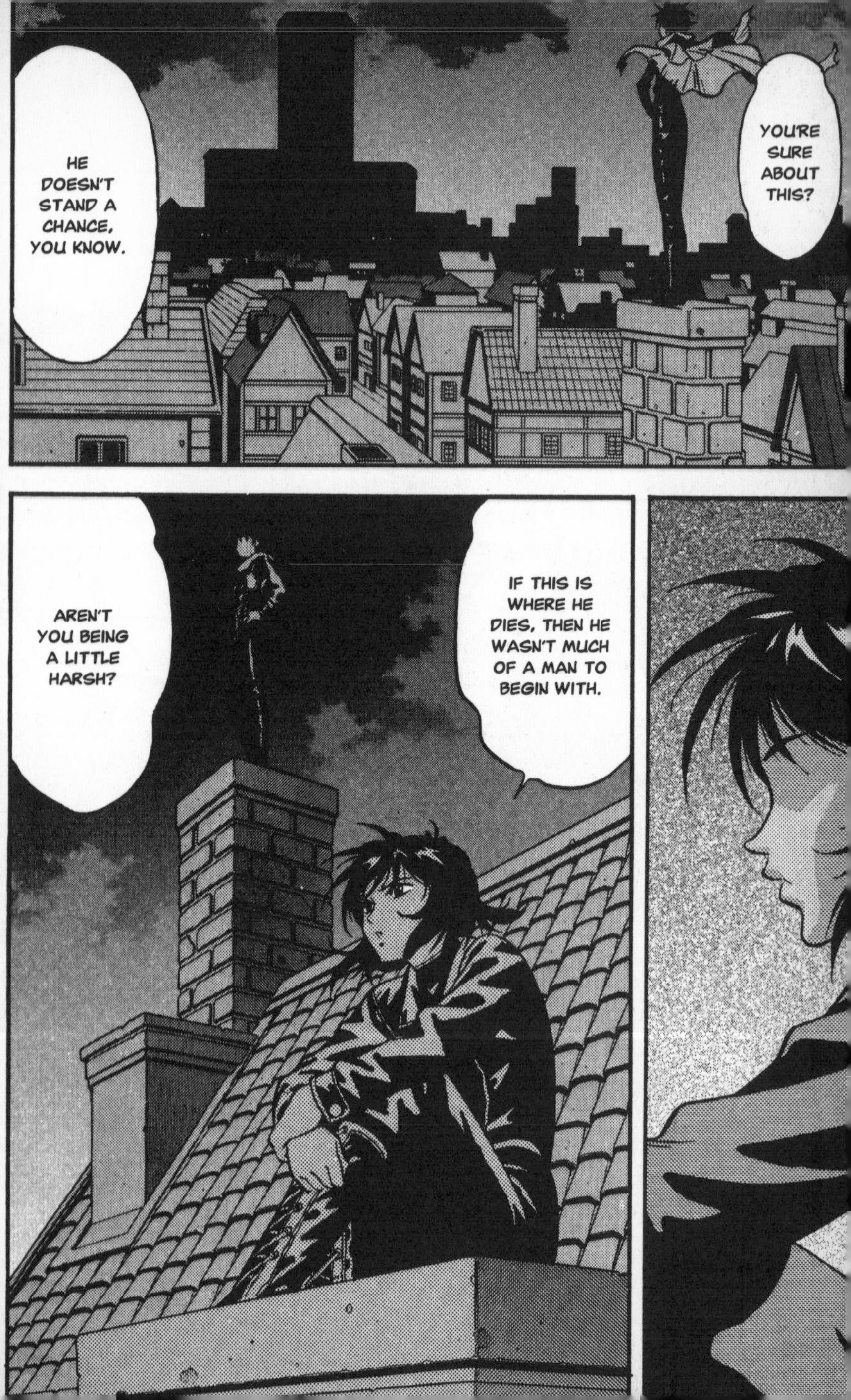
YOU'RE SURE ABOUT THIS?
HE DOESN'T STAND A CHANCE, YOU KNOW.
IF THIS IS WHERE HE DIES, THEN HE WASN'T MUCH OF A MAN TO BEGIN WITH.
AREN'T YOU BEING A LITTLE HARSH?

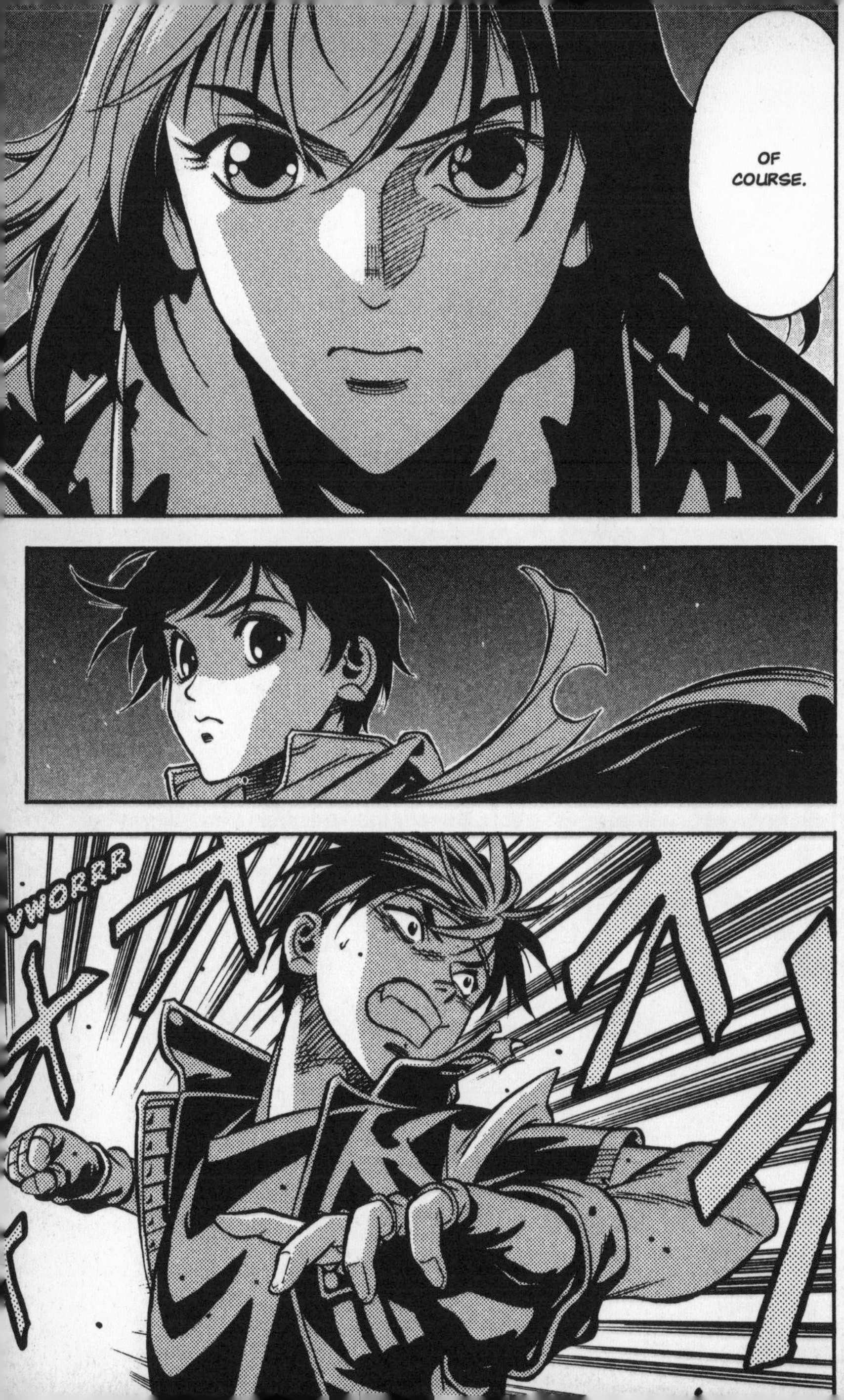
OF COURSE.
VWORRR

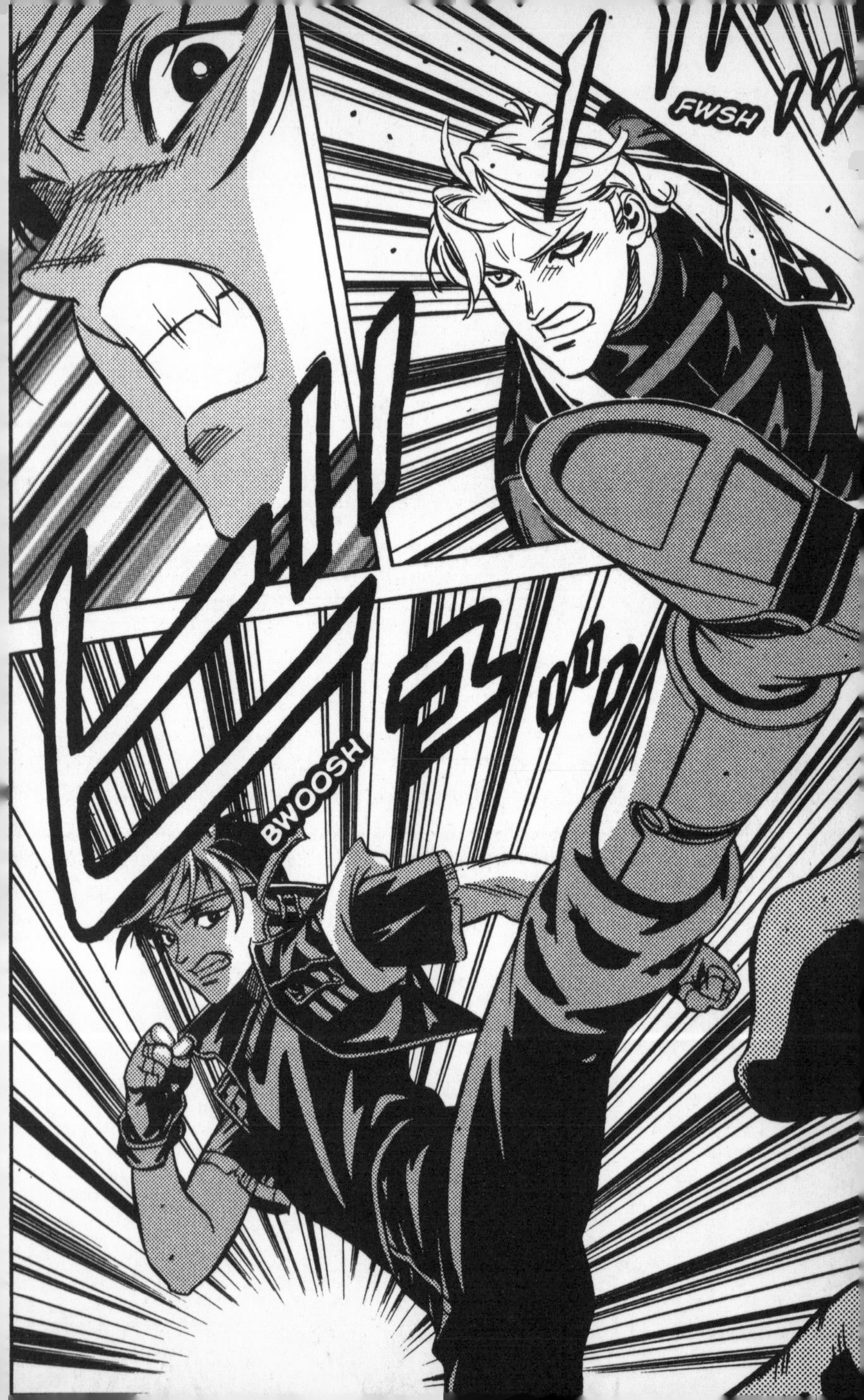
FWSH
BWOOSH

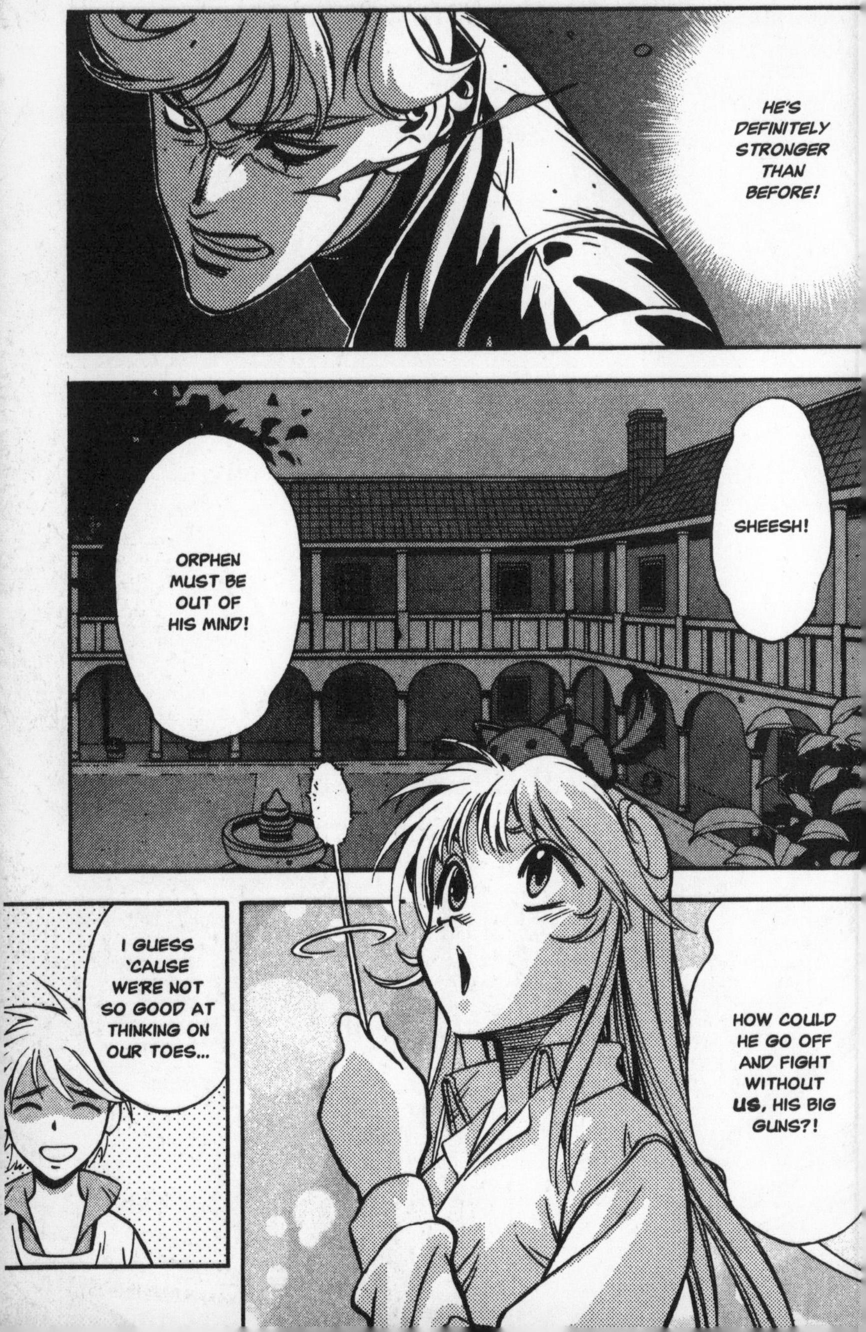
HE'S DEFINITELY STRONGER THAN BEFORE!
SHEESH!
ORPHEN MUST BE OUT OF HIS MIND!
HOW COULD HE GO OFF AND FIGHT WITHOUT US, HIS BIG GUNS?!
I GUESS 'CAUSE WE'RE NOT SO GOOD AT THINKING ON OUR TOES...

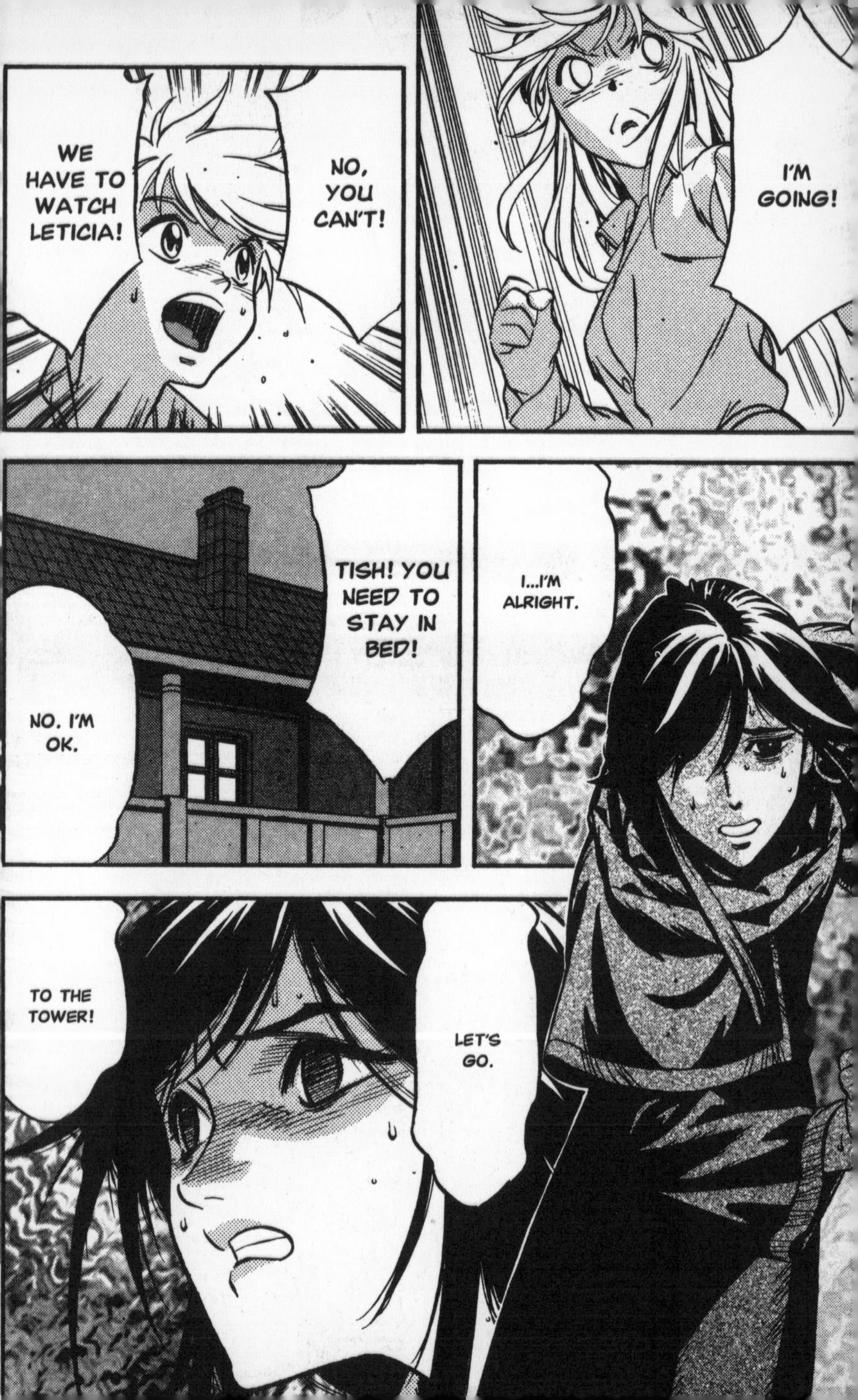
I'M GOING!
NO, YOU CAN'T!
WE HAVE TO WATCH LETICIA!
I...I'M ALRIGHT.
TISH! YOU NEED TO STAY IN BED!
NO. I'M OK.
LET'S GO.
TO THE TOWER!

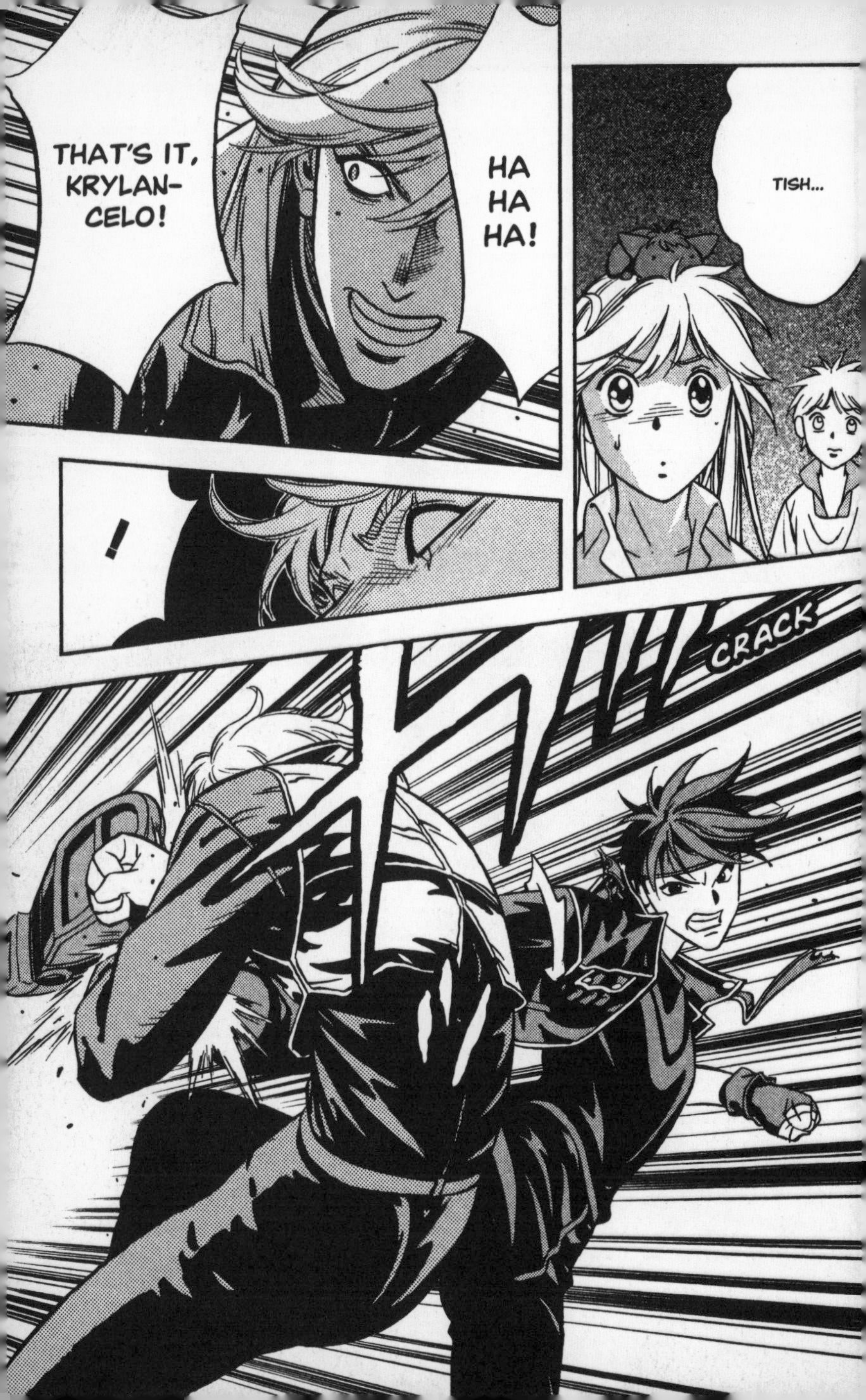
HA HA HA!
THAT'S IT, KRYLAN-CELO!
TISH...
!
CRACK

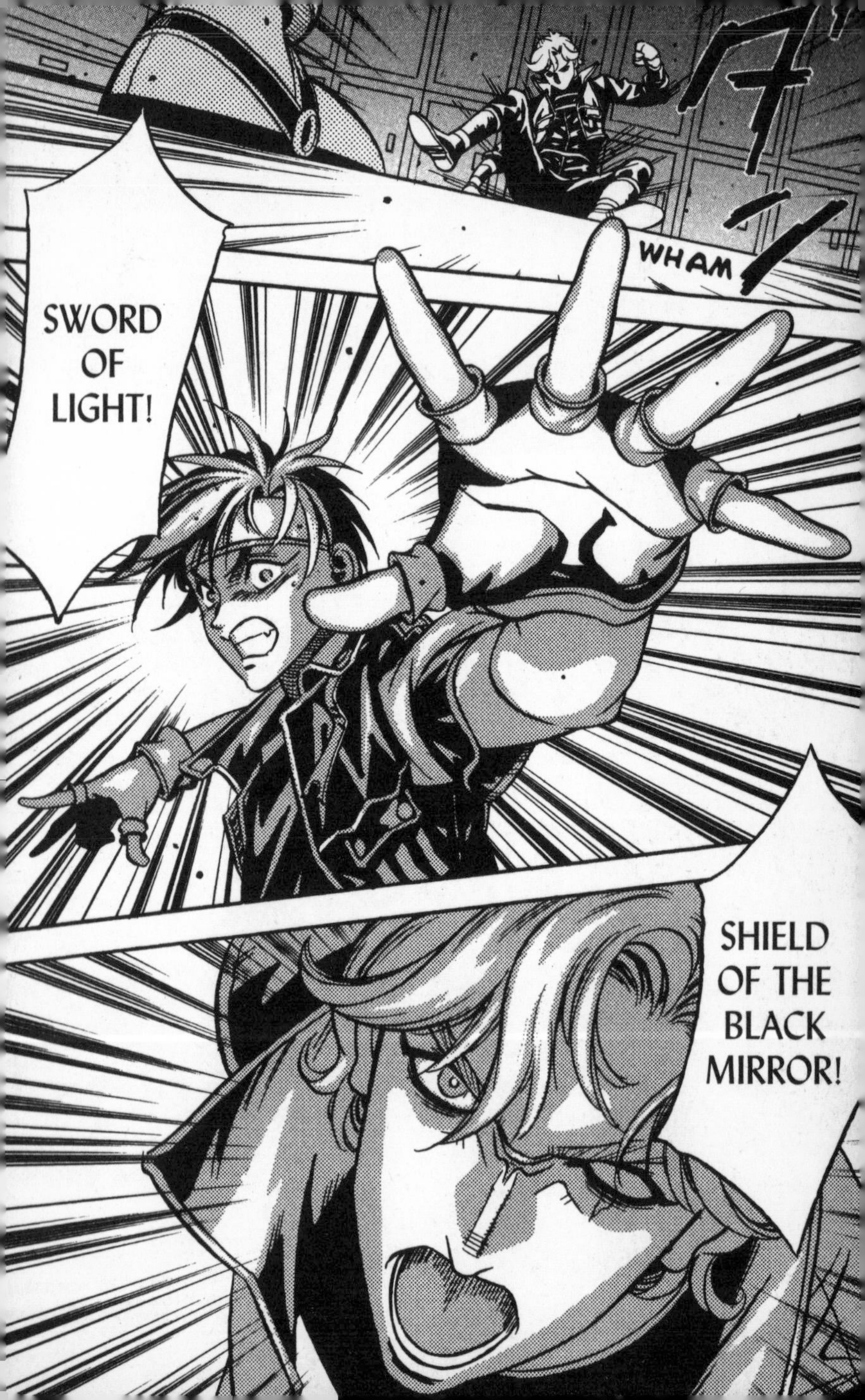
WHAM
SWORD OF LIGHT!
SHIELD OF THE BLACK MIRROR!

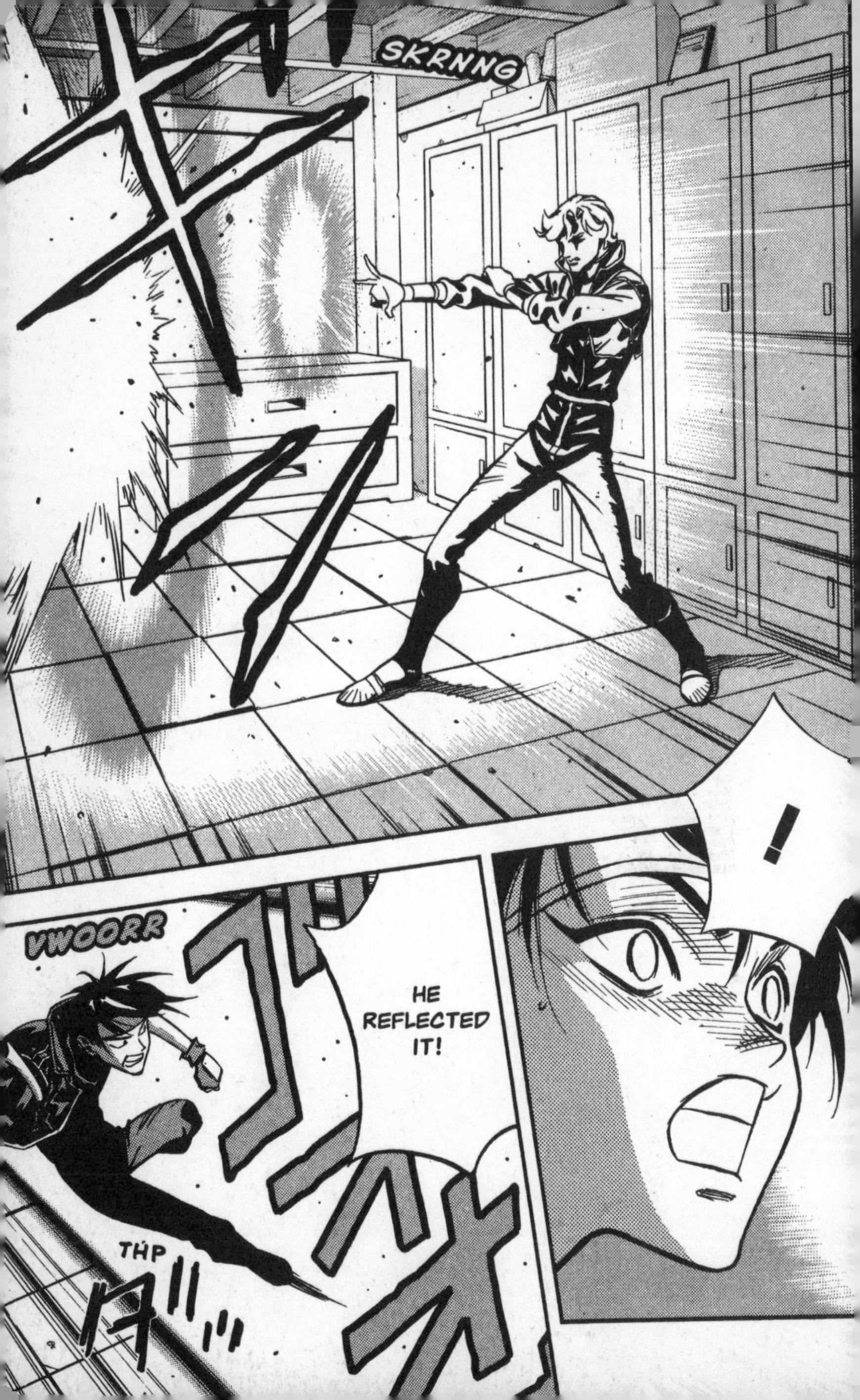
SKRNNG
!
HE REFLECTED IT!
VWOORR
THP

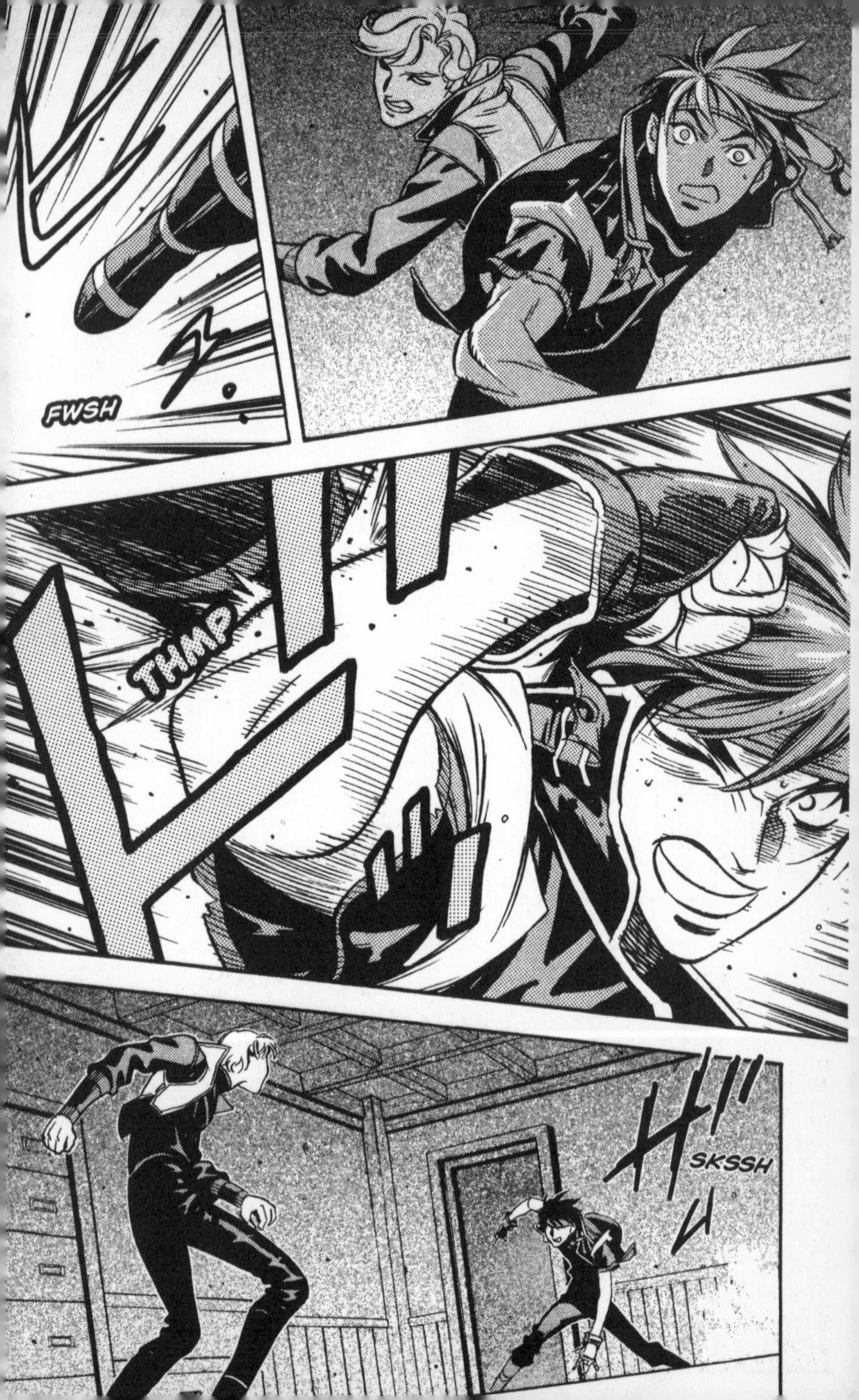
FWSH
THMP
SKSSH

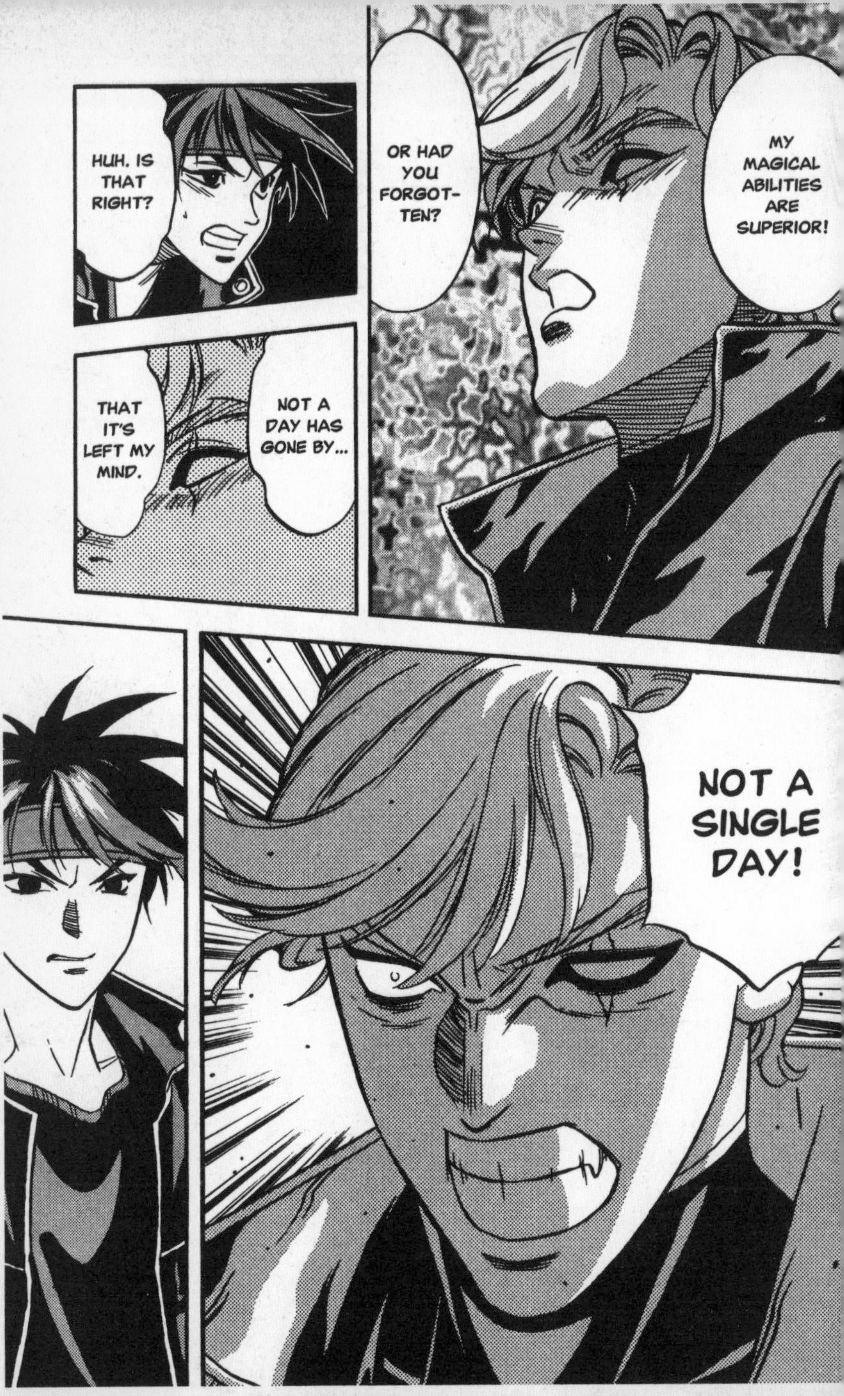
MY MAGICAL ABILITIES ARE SUPERIOR!
OR HAD YOU FORGOT-TEN?
HUH. IS THAT RIGHT?
NOT A DAY HAS GONE BY...
THAT IT'S LEFT MY MIND.
NOT A SINGLE DAY!

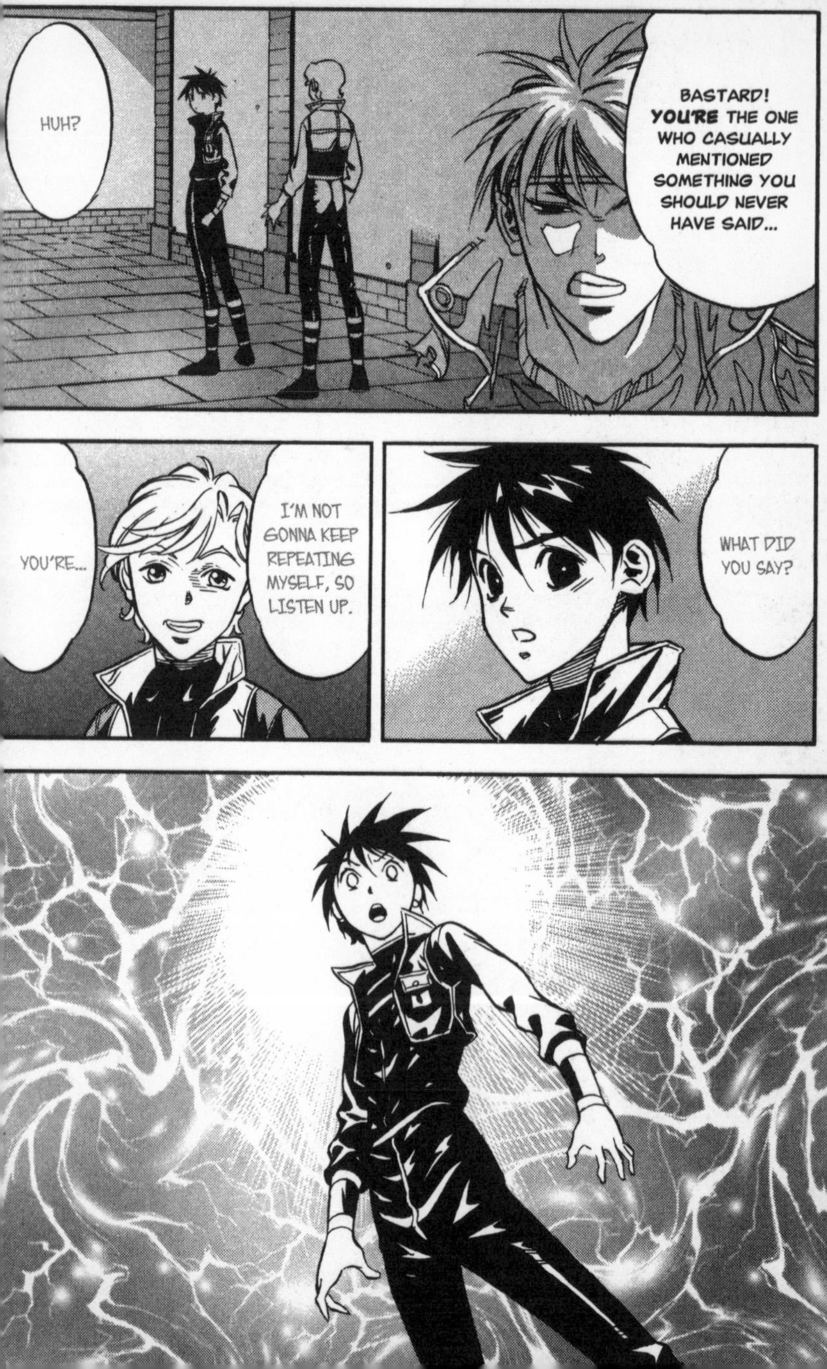
BASTARD! YOU'RE THE ONE WHO CASUALLY MENTIONED SOMETHING YOU SHOULD NEVER HAVE SAID...
HUH?
WHAT DID YOU SAY?
I'M NOT GONNA KEEP REPEATING MYSELF, SO LISTEN UP.
YOU'RE...

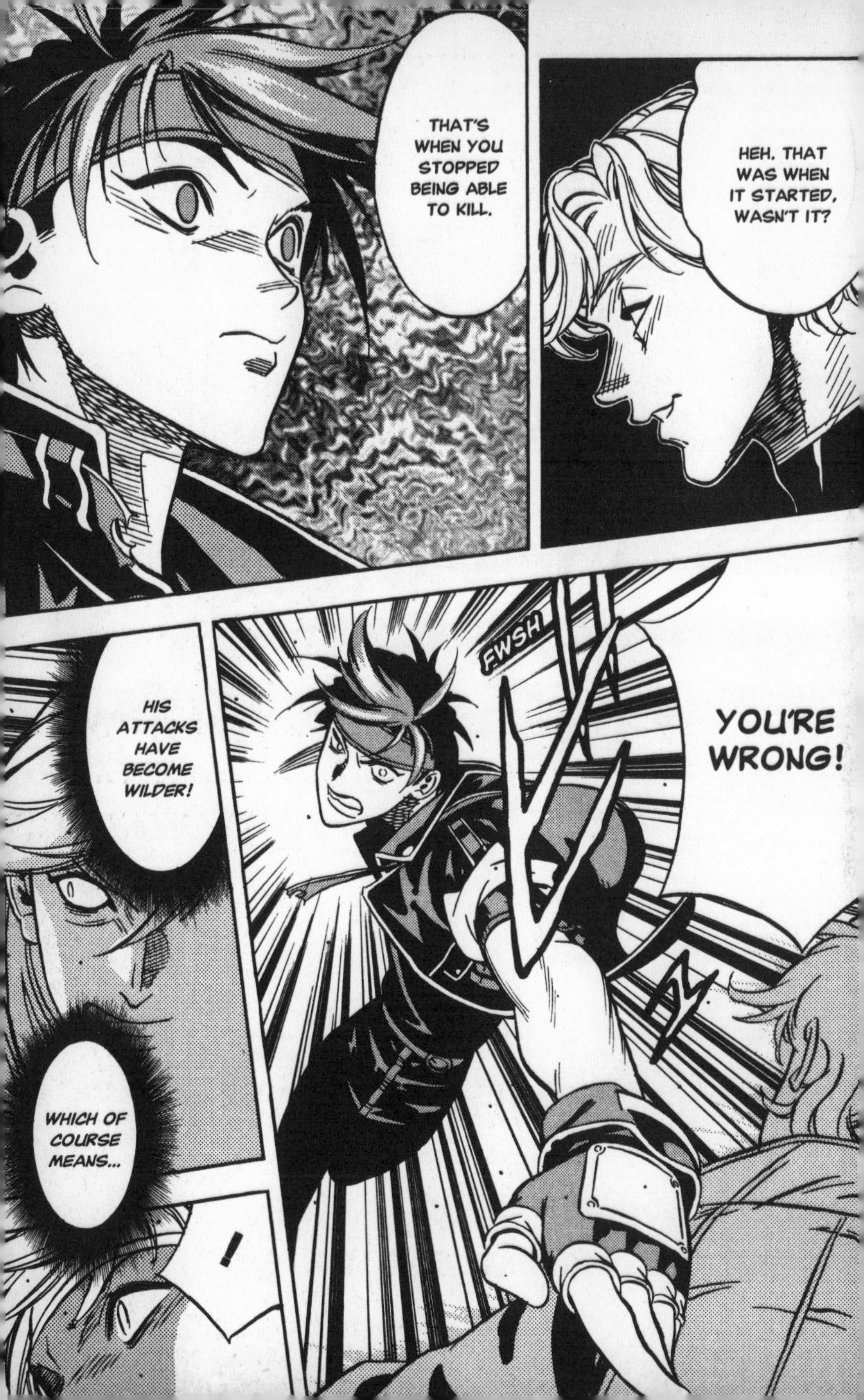
HEH. THAT WAS WHEN IT STARTED, WASN'T IT?
THAT'S WHEN YOU STOPPED BEING ABLE TO KILL.
YOU'RE WRONG!
FWSH
HIS ATTACKS HAVE BECOME WILDER!
WHICH OF COURSE MEANS...
!

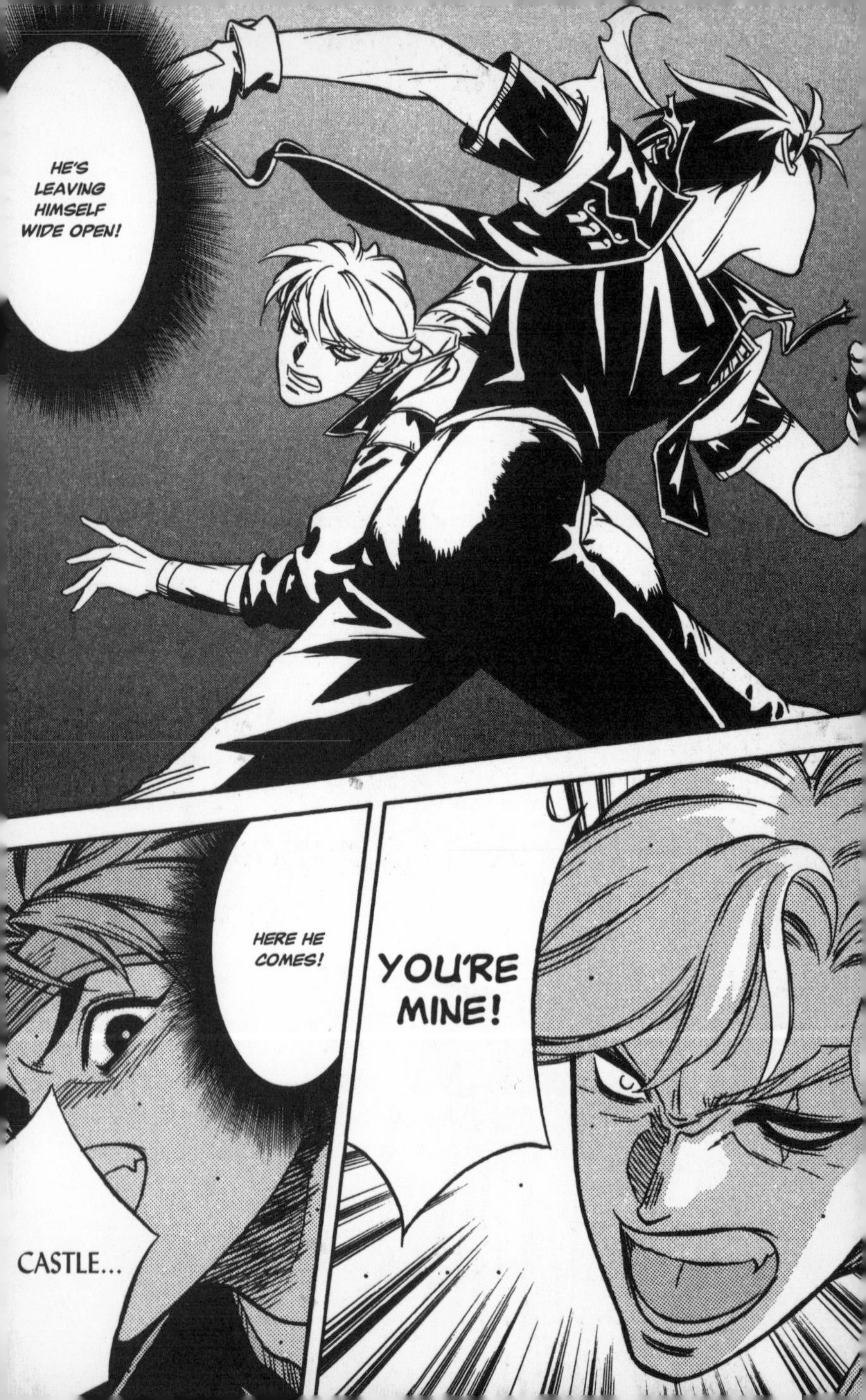
HE'S LEAVING HIMSELF WIDE OPEN!
YOU'RE MINE!
HERE HE COMES!
CASTLE...

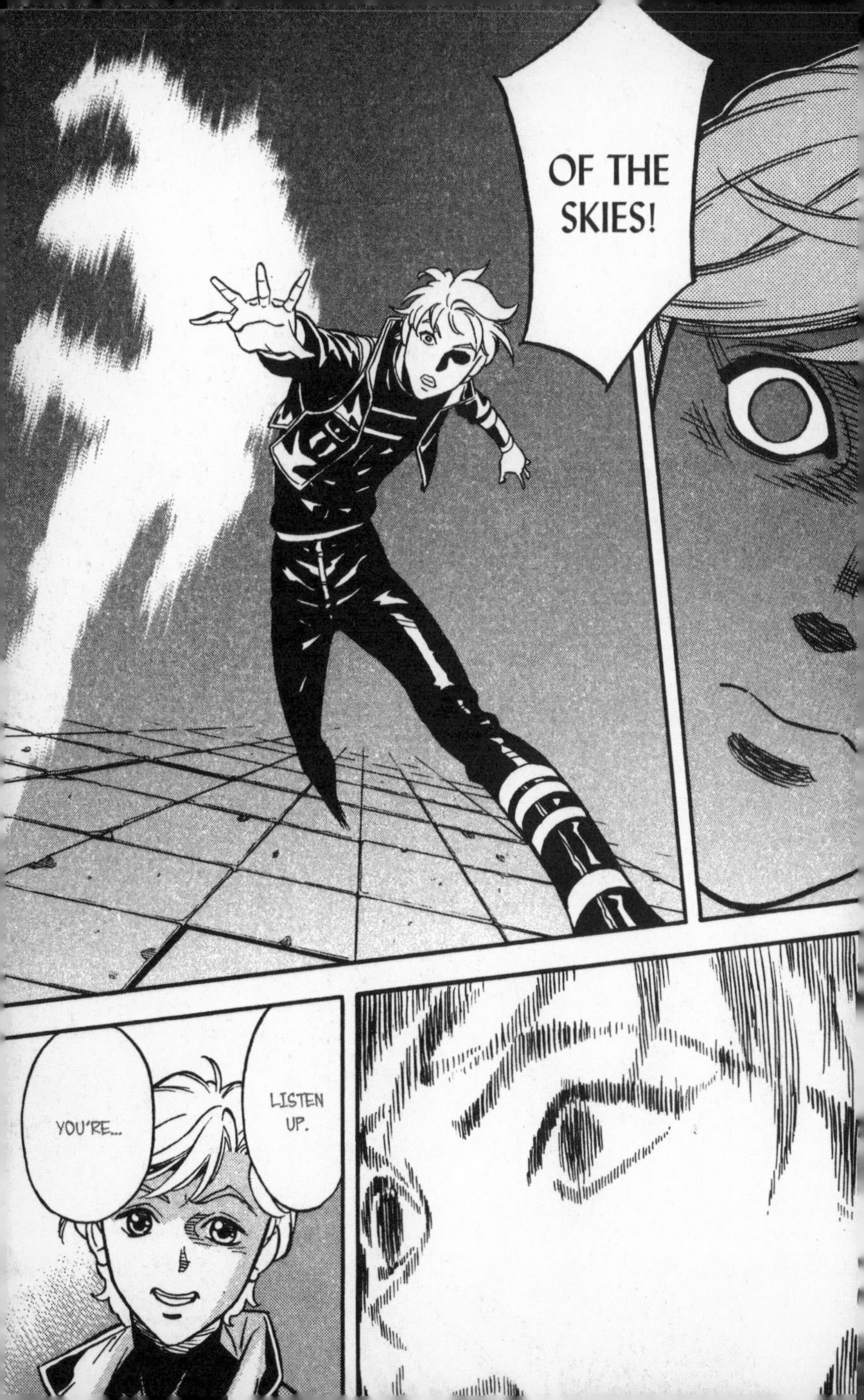
OF THE SKIES!
LISTEN UP.
YOU'RE...

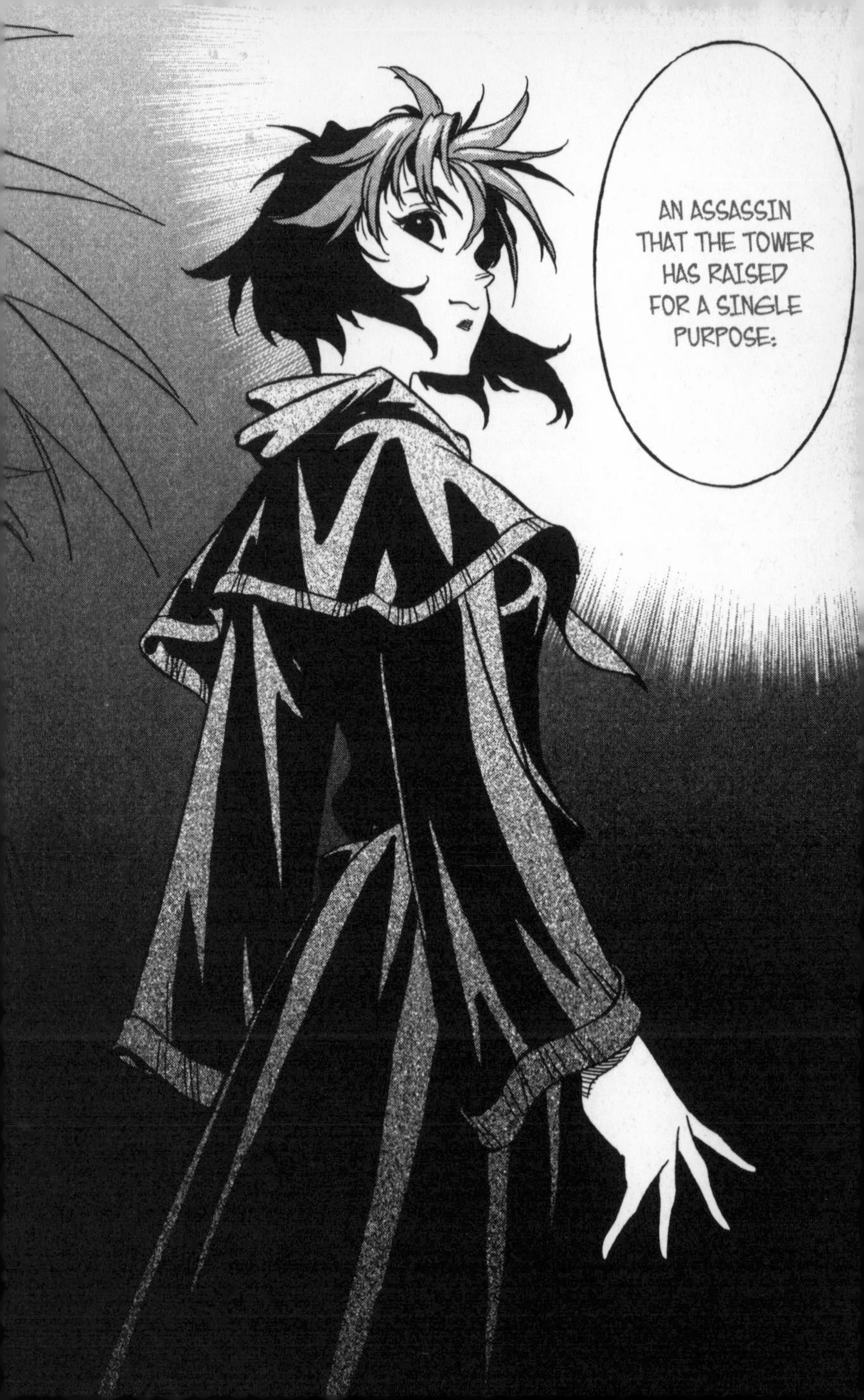
AN ASSASSIN THAT THE TOWER HAS RAISED FOR A SINGLE PURPOSE:

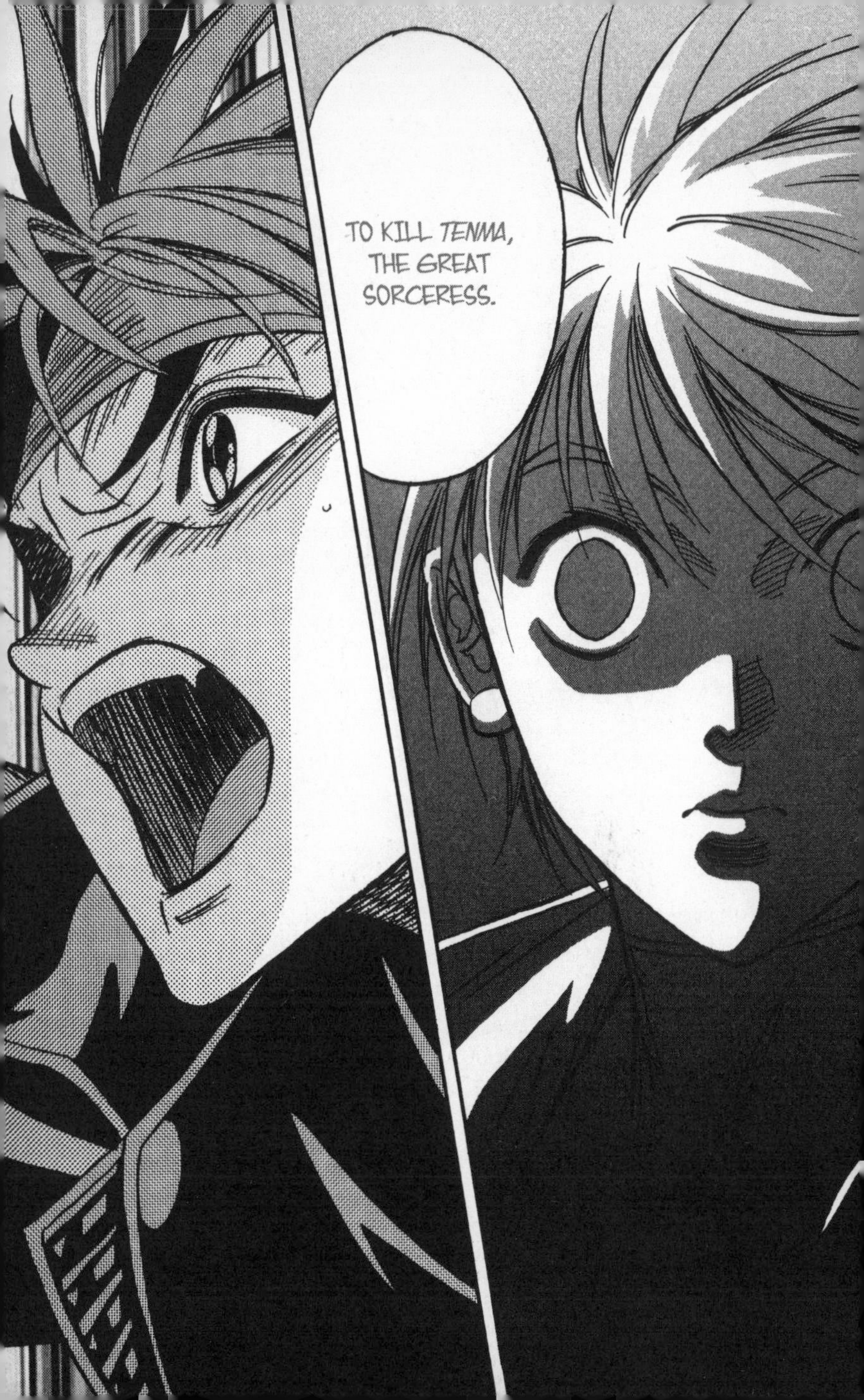
TO KILL TENMA, THE GREAT SORCERESS.

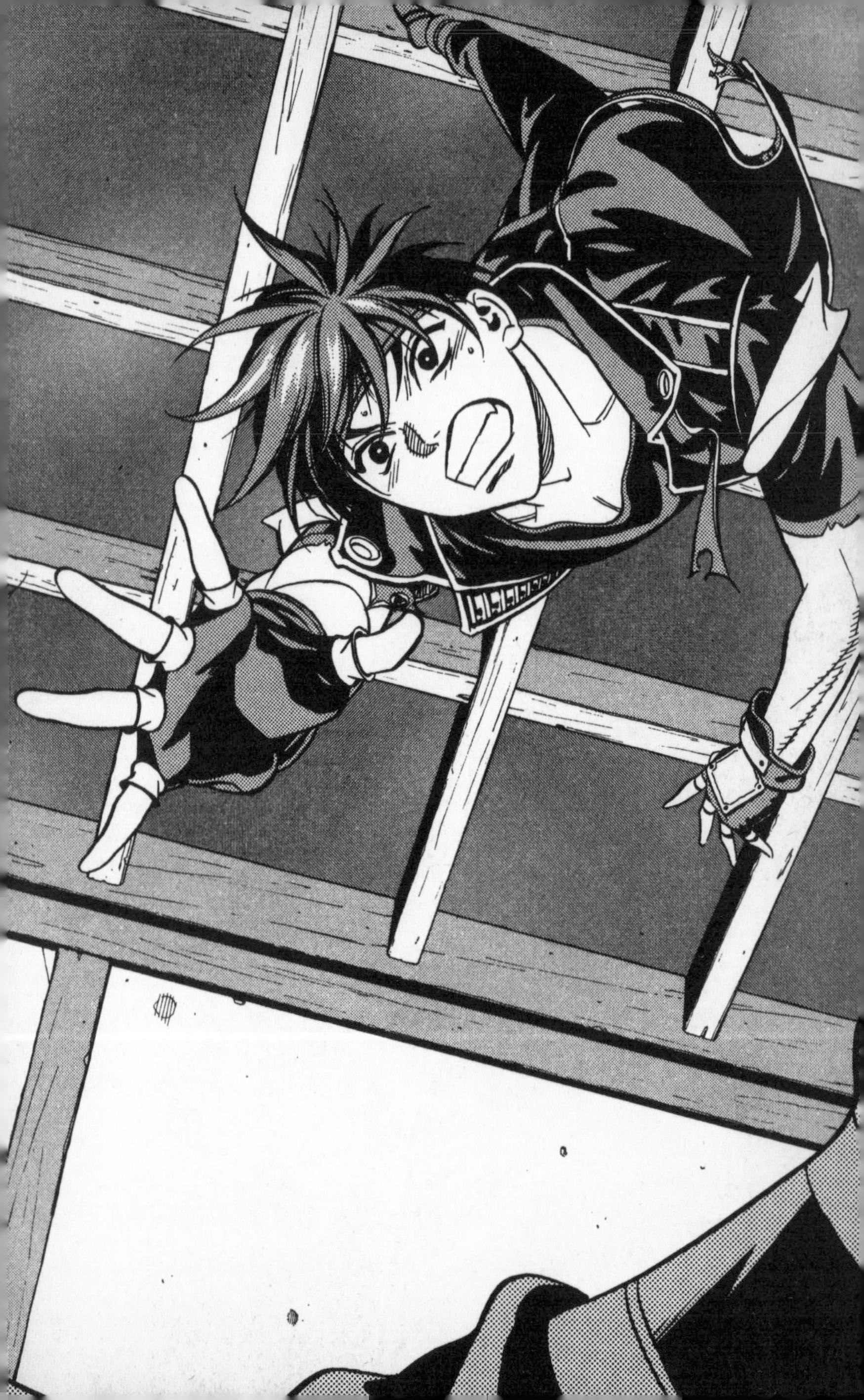

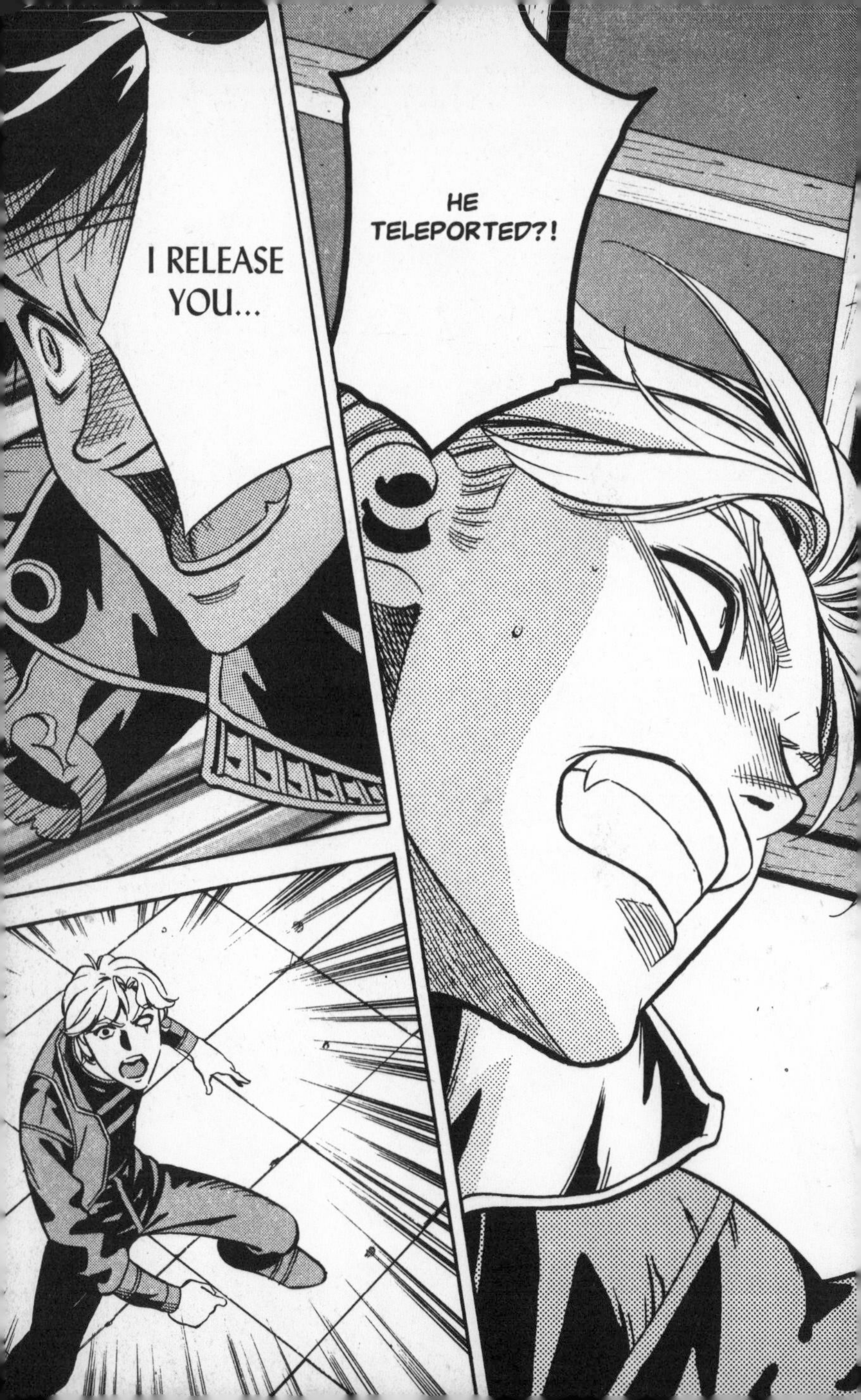

HE TELEPORTED?!
I RELEASE YOU...

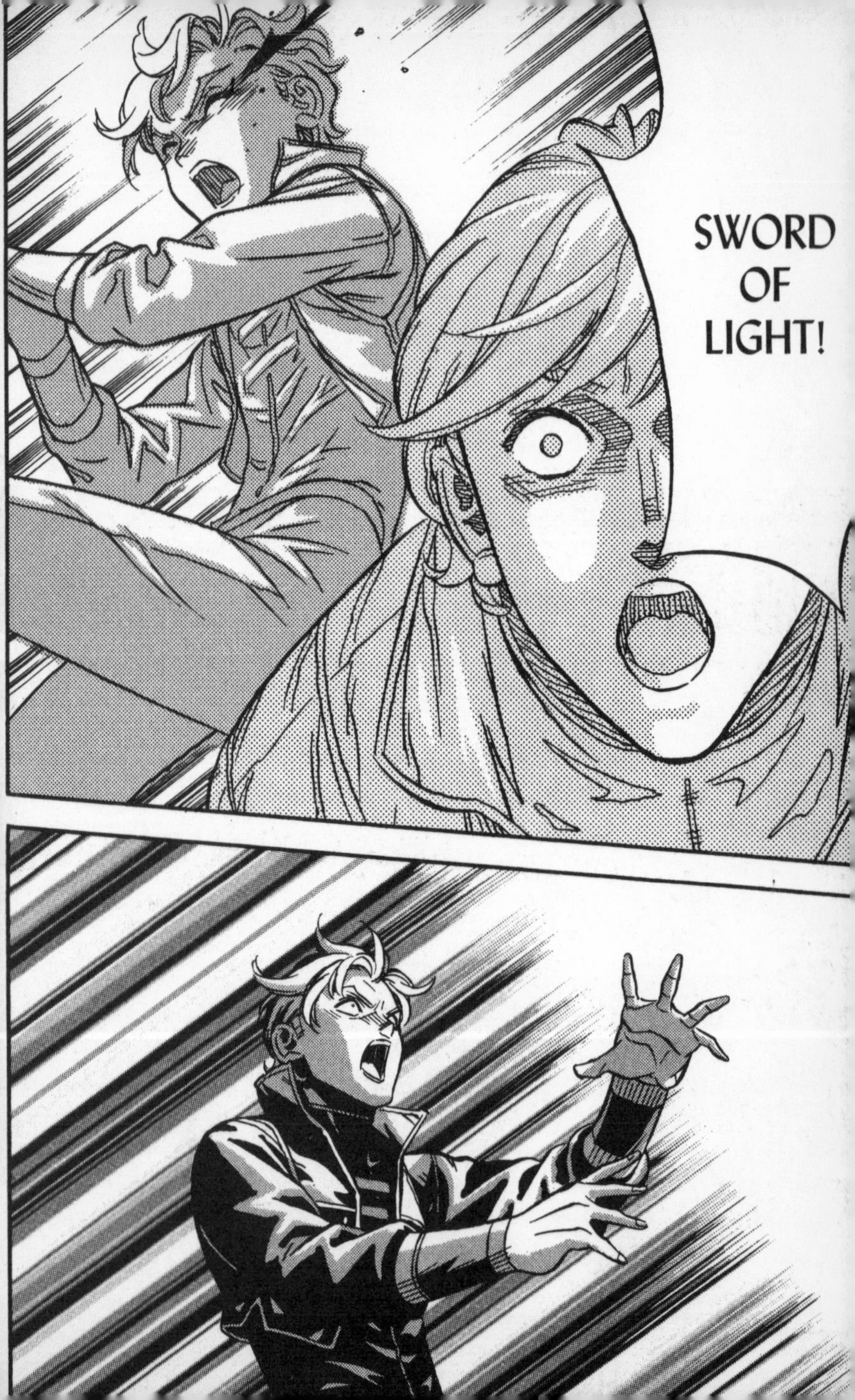
SWORD OF LIGHT!

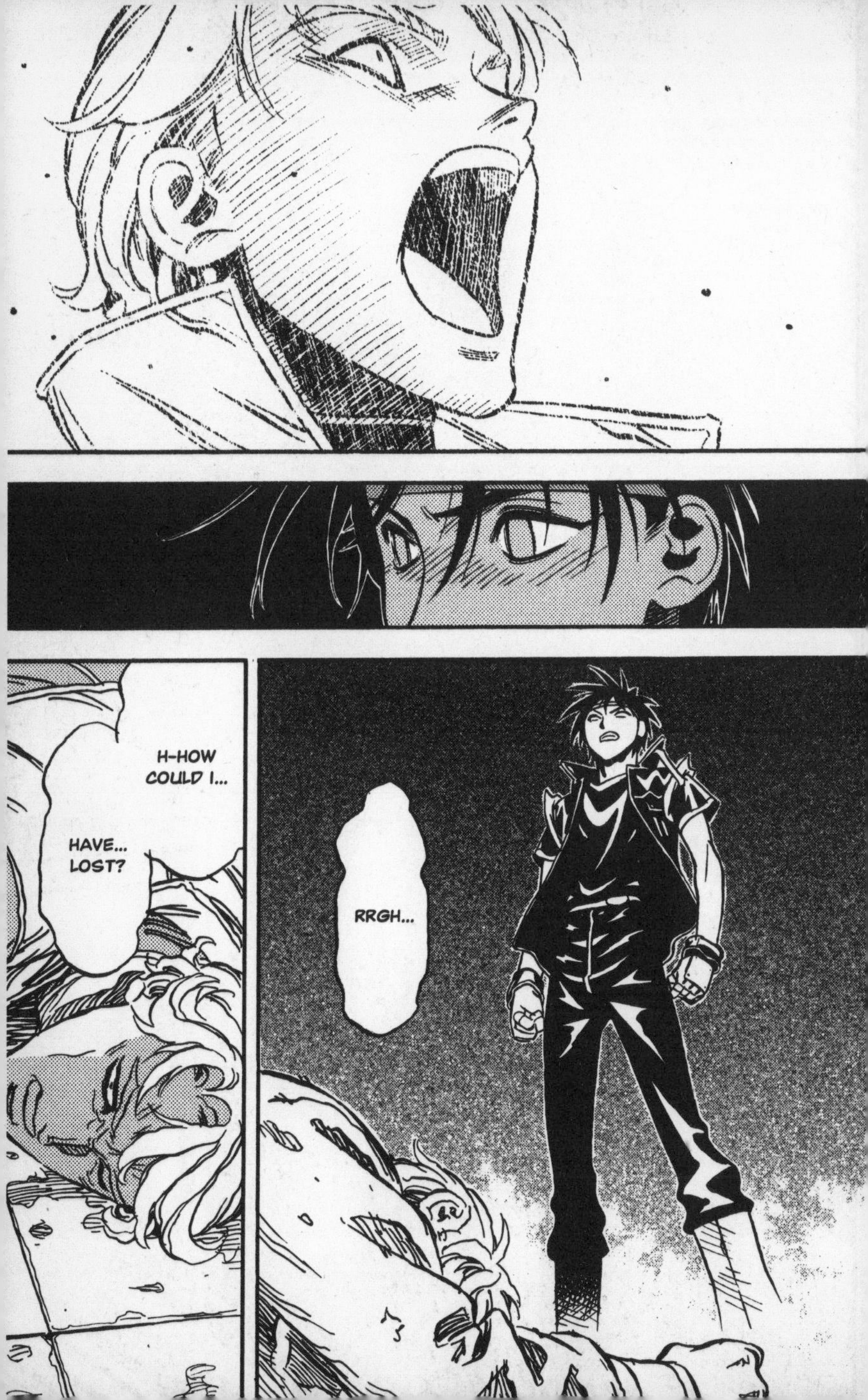
RRGH...
H-HOW COULD I...
HAVE... LOST?

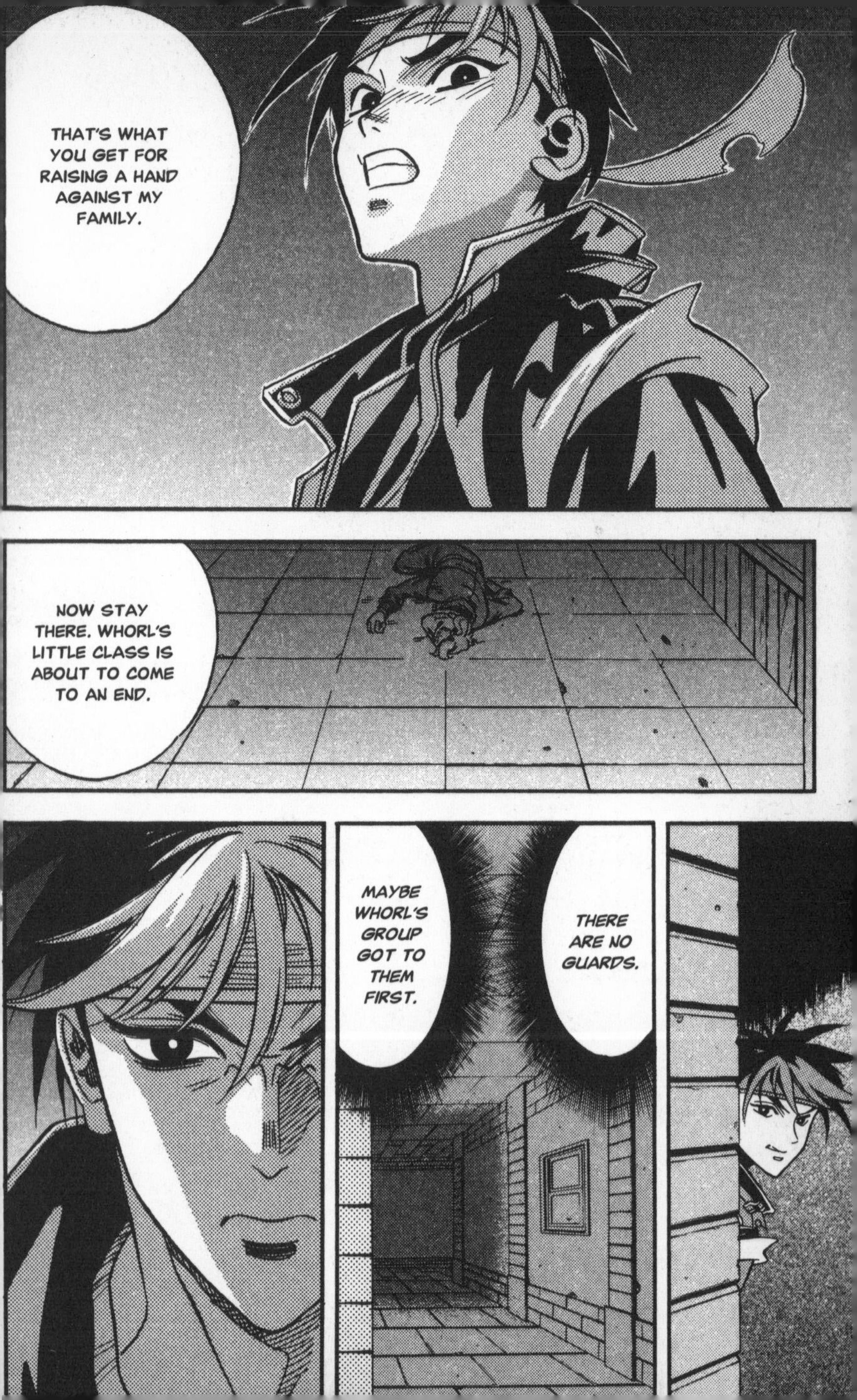
THAT'S WHAT YOU GET FOR RAISING A HAND AGAINST MY FAMILY.
NOW STAY THERE. WHORL'S LITTLE CLASS IS ABOUT TO COME TO AN END.
MAYBE WHORL'S GROUP GOT TO THEM FIRST.
THERE ARE NO GUARDS.

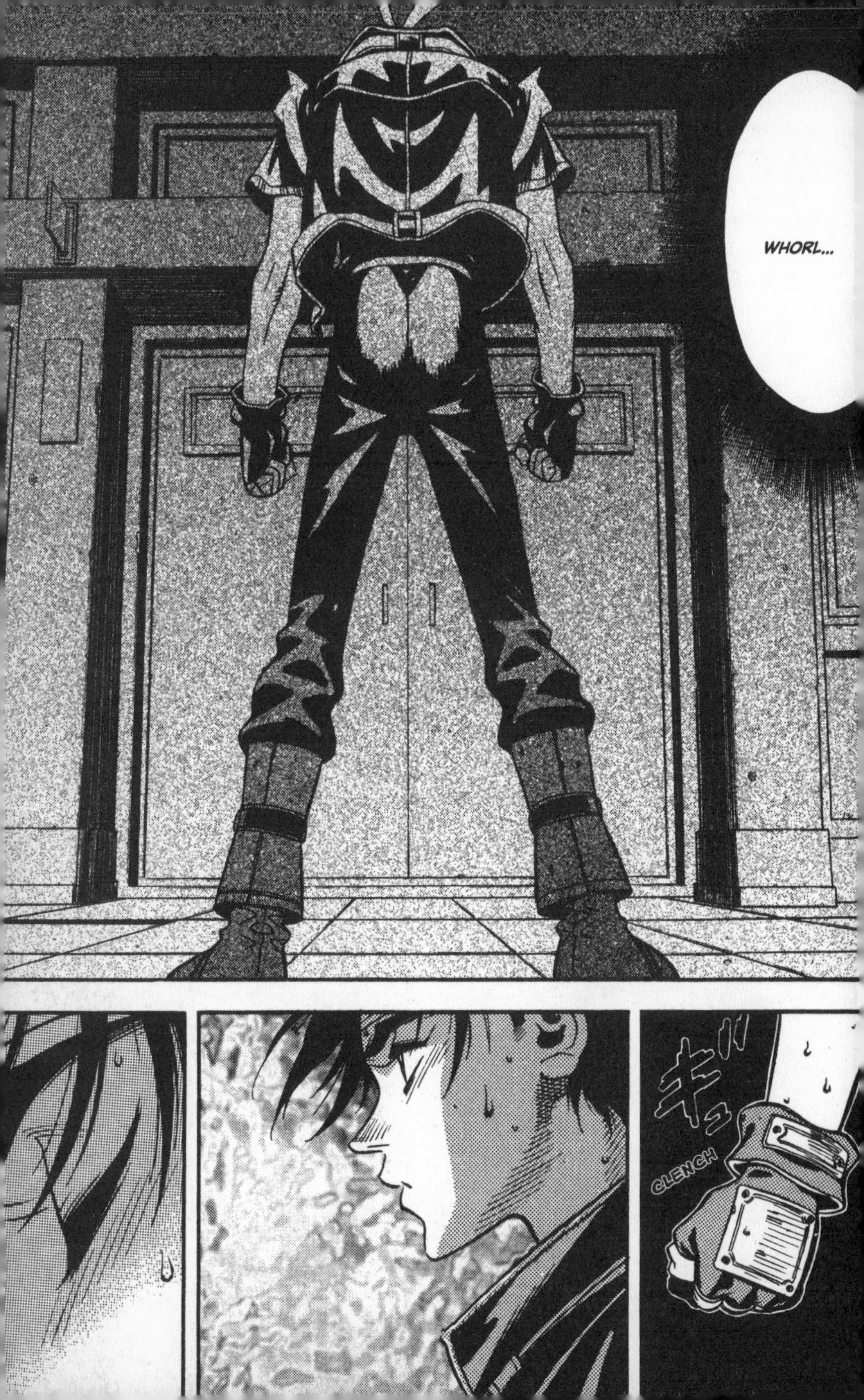
WHORL...
キュ
CLENCH

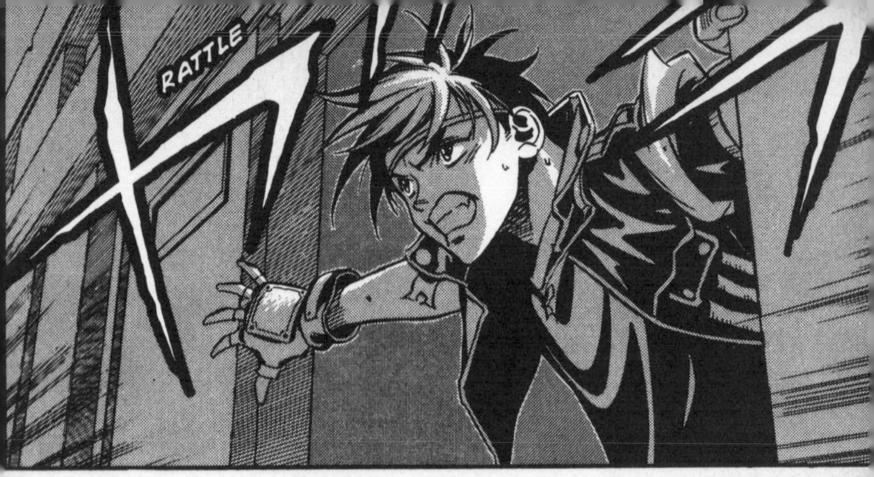
RATTLE

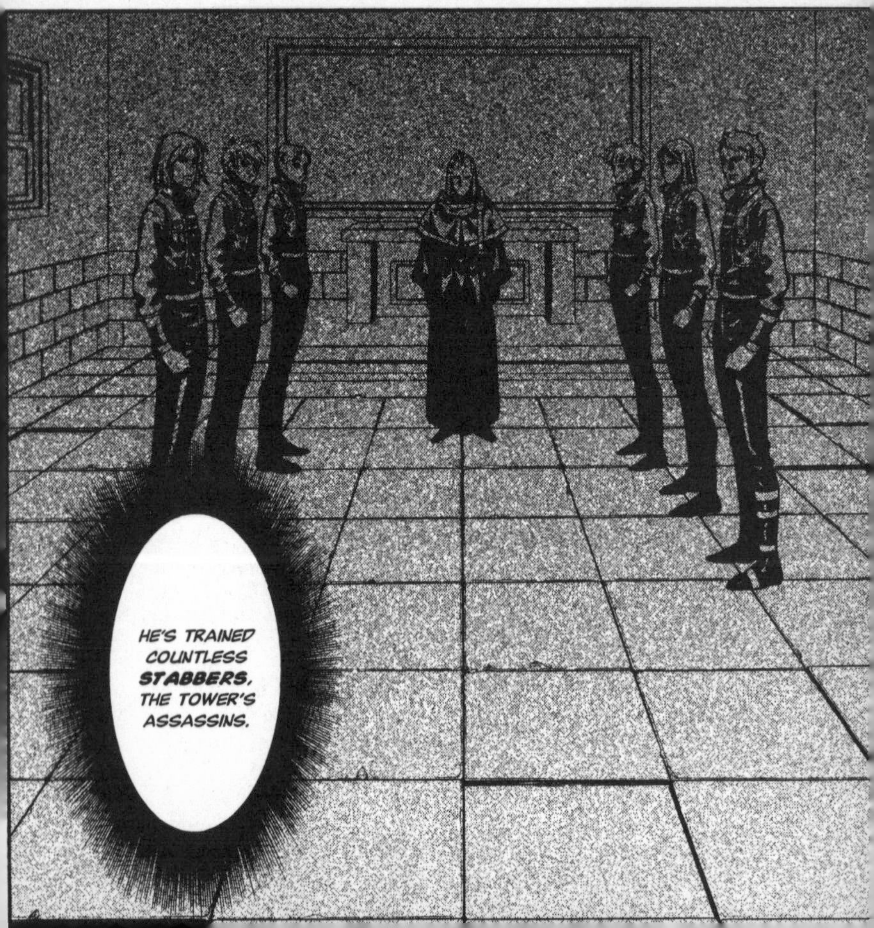
HE'S TRAINED COUNTLESS **STABBERS**, THE TOWER'S ASSASSINS.

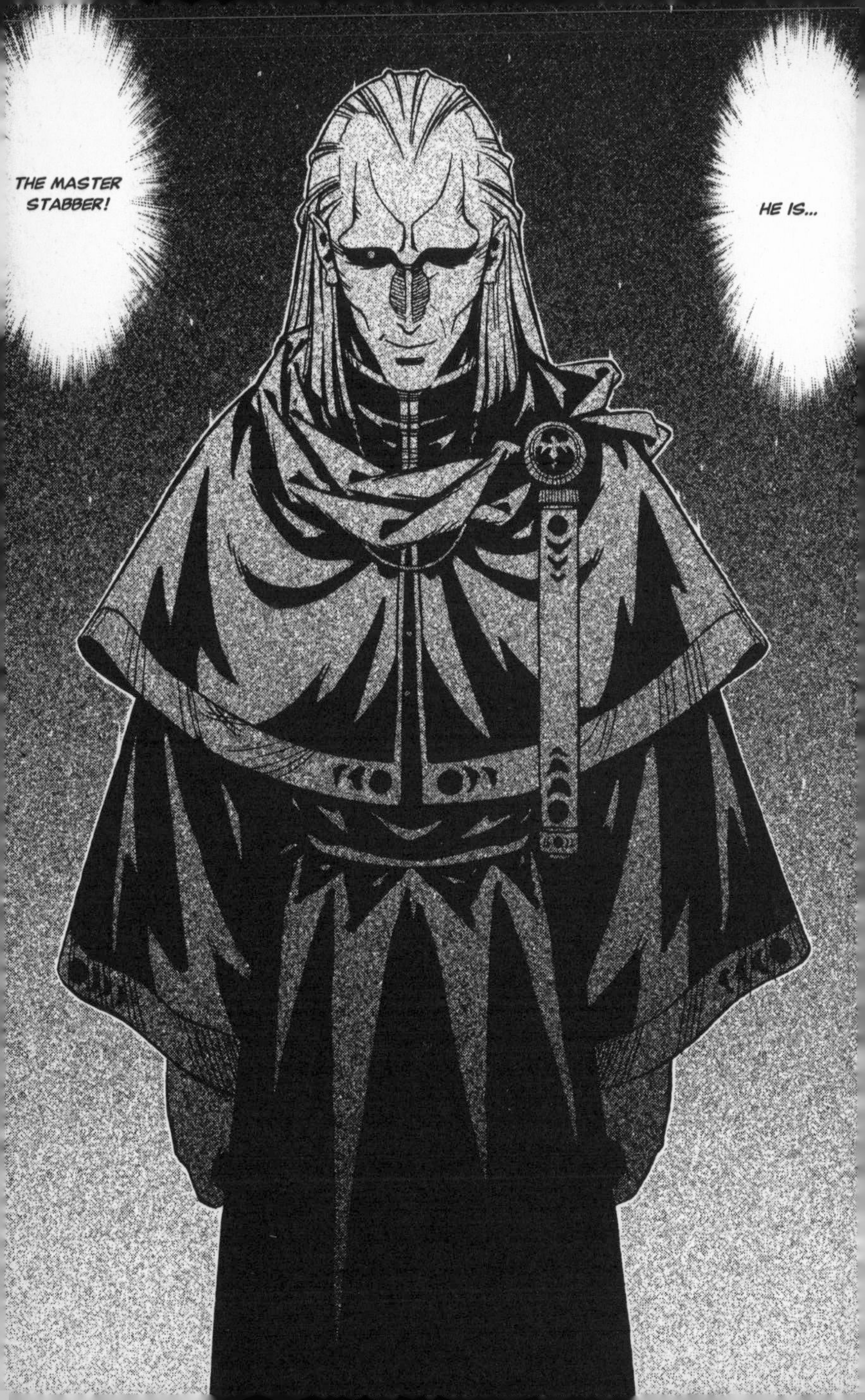
HE IS...
THE MASTER STABBER!

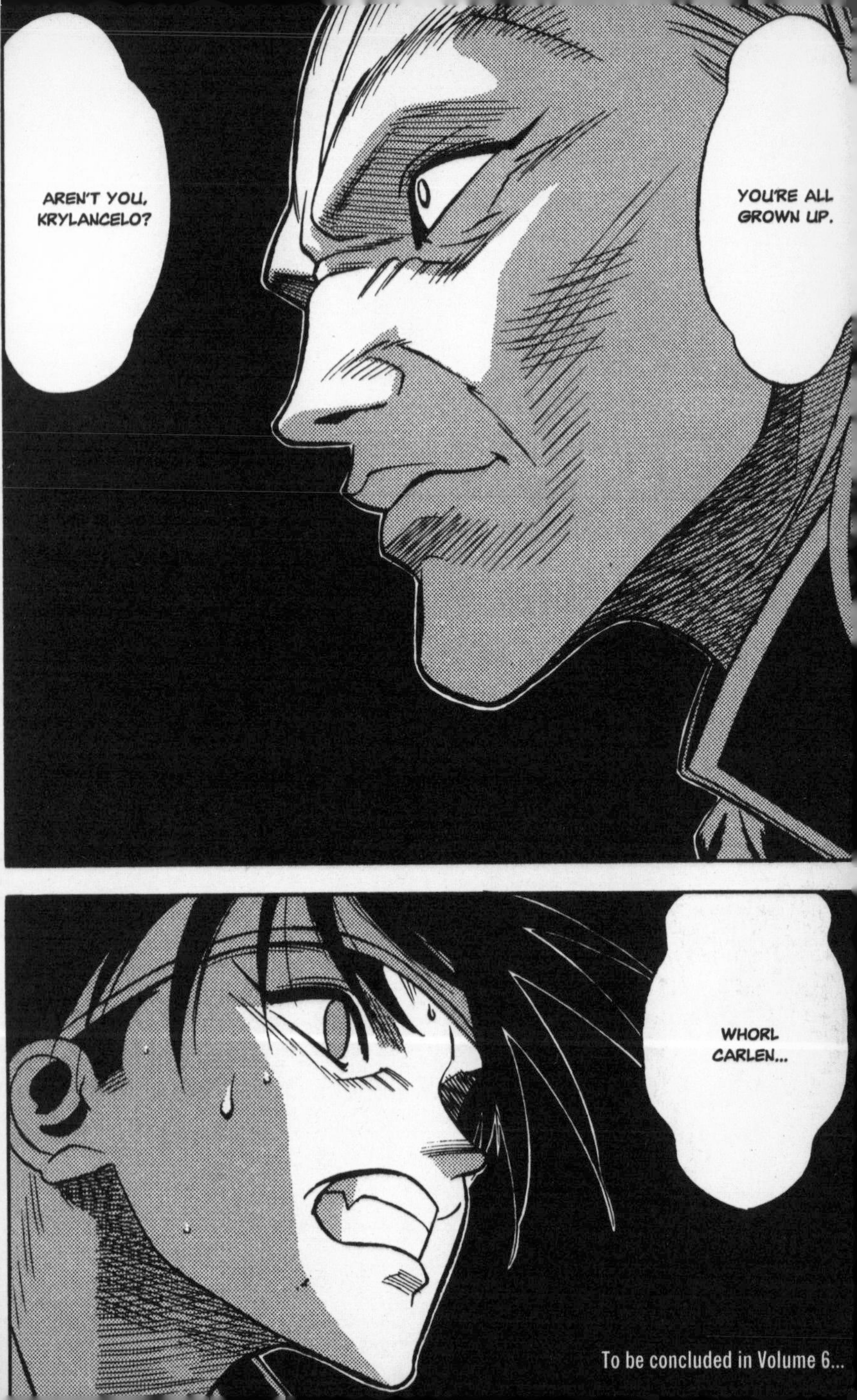
YOU'RE ALL GROWN UP.
AREN'T YOU, KRYLANCELO?
WHORL CARLEN...
To be concluded in Volume 6...

ORPHEN

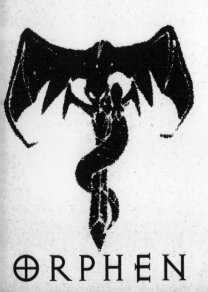

Orphen Volume Five

© 2001 Yoshinobu Akita/Hajime Sawada
© 2001 Yuuya Kusaka
Originally published in Japan in 2001 by
KADOKAWA SHOTEN PUBLISHING CO., LTD., Tokyo.
English translation rights arranged with
KADOKAWA SHOTEN PUBLISHING CO., LTD., Tokyo.

Editor JAVIER LOPEZ
Translator BRENDAN FRAYNE
Graphic Artist SCOTT HOWARD

Editorial Director GARY STEINMAN
Creative Director JASON BABLER
Sales and Marketing CHRIS OARR
Print Production Manager BRIDGETT JANOTA

International Coordinators TORU IWAKAMI & MIYUKI KAMIYA

President, CEO & Publisher JOHN LEDFORD

Email: editor@adv-manga.com
www.adv-manga.com
www.advfilms.com

For sales and distribution inquiries please call 1.800.282.7202

ADV MANGA™ is a division of A.D. Vision, Inc.
5750 Bintliff Drive, Suite 210, Houston, Texas 77036

English text © 2006 published by A.D. Vision, Inc. under exclusive license.
ADV MANGA is a trademark of A.D. Vision, Inc.

ISBN: 1-4139-0270-7
First printing, May 2006
10 9 8 7 6 5 4 3 2 1
Printed in Canada